*For Solomon's Grandchildren,
his life in the new world...*

The Blackwoman's Guide To Understanding the Blackman™

Copyright 1990 by Shahrazad Ali

First Edition Released 1992

Library of Congress Cataloging-in-Publication Data

Ali, Shahrazad, 1947-
    The Blackwoman's guide to understanding the
    Blackman / written by Shahrazad Ali. — 1st ed.
    p. cm.
    ISBN 0-933405-03-0 : $10.00
    1. Afro-American men. I. Title
  E185.86.A39 1992
  305.38'896073—dc20   92-4982
                                      CIP

Published by
Civilized Publications
2019 S. 7th Street
Philadelphia, PA 19148

Wholesale Rates Available

The survival of the Blackman is in crisis.
He is dying a shameful unnatural death.
He is rejected by his woman
and detached from his own seed.
Slavery fractured his birthright ego
so he fails as husband, father, and son.
His problems are too big now
So he has no value for life,
And no matter how hard he tries...
he just can't get it together —
And without divine intervention
he will continue to self-destruct.

THE BLACKWOMAN'S GUIDE
TO UNDERSTANDING THE BLACKMAN

* All biographical data in Chapter 12 can be documented for verification in Black Bookstores, and at the *Schomburg Center for Research in Black Culture* in Harlem, New York. Much of the information is from eye-witness reports. The author suggests that readers do their own investigation using the above cited sources.

FOREWORD

While the scabs on the wounds inflicted by *The Blackman's Guide to Understanding the Blackwoman* are barely healed, we now embark on the second phase of this purification process to expose and dissolve selected behaviors that destroy love and stifle respect between Blacks. Of course it is impossible to include, in any writing, all of the idiosyncrasies of 30 million African-Americans. This makes it difficult to access specific conditions because of their resemblance to stereotypical accusations. Insistence that both sides of the story, the good and the bad, be told simultaneously, further complicates any effort to address problems which by virtue of importance have isolated priority. The need to explore all aspects of Black life is overwhelmingly welcomed — unless the exploration points the finger at individuals guilty of creating the problems by how they behave.

It is extremely important for the reader to understand clearly that the sole purpose of this study is to continue to examine the underlying causes of animosity between Blackmen and Blackwomen. It is not an attempt to insult or publicly ridicule the Blackman. Nor should it be dismissed as superficial or typical male bashing. Recent experience has proven that confronting brutal truths about personal motivation is painfully embarrassing and usually met with gross denial. Many of the segments in this book contain information that appears to rival or contradict data presented in *The Blackman's Guide to Understanding the Blackwoman*. This is done intentionally to reveal concurrent opposing behaviors between Blackmen and

1

Blackwomen, which ironically accelerate the demise of an already fragile union.

Regrettably, a recent University of Chicago study concluded that by the year 2000, seventy percent of Blackmen will be unemployed, on drugs, in jail — or dead. The predictions are grim and seem self-fulfilling. The background reasons for this sad reality, all provable, are the bloodcurdling events of slavery, lack of opportunity, poor education, drugs, bad breaks and set backs. These obstacles are 100 percent the responsibility of the perpetrators who created and foster special systems of human dejection. This misery is referred to in the African-American experience as racism, or *outside* intervention. A root cause of the resultant discontent *inside* this tattered community is the disorganization of the shattered Black family. This secondary aspect of the problem, according to frustrated members of the group, is the failure of Blackmen to accept and deliver on their obligations as husband, provider and father.

Decidedly, the Blackwoman has failed miserably on the homefront. Many months have been spent aggressively attempting to apprise Blackwomen about how this failure manifests. Predictably, this deduction was not accepted happily. Pedestals toppled and were replaced with sobering realities. Complicated unpleasantries were acknowledged to pave way for progress. On the flip side of this dreadful predicament the Blackman must now study and recognize the mismanagement of his masculine authority. His blunders, as colossal and unintentional as his woman's, equally splinter the Black household.

As head of the Black nation in America, whether he admits it or not, the Blackman is solely responsible for any liabilities existing among Blackwomen and Black children. Reportedly, the Blackman has never taken proper charge of his own life, the life of his woman, or his children's. He has allowed himself to be overwhelmed by the strong wording of contemporary opinion, and the unpopularity of addressing his own needs. All of the cries of "racism" have become a convenient crutch he leans on to explain his perpetual crippled leadership — in and out of the house.

While many of his negative habits are merely reactions to the ill-fated approaches of his woman and his mother — this has already been discussed in *The Blackman's Guide to Understanding the Blackwoman*. This new study is devoted entirely to the greater problem — the irresponsible leadership of Black-men, and how they got to be the way they are. Although this book does not cover every aspect of African-American history, it does include factors contributing to the decline of the Black-man's leadership potential. It also explains how Black male teens, unfamiliar with past and modern history, become dis-placed and reckless in the world. This book is merely a mirror, a galloping reflective account of the Blackman's last 19 decades in America. It chronicles condensed events and trends ordinar-ily unknown which must be considered when dealing with him, and making judgments about his condition. His mind was tampered with, and brainwashing schemes must be discussed and understood.

As before, I do not expect all Blackmen to accept the accuracy of this report. But mass denial among them must not constitute cause to reject or disbelieve the contents of this work. Public confession is not necessary for improvement. Readers must realize that here is a man who claims he is victimized by entrenched racism, slanted justice, media attack, multiple drugs and accessible weapons — compounded with charges of genocidal conspiracy out to destroy him — yet he has done little to ward off the results of such conclusions. He has been screaming "foul" for umpteen years trying to bring attention to his unfair treatment. And he now dizzily wanders around crying "racism" at the slightest provocation, but still swears that the possibility of a diverse multi-cultural society exists.

This book contains new perspectives. The suggestions made are not written to endorse or promote negative racism, instead, they prove historically that the only successful multi-cultural society is one where each race retains economic and spiritual individuality. Anything else creates confusion and resentment between nationalities. And subsequently has landed the Blackman in his present predicament — endangered. And some say unhelpable due to his insistence in doing things his own way — the wrong way for his survival. His pride is tissue-paper thin, blowing in the wind.

Hopefully every Blackman will read this text and voluntarily place his nose to the grindstone of reconciliation with his manhood, and proper evaluation of his political dreams. He must commit to save himself at any cost, with minimal tears and moderate ego damage. False pride and stubbornness have no place when one is contending for self-preservation. And yes, the effects of slavery still rank as number one in the dismemberment of the Black home and displacement of the Blackman; but the number two problem stems from contributory neglect of an internal nature that takes the form of a) disunity, b) distrust and, c) bad choices.

Tragically, the number one problem cannot be reversed, but number two can be repaired. This is not shifting the burden, just smoothing it out a little to make it more manageable for correction.

Blackman, I have faith in you.

As-salaam-alaikum,

Sister Shahrazad Ali

Chapter 1

BABYHOOD AND PUBERTY

Adult Blackmen over the age of 40 have similar childhood backgrounds. They remember their past somewhat fondly at times, and whatever complaints they recall are seemingly small unpleasantries when compared to the horror reports and wayward status of Black male youth today. The majority of them were taught proper table manners, how to behave in public, respect for elders, the importance of attending church, neatness, household chores, control of his mouth, to be nice to girls, to fight only if aggressed, the value of education, modest goals, moral convictions, obedience to parents, reasons to reject alcohol and tobacco and why they shouldn't talk back.

As a small boy he played with ropes, chinese checkers, puzzles, cards, dominoes, marbles, bikes, scooters, blocks, kites, wagons, electric trains, balls, trucks, guns and cowboy hats. His make-believe heroes were Superman, G.I. Joe, The Lone Ranger and Tonto, The Cisco Kid, Batman, Zorro, Roy Rogers and Davy Crockett and Daniel Boone. He learned of them from comic books, television and radio programs. He was aptly entertained by Howdy Doody and Pinkie Lee. He read Snow White, Little Red Riding Hood, Goldilocks and the Three Bears, The Three Pigs and a host of nursery rhymes like Hickory-Dickory-Dock, Little Miss Muffet, Humpty Dumpty, London Bridges and Jack and Jill. Television showed him moving pictures of Superman and he watched Father Knows Best, Ed Sullivan, Ted Mack Amateur Hour, Beat the Clock, The Price is Right, Queen for a Day, Alfred Hitchcock, Roy Rogers and Dale Evans, Topper and Perry Mason. He heard other stories about Paul Bunyan and John Henry. Included in his visual were other shows all featuring brave, handsome, white male performers with glamorous female starlets — mostly with long yellow/blonde flowing hair and sky blue eyes. He committed her features to memory and she was the first woman he drew a picture of in school.

He loved to go to the movie theatre to see gangster, western and war flicks. Tarzan was Bwana and King of the Jungle. Every action, every emotion, attitude or moral judgment was demonstrated for him on the big screen, in black and white or color cinematography, with every situation featuring caucasians conducting their business and social affairs. Lana Turner, Doris Day, Dinah Shore, Marilyn Monroe and Debbie Reynolds were just a few. Rock Hudson, Elvis Presley, Troy Donahue and Clark Gable premiered as the top male actors. If the Blackman saw himself on T.V. it was as the cook, the waiter, shoe shine boy, dish washer, baggage carrier, car washer, maid or babysitter — always, but always in the employ of wealthy whites. If he wasn't sweeping the floor or running from ghosts he was seen dancing a jig grinning as wide as possible and stretching his eyes to the limits to show the most white or making other facial contortions designed to be funny and show him up as ignorantly playing the fool. Some played in big bands and grinned along with the music but never spoke. He may have had the rare opportunity to see A Raisin in the Sun, Imitation of Life, Rochester on the Jack Benny Show, Amos-N-Andy and the Kingfish, Carmen Jones, or Green Pastures, or Stepin' Fetchit with Shirley Temple. He did not seem to wonder why he wasn't featured in key roles in the movies or on T.V. T.V. was fairly new during his childhood and it was basically understood that white people were in charge of T.V. land. Then he was introduced to Uncle Remus and The Tar Baby, Buckwheat and Alfalfa, Little Black Sambo, Aunt Jemima on the Pancake Box, Uncle Ben's Rice, and a host of other "Mammy" products from syrup to shortening. He was aware of many outside influences that did not look like him but his life had structure and his community was in agreement on certain behavior codes and in-home values.

In the South the differences between him and other races were more pronounced and he was instructed and reminded with public signs that not only was he unalike but had to move about in the world carefully. One of the main reasons he was

6

taught to read was so that he did not accidentally go in the wrong door, drink from the wrong public water fountain or get caught in certain areas after the sunset. His mother taught him to fear and be extra polite to whites as a way to protect himself, and she warned him of improper conduct, especially around white women and little white girls. He was taught to lower his eyes and never look them directly in the face, to remove his hat when addressed by them and never walk too close behind, beside or in front of them — lest he be charged with being disrespectful. There was a penalty that went with disrespecting a white woman so he must always keep his distance. He was warned that even an accidental glance could cost him his life. His parents and grandparents advised him to be friendly, smile, helpful and do what he was told to do, use good manners and be proud if whites recognized him or approved of his work. He was educated in a mode of behavior to save his life. He eventually heard stories about what whites did to Blacks if they were in the wrong place at the wrong time. But he was not bored because Blacks had their own sections of town and recreation outlets which they could freely frequent and which were sometimes visited by whites at will, but he was strictly forbidden from ever trying to patronize theirs. He learned to dance for whites.

No matter where he lived whenever it was time to have a party they had fun. His father, if present, earned about $1,000 to $3,000 a year in income although he usually never knew it. Provisions were made for him and he witnessed attempts to make sure he was not hungry, so other than owning a television set, there was little to compete with his family or their status in life. He was relatively comfortable in most cases and didn't realize for the most part if he was rich or poor since his Black neighbors and friends all appeared to live the same way he did. Many of their guardians maintained single parent households. It was not that unusual at the time. If one of his friends lived with both his mother and father he was revered as quite special. Many of their mothers had men friends who visited, stayed overnight or lived with them periodically. He was taught to respect his mother's man and refer to him as "Mr. so-n-so," and to make few demands on his stand in father and he often knew little if anything about his own biological daddy. It wasn't discussed much in his presence, and if the missing father showed up in town or in the neighborhood for a visit, it was considered a big deal and something to brag about. He was somewhat stifled regarding questions about his father. If he was told anything at all it was some flamboyant reputation attached to his father, or he was given an overly negative historical account about how no-good he was. He was routinely shipped, especially during summer, either to the North or "down" South, to visit with relatives — where the house rules were the same and if he did something wrong the whipping hurt just as bad.

Often he witnessed his mother fighting with, or being "beat-up" by one of her male friends. He got used to the stale smell of whiskey on Friday and Saturday nights. There was little he could do about it but it made him dislike these unpredictable strange men who were too big for him to fight — or defend his mother from. Many times this frustrated anger was directed and blamed on his AWOL father. He later learned to milk his mother's "man" for spending change or other minute benefits to forget what happened or to stay out of the way when he was visiting.

He was also exposed to other elements in his community. The drunks, the slick haired finely dressed number men, their runners, the fast loose women reeking of heavy perfume, wigged down in tight dresses with luscious exploding bodies, the holy-rollers piously dressed in all white or strict black suits, the impeccably dressed gamblers, the owners of flashy colored bulky cars, and the neighborhood retard or cripple. He knew a little about everybody's business just as they knew about his. Many of these images struck him as exciting and represented fun and freedom topped with money. He would listen hard when the grown-ups talked so he could learn about the fast life and community gossip. If he got caught listening he could count on getting wopped in the mouth or sent outside out of ear shot. Even if he did not live around such characters he heard about their existence and they were role models of a sort and helped him have good dreams of growing up and wearing fine clothes and being successful in the street life. Cool without working hard.

Much of the reality of life between men and women was kept from him. He learned certain things about sex in whispered conversations among his friends. Getting a kiss was considered a big thing. Grown-ups kept grown-up things out of his face private. As far as he knew, being a boy, when compared to being a girl, other than the fact that he had a "weenie" and she had a "poon tang," only meant that he had to do heavier chores around the house, take out the trash, run errands, carry large packages, stay out a little later and he could travel further away from home on his bike or by foot. He didn't have as many clothes as the females around him and he could relieve himself any place he chose while the girls needed a pot, a room with a toilet and a door. He could also play rougher games and contact sports. His home life became his routine. It ran smoothly enough. And had dependable systems. He always saw his mother going to or coming from work, food shopping, cleaning house, paying bills, cooking, negotiating with store vendors, participating in church, praying on her knees at home, humming spirituals, picking out his clothes, arranging furniture, talking on the phone — and she was always still up when he went to bed, and already up when he rose in the morning. He didn't quite understand how she did all this and he wasn't quite sure what he was supposed to do since it was visibly apparent to him that his mother took care of practically everything including all his needs. He knew he had to do what he was told but other than playing, doing a few duties, going to school, and having a few squabbles with his peers he didn't know what else to do.

If he was really poor he learned early to be ashamed of his condition. He never liked being different because being different kept him from having certain things and feeling good about himself. The toys or games he wanted were usually attached to the value of them placed on him by others in his peer group. Many of their mothers were on welfare or some kind of public assistance, received a type of food stamp coupon and predictably ran out of money and food before the end of the month came. Welfare checks traditionally arrived on the first day of each month and always generated much activity and bustling excitement in the area. The check amounts varied from about $12/month to about $200/month depending on the number of dependent children in the household — North, South, East or West. Because of the strict stipulations set up by the government in order to qualify for welfare he often confusingly witnessed his mother hide an appliance, the telephone, a radio or T.V. set, a record player, etc., or any item the visiting, generally white, social worker might deem as an "extra" and reason enough to reduce or cut off the welfare support check. The "workers" attitude was that if a family was on welfare they were not to have anything considered a luxury — other than food, basic clothing and furnishings. And there were guidelines on even that. The furniture couldn't be too fancy and the clothes couldn't be too fashionable. There was a distinct "welfare look" and when a family stopped looking like they were on welfare they were cancelled out of the program. Sometimes his mother had to "hide" her man (maybe his father) outside the house, under the bed or in the closet, so that the "worker" would not catch a man in the house. Word always spread like wildfire in his community if a "worker" was seen or rumored to be in the vicinity. His memories of the shame attached to welfare poverty are not pretty. The more industrious ones ran errands for neighbors or shop owners, carried groceries, swept steps, emptied trash or sold newspapers to provide themselves with spending money. He was highly motivated to get his hands on some change and selling soda bottles was not out of the question at 2¢ or 3¢ per bottle refunded. Earning enough money to buy an ice cream cone, some penny candy or go to the movies was sufficient to boost his pride. Little discussion of his future or the kind of work he would do when he grew up occurred.

If he lived with both his parents things tended to be considerably better. They might have a car, go on real vacations, get dressed up every Sunday, attend a modern school away from the neighborhood, get new clothes seasonably, visit the dentist or doctor, eat out in a restaurant, go to camp or go out of town often on the train or bus to participate in activities with other two-parent children. These parents made his life as comfortable as possible and he was programmed to achieve. He got a chance to learn from his father or his father's work. They were small lessons but they helped him make social transitions to adult expressions of masculinity and responsibility. Some of the memories are connected to a particular "whipping" he got for doing something wrong. Unless he was brutalized, Blackmen recall these memories fondly and make jokes about what happened.

In the two-parent household he was more so indoctrinated with the idea that he was just as good as anyone else, he could do anything as long as he got a good education, and that he must grow up and be a credit to his race and make his parents proud. Under no circumstances must he be prejudiced — against his own kind, whites or anyone else. His home life was positive as he was programmed with ideas about his future success. Little mention was ever made about the specialness of his being Black, and no information about his proud Black heritage was imparted to him, and no mention of slavery was ever made. He was told he was a negro and, other than his immediate family history, his ancient past was blurry and unfocused on any unique roots or personal background. He was instructed to be a good American. In some homes he received a vague explanation about whites disliking Blacks because of their skin color , that they were just prejudiced against the coloreds. And every book he read from the first page to the last contained white children or white families with white neighbors. None of the books were about him.

During his earliest childhood he is exposed to other routine experiences. Each Christmas he was taken to town to go window shopping and sometimes permitted to take a snapshot picture sitting on the wondrous lap of "Santa Claus," a mystical character who granted wishes for good little children on Christmas morn. Santa was always white in every picture or decoration. The Black boy's eyes would light up with excitement mixed with a little fear as he was led through heavily adorned stores with twinkling lights, puffy white cotton, sparkling glitter, evergreen trees with all sorts of candy canes and brightly wrapped gifts. There was silvery tinsel, tinkling bells, little white elves as Santa's helpers and holiday songs playing over speakers in stores and on the streets. Decorating the Christmas tree with glistening balls, angel hair that seemed to draw him into its maze and flashing colorful lights was the most beautiful sight he had ever seen. Even the poorest families had a Christmas tree and most of them had wreaths or lights in the window.

The Black boy also saw little white children in white flowing gowns with white feathered wings on their backs with a silver halo over their heads — hanging from the ceiling in stores, perched on lawns, in windows and as table centerpieces. He was told that these lovely creatures were angels sent from heaven to celebrate the birth of Christ Jesus. Then, ohhhhhh, the nativity scene featuring a docile looking, gently hooded, serene, pale skinned white woman identified to him as the saintly mother of the Christ child. Next there was a strong looking bearded white man whose name was Joseph, the father of baby Jesus. And of course there was baby Jesus himself, peach colored cheeks, tiny blue eyes with perfectly formed glistening white limbs. A divinely beautiful little white baby in a manger in a barn representing the King of Kings — sent to save the world. The three shepherds arrived on camels from the East, with a huge star over the stable barn where Jesus had just been born and wrapped in swaddling clothes and lain in a bed of straw.

This glorified mysterious dramatic story mesmerized his attention and hypnotized him into believing the story and to always honor this saintly family — above all others. He was taught that this was the "real" meaning of Christmas. Silent night, holy night. Santa Claus was like the icing on the cake. Intermingled with the spiritual and religious connotations, Santa guaranteed that every parent would teach the Christmas story to their children. Faith and fun, what could be more innocent? Santa and his elves, a fat jolly old-timer also called "Saint Nick" enjoyed a reputation of being the first always smiling, kind and good doing whiteman the Black boy had ever met. Santa, for many years, was allowed to take the credit for gifts of happiness to him. Presents and toys purchased with hard earned Black dollars, even going into debt, was attributed to the beneficence and goodness of a jolly old whiteman in a red suit with a white beard who travelled in a sled that flew across the sky pulled by reindeer — led by Rudolph with a shiny blinking nose. It was suggested to the Black boy that if he put out cookies and milk that Santa would eat them during his visit after he tumbled down the chimney to put gifts under the tree. For many years the Black boy believed this story, and by the time he was told, or found out on his own that Santa was just a fairy tale made up to entertain him, the Black boy had spent many a night dreaming about Santa and swooning to the words of "Twas the Night Before Christmas." He was very susceptible to imaginary heroes who treated him good. Every Black boy in America was taught the same two aspects of Christmas — Christ Jesus' birth and Santa Claus. Being so impressionable he believed the people he trusted. And trusted the people he believed in. Baby Jesus and Santa Claus... and his mother — who endorsed them both.

At another time of the year he was introduced to Valentine's Day. A day he is told means love. This love was best expressed with a red shaped symbol to replicate the heart which was sometimes pierced with an arrow looped across it, or accompanied by one or two chubby little white babies called cherubs. The cherubs had a tiny bow and arrow which they were able to shoot into the heart of couples to make them fall hopelessly in love with each other. The heart became his idea of love. He was never told who St. Valentine was. And his parents didn't know either. But all of them knew about Cupid and his little bow and arrow spreading love and heart shaped boxes of candy and pretty red and white greeting cards which he distributed on a miniature level among his closest school friends.

Then there was St. Patrick's Day. A day about a white saint and a day he was to wear something green to commemorate St. Patrick. Along with St. Patrick came a bunch of little elderly white midgets in green suits with pointed green hats and curled toe green slippers called leprechauns — mischievous little fellows who played pranks on unknowing bystanders. It had something to do with Ireland and the Irish people who celebrated their folklore with gutsy ales and other festivities.

One of his favorite holidays was April Fool's Day. Few Black parents knew how this holiday originated but they did know that it was a day to play tricks on friends or make a joke of some sort, and when the person falls for the act or information — the culprit calls out "April Fool." A bit of lying and devilishment all in the name of fun. The Black boy would run around the neighborhood, the house and the school yard yelling "April Fool, April Fool" after he played a successful trick on someone. How entertaining.

George Washington, the first President was the father of his country and Betsy Ross sewed the first American flag. He knew about the cherry tree, too. In the midst of these came Mother's Day and Father's Day. If his mother was alive he wore a red rose on his lapel, if she was dead he wore a white one. This procedure was repeated on Father's Day also, which never got as much attention as Mother's Day. Throwing in Ground Hog's Day, Veterans Day, Labor Day and May Day, the next major holiday he was taught was Thanksgiving. Blessed Thanksgiving decorated with colorful fall leaves and beautiful fruits and vegetables protruding out of a "Horn of Plenty" – kind of like a basket shaped like a long funnel. Thanksgiving was explained to him as the day when a small group of friendly white settlers came to America and sponsored a big sit down dinner for the native Indians and taught them how to bake bread, set a table and eat pork. This represented the exchange of goodwill between the whites and the Indians and their agreement to share cultures with each other. A multi-cultural festival of respect. This grew to include donating gifts of food for the less fortunate. The first Thanksgiving was described as a merger and a peaceful unification initiated by whites. He was taught a great deal of detail about the European pilgrims but given only superficial notations on the Indians. Plus, he knew the Indians were not really the good-guys because in the movies the Indians always wanted to fight and kill off the settlers and he loudly cheered when he heard the familiar trumpet sound of "Dum-tee, Dum-tee, Dum-tee-tum" as the organized white troops charged in to kill the Indians and defend their fellow immigrants. He felt good every time a calvaryman slew an Indian and got him back. The Black boy participated in school plays about the first Thanksgiving in school and wore pilgrim clothes or Indian feathers. His teachers didn't mind that he was left out of every story, every holiday and every celebration or tradition or routine ritual recorded by Americans. After all, what difference could it make? The important issue was the celebration of the event itself and all children should enjoy them and respect their country.

The Fourth of July was special to him because it signaled a picnic, nighttime fireworks and celebrations at school. He would happily don his red, white and blue hat he made in class, or proudly wear his own hand-drawn American flag on his shoulder or shirt pocket, and he could recite the Pledge of Allegiance to the United States of America with his little hand held over his heart. He would swear with all his youthful honesty that he would support his country and all it stood for. Status quo, unknowingly included. He was told to be proud of the day the Declaration of Independence was signed. Of course, he didn't know what Independence meant and no detailed explanation followed from his teacher or parents. At home, the 4th of July took on a lesser patriotic meaning and featured barbe-que pork ribs, hot dogs, burgers, potato salad, cakes, pies, baked beans and maybe even some homemade ice cream — all eaten in the back yard, out front, or at a public park for a fun-filled picnic. He loved the firecrackers, the happy sparks of twizzlers and the fiery blast of cherry bombs. The colorful parades with balloons and all were the most fun of all.

On Easter he knew he would probably get some new clothes, get dressed up, go to church, walk around downtown or at home showing off his new threads. He might attend a movie, go to a carnival or amusement park, take a long exploring bus ride with his "pass" and eat a snack while out. He was taught in church and at school that Easter is the day that Jesus rose from the dead three days after he was killed on a cross the previous Friday (Good Friday). Jesus had been nailed to the cross through his hands and feet until he expired from blood loss and unbearable pain. The Black boy was shown in books and read to out of the Bible about how Jesus wore a crown of thorns, was offered briny vinegar water to drink, and suffered through it all with dignity and everlasting strength. The actual pictures of the crucifixion drawn or painted by European artists were shown to him at a very early age, and represented the first gory sight of a dead white man presented to him as reality. He saw white men killed in the movies but he knew they were just actors and not dead for real. He was told that Jesus, in his unselfishness, died for his sins and those of the entire world. Easter was the first holiday in which the Black boy learned more about religion, and also was the first occasion that he got a chance to hear God speak. There were always T.V. Easter special or movies at the theatre depicting the death of Jesus. In the movies God was always portrayed as having a big booming baritone voice that thundered from behind the clouds or sun. God always spoke to make vibrations in the air and cause fear every time he talked to earthlings. The big God in the sky also was invisible, he could recognize Jesus, Mary, Joseph and the 12 Disciples by sight, but it was a mystery to him as to what God actually looked like — so how would he recognize Him? Church had taught him that Jesus really represented the Father, the Son and the Holy Ghost, so they would all have to look alike so Jesus, the slender white male with the pale brooding eyes, shoulder length thick dark brown hair and keen nose was also God. Thereafter, whenever confronted with biblical photographs he was able to pick out God from the rest of the white people and could even recognize him in the Last Supper portrait. Jesus/God had very distinctly different features from the other guests at the table. He recognized Jesus on Church fans, Bible School cards, calendars, wall hangings and greeting cards. He became comfortable that he could recognize his savior. It had already been explained to him that he must not sin. Sin was described to him briefly as lying,.cheating, stealing, doing any kind of wrong.

Drinking, using drugs, sassing, staying out all night, not saying his prayers, not going to church or being plain disobedient meant going to hell. The hell place contained every horror imaginable. It had everlasting scorching flames, fire that would never go out, a big boiling pot with smoke all over the room. In this hell place was another white man in a red scuba diving type suit with red horns on top of his head. He had a long tail with an arrow at the end of it and a permanent evil scowl on his face. This devil was designed to scare him into doing right, obeying the Lord and refraining from sin. Hell was not the place he wanted to go after he died. The stories about hell frightened him. The fact that hell was deep underground made him feel no better. (And if it rained while the sun was shining he was taught that this meant the devil was beating his wife.) He had not previously been told that the devil was even married but he believed it anyway.

Simultaneously with teachings of Jesus' death, rising from the dead and floating slowly up into the sky; he was taught about Easter bunnies. They laid colored hard boiled eggs that came in cute little baskets with green straw and all sorts of chocolate and colorful goodies to eat. He knew nothing of the reproductive system of mammals and whatever he knew about chickens laying eggs was suspended because the Easter bunny was so much more fun. He liked the new games of hiding the eggs and finding them, dyeing them with bright colors, putting designs on them and writing his name on them. And of course, he got to eat all he could hold. Candy chickens, jelly beans, marshmallow rabbits mixed in with all the other special goodies hidden in his basket. Sometimes he even got his own stuffed bunny plaything. He saw real rabbits in books or in school but he didn't care if bunnies laid eggs or not – he enjoyed the goodies. The Tooth Fairy was a pretty good idea, too. If he lost a tooth he could put it under his pillow and in the morning he would have money in its place — and the tooth would magically be gone.

He grew to look forward to these yearly festivities and the symbols and myths surrounding each holiday which were reinforced in school, in church, and at home by his mother and sometimes father, too. The predictability of them made him secure. Everybody knew about them, everybody celebrated them and everybody liked them. What a comfort. At least life had some good points that he could look forward to every year and benefit from.

Stories supporting these holidays were ingrained in him

before he left kindergarten. Of course he celebrated the major holidays at home even before he got to school, but school explained them in more detail and absorbed his participation on another level as a requirement. School expanded on the meanings and their value to his development. School supported this process by plastering pictures on the walls, on the blackboard, in the halls, windows and cafeteria. He was prompted to draw a portion of each story about each holiday and then join in class celebrations usually in the form of a party. His mother and his teacher stood as the main authority figures in his life. From kindergarten on he was fed more and more details of these holidays so as to firmly implant them in his brain. Kindergarten means children's garden. A garden to grow the child's mind into certain fertile ideas for readiness to take steps toward adulthood and self-sufficiency. The Black boy was surrounded with seeds of information alien to his history and lifestyle. These ideas were implanted in him at a very early age. And he was abruptly weaned from any suggestions that might bloom into self-worth or self-value. His growth was non-political towards his own kind. He was bred to ignore his own presence on the earth.

Prior to his formal education several other fictional personalities were introduced to him of skeptical value. If he got particularly out of hand, or if his mother or another adult taking care of him needed to control him after threats or spankings had failed, they would evoke a few other monsters especially designed to make him behave:

1) The Boogeyman — an ugly, mysterious man who scares, kidnaps or kills bad little children.

2) A Ghost — a dead person who comes back from the dead to "get" him and do him terrible harm by scaring him senseless.

3) The "Monster" — a horrible type of creature with dis torted features who would claw his skin or gobble him up if he was bad.

All of these characters existed in the dark when the lights went out. They were all used when applicable to scare the Black boy into behaving in a desired way. Although thought to be temporary in value and usage, this tactic was never quite forgotten by the Black boy. Their existence was seemingly forgotten by the Black boy. Their existence was seemingly validated on a holiday like Halloween when the witches and goblins came out from somewhere to scare little children. On Halloween he got to dress up in a funny or scary costume and go out "trick-or-treating" — which meant he went from door to door of strange homes saying "trick or treat" and would get some kind of morsel of candy, fruit or snack. He loved to wear a mask or paint his face. This Halloween holiday was also gaily celebrated in school with costume parties and refreshments. If he received no treat the tricks surfaced in writing on people's cars or house windows with soap, throwing eggs or turning over trash cans or some other prank designed to hassle households who did not provide "treats."

Interestingly, all of the holidays the Black boy was taught about contained various aspects of fear and the supernatural. They also instilled certain ideals and imprinted Western values in his head all rooted in expressing gratitude, honor and respect for white males. Additional to the festive holidays, during his first few years of school, he learned about Abraham Lincoln, a former American president who freed the slaves. His little brain was too undeveloped along with his short attention span to give him any long drawn out political explanation about ole' Abe and his real position on slavery. No one told him that Mr. Lincoln made a strictly political decision that public relations-wise awarded him the misleading credit of freeing the slaves. This was the first major mention of slavery he ever heard of. He was programmed with the impression that Negroes were happy slaves and needed the master to take care of them. He was told stories about how the slaves sang while they worked and danced all night. Nothing was mentioned to him about how Negroes became slaves or where they originally came from. He was just taught to be grateful to ole' Abe for setting the slaves free. Lincoln, a tall white man, but nice as Johnny Appleseed.

Christopher Columbus was always highlighted for his masterful discovery of America which he accomplished in 1492 by sailing across the ocean from England in three ships supplied by his queen. It was quite easy to teach the Black boy about boats floating on water with a great captain at the helm. Teaching Black boys to be grateful to Columbus is one of the worst travesties of misrepresentation ever inflicted on him. Telling him to respect and honor Christopher Columbus Day is like teaching a Jewish child to celebrate Adolph Hitler Day. It is that far from the truth. This falsified historically incorrect information is still taught to the Black boy today despite serious scholars announcing that Columbus introduced Western Colonialism, capitalism and slavery on the North American continent. Furthermore, studies show that he was already entertaining a few pre-Nazi theories on the natural supremacy of the white race, proceeded to inflict genocidal practices on the native Indians — who were already set up and functioning in their own civilization when Columbus first docked. Ol' Chris was eventually debunked and jailed for unscrupulous politics.

Every notable or famous individual that the Black boy was introduced to — be he real or imagined — was in the personhood of a white male. Thus he completed nearly 13 years of public school education acknowledging that every commendable action or intellectual victory was attributed to the white man. Nobody ever taught him during his formative years of the Blackman's place in history or his record of achievements. He had no knowledge of his own people or their contributions to math, science, medicine or art. His own parents rarely mentioned Black history to him. His church did not place Blacks in any biblical context, and it was subtly suggested to him that being "colored," "a negro," or "Black," was something bad and undesirable. And if somebody insulted him by calling him "Black" he was always ready to fight about it. He wasn't Black and he didn't want anybody trying to say he was. Black was a bad word only used in anger and hatred against another negro.

This system of loading the Black boys brain with foreign data put into motion an adult Black male who left home to confront the world and his destiny with absolutely no knowledge about his past, with a white man's name, an Anglo-Saxon religion, and a memory dedicated to Western values that would plague him for generations to come. This intentional cover-up laid the foundation for the confusion and displacement that would eventually lead to his present endangered classification. The ultra critical years between 1940 and 1990 produced the current perilous legacy of the Blackman, his sons, and his grandsons. This book is about the damaging effect of the brainwashing that the Blackman was subjected to during that 50-year period. And it represents the first contemporary debriefing session he has had since slavery.

NOTES

Chapter 2

IDENTITY

Trying to identify the Blackman or to get them to uniformly identify themselves is quite complicated. The cause of this complication is his overall unfamiliarity with his exact origin, aims and purpose. Some of them spew various definitions and views about who they are. Over the past 50 years or so they have changed their titles several times, so it is obvious that they are periodically undecided about who they are, and unable to settle on a word that aptly portrays who they wish to be. They have been called niggers, nigras, or nigrahs and claim that they do not like this label. They still tend to use this term with each other vacillating between using it to express fondness or as an insult. Later they referred to themselves as colored. By order of the more educated among them they settled for Negro for a short time. As years passed they outlined another reference — contrary to their previous position of claiming they hated the term — they, after much prompting, preferred to be recognized as "Black." As the years progressed and they became more politically astute they selected the modern term of Afro-American. Their latest preference is to answer to being an African-American, or just African. He does not seem to be primarily concerned with locating the place of his beginning. He seemingly is satisfied with settling on the African continent as his homeland. It has proven impractical to question them as a group regarding their identity and the closest they come to being unified is to collectively state: "I am a Blackman," and they deem this answer to be sufficient to define, for their women and the world, who they are and what their needs consist of.

Obviously this system of vague explanation has not worked. Any cohesiveness he has tried to have regarding his identity usually remains within elected geographical areas of inner cities and tends to stay confined within those bounds — recognized and known only to the community inhabitants. He has been so excited about his physical freedom for the past 35 years or so, that he feels no compulsion to study or gain knowledge about how his slave history impacts on his current behavior. This is strange indeed since most academicians agree that a knowledge of one's history makes life more valuable. It puts controls on negative actions and allows sane choices to be made according to the potentialities available to a person with a certain kind of background. He has chosen to skip a detailed study of what happened to him during slavery. This study should be performed, not for blamability on the perpetrators, but to debrief himself and rid his subconscious of any psychological emasculation resulting mentally or genetically from that experience. An experience that was so devastating that its latent memory has seemingly contaminated his sperm, and deranged him rendering him unable to even think himself out of his misery. His rantings about being proud to be Black runs in what is now becoming a predictable pattern. He tried to recognize his identity in the 20's and 30's, tried again in the 60's and 70's, and is approaching his third, therapeutic purge, in the 90's. Each generation unavoidably feels the frustrating pangs of unresolved conflicts left unattended by their predecessors — they want answers. Youthful Black males are starting to crave information and public acknowledgement of his African culture. What is culture? Some say culture is a system of preserving historical social ideas, traditions, memorabilia and basic principles by which a people live. Culture contains rites, qualifying tests and other values passed from one generation to the next who are emotionally connected by nationality, including skin color. Culture serves the purpose of functioning as a moral compass to direct and monitor people to keep them on the right track to preserve their ideas. Using this definition, it is plain to see that the Blackman is not earnestly trying to adopt his Black culture. In fact, he is far from it. His definition of culture has become a stew pot filled with a smorgasbord of unharmonious ideas and practices that so far have only inspired a few Blackmen to wear African clothes, a kente cloth scarf, fezzes, ethnic jewelry or slogan t-shirts. As usual, many of them are starting to express their dissatisfaction angrily. They are not really hostile, but they feel like their ego has been damaged, or that they have been punked out in front of the whole world for not getting what they think they deserve, and what they have been fighting for. They are an overly sensitive emotional group so they derive s short lived surge of power from talking rough to non-Blacks in authority.

Next he says he wants to reclaim his righteous character. So what is character? Character is a gradual process of development guided by specific attitudes, philosophy, ethics and a clear sense of right and wrong. It must first be planted in an individual by the mother and cultivated on a daily basis. It preferably should be endorsed by the father and recognizable in the surrounding community. The Blackman has not had the benefit of these interpersonal systems so it is no great wonder that adult Blackmen do not possess similar recognizable traits of character. Their behavior and practices have been developed from a conglomeration of foreign ideas he has been surrounded with since birth so he has been unable to settle on a definite scope of Black male characteristics. And he has wasted an entire generation being indecisive and unorganized resulting in no establishment of traits for himself — or his now unruly offspring. Instead, he has spent the last 40 years trying to find work, himself, and a mate, while experimenting with opposite ideas. He spent money on the side trying to have a good time.

According to this study, the biggest breakdown of any sensible character values, as vague as this may seem today, occurred in the 1960's. This period of the Blackman's life signalled a change in his priority schedule and a reorganization of traditional and basic social practices. Little beknownst to him, the 1960's also provided him with the last platform he would ever have to design plans to ensure he and his family of having a prosperous and praiseworthy future. And he blew it.

His children today, especially the sons of these Blackmen, have never been told about what happened during that time, or of the political and permanent ramifications of the lifestyle choices made by their parents. It must now be explained to them so they can understand how and why the Blackman wound up in his current condition. These same sons must start a tradition of holding each previous generation of Blackmen accountable for their collective efforts towards progress and survival. They ought to examine any previous mistakes and focus on improving those areas. It is pointlessly futile for each oncoming generation to have to start back at square one trying to repair the exact, or worse, conditions endured by their predecessors. None of the problems are new, yet no evaluation is ever made on the feasibility of the typical solutions used to better the overall quality of life for African-American peoples. The reason this has never been done is due to the disunity among Blackmen from coast to coast. This has kept them stuck in the stage of bickering about who, what, when, where and how. They haven't addressed the commonality of obstacles that all Blacks face daily.

The early 1960's are chosen as a starting point of error for Blackmen because it was during this era when all Americans, white and non-white, were embroiled in issues inspiring tremendous emotional upheavals in personalities and lifestyles. New ideas surfaced at frightening speed and new trends developed almost daily. Whites were busy tussling with the police in the streets rebelling against the Vietnam War, they had publicly discovered drugs and sex, and were showcasing their artistic flower child campaign and organizing on campus to protest for peace. On another level white women were gearing up for the Women's Liberation Movement to struggle against unfair treatment in the workplace, in the home, and in their personal relationships. White men were in an unusual tizzy about their women burning their bras, abandoning the kitchen — and not having their dinner ready when they got home from work. American soldiers were dying in rapid numbers in a war that emerged as making no sense at all, and literally volumes of European values, formerly uncontested, were being replaced with new, sometimes outrageous and often immoral behaviors, supposedly rooted in freeing up the inner-self for the pursuit of individual satisfaction. White boys of draftable age created, for the first time in America, a climate which prompted others to say NO to requests placed upon them by the government and the nation. Their refusal to fight in the Vietnam War represented the first major issue that put the government and the people at odds against each other. The breaking of this tie, and the survival of those who declined to obey, signalled a new option for anyone who preferred to maintain individual choices or opinions about every aspect of daily living. Youth started to reject and refuse many of the values their parents had maintained throughout their entire life. It was a new day.

24

The Civil Rights Movement, such as it was called, began exploding. Blackmen sprouted voices and long suppressed complaints were finally noisily announced. Several surfaced as makeshift bargain basement leaders expounding new theories of action to obtain rights and benefits of living in America. White women and girls commenced to join the civil rights protests and for the first time functioned in close intimate contact openly with Blackmen. Their presence drew the attention of the Blackman and interracial sexual involvements milked much of their energy and reduced their anger at "all" whites considerably. His expanding ideas incorporated his wardrobe, too. In the grass-root units they began to wear African symbols while others adopted the absurd flair of "Superfly" (a popularized fictional Black pimp). They sported the Afro hairstyle (a kind of rounded bouffant look), and danced to good music in a flurry of new nightclubs and social spots. The excitement was kept aflame with new words like "honky," and "pigs," echoing from the parched throats of Blackmen. Other words contained demands for freedom and justice and equality. He also beckoned for recognition, integration, and acceptance. He did not know that the difference between those two sets of requests were as opposite as night and day.

Blackmen were creating their own stimuli to help them throw off the yoke of racism and self-incrimination they had slept with for over 100 years. The revolutionary mobs roaming the streets inciting spontaneous ghetto rebellions rewarded him with T.V. sets, stereos, couches, lamps and other items captured by vandalizing local merchant businesses — all of which were blamed on racism. President John F. Kennedy sent the first troops to Vietnam which turned out to be a bottomless pit demanding thousands of recruits shipped daily to feed its fury. The anti-war protests were staged mostly by college age white males who didn't want to fight.

Blackmen hungrily bit into new ideas and swallowed morsels and tidbits of principles and attitudes taken from several sources existing as new options. The uninterrupted ability to make these choices created in him a sort of cultural shock. He was emotionally set free, not psychologically, but emotionally. He was free to feel any kind of reaction about a variety of standards and responsibilities — plus — he could act on his choices, and he could endorse or abstain on any situation he encountered. Many European establishments let him in and it was likened to being turned loose in Disney World — the wonders of an integrated society never ceased. He dove in and his woman and children followed. Few of them realized that the decisions they were on the brink of making would stifle their development and progress for untold years to follow. He chose to carve himself out a new identity, one forged out of the new freedoms the white people were experimenting with, and one based on the expected benefits the civil rights leaders had promised would be forthcoming. From that moment, and at every juncture since, he established no national agendas or formats to involve the masses of Blacks in united progress. He virtually regressed, and reacted as his ancestors did during a big slavery breakout — the slaves scattered — in all different directions to become absorbed into existing lifestyles, and blend in with the scenery. So they all went in different directions to pursue disconnected unrelated self-survival goals. No thoughts or plans were given to the future and they were woozy with the hallucinations created by the slight improvements generated by the Civil Rights Movement, and believed that many of their grievances were settled, in the process of being settled, or would fade away in due time. Based on this kind of faulty, pie-in-the-sky, promised land misinterpretation, the Blackman selected one of the following paths:

1) Went to college or trade school and pursued education.

2) Joined the Civil Rights industry.

3) Signed up for the military, went to Vietnam or travelled.

4) Accepted a position to work inside the system.

5) Became an outspoken political leader of the times.

6) Aligned himself with one of the popular ethnic organizations.

7) Became an artist, poet, actor or entertainer.

8) Got high, dropped out completely, or turned to crime.

9) Developed a lifestyle firmly rooted in the imaginary benefits of social integration.

10) Built a life based on the rules, traditions, and values of European culture and became an ordinary Joe, an unconcerned Negroid.

The results of these choices are as follows:

1) *Pursuit of Education*

Blackmen who chose educational pursuit or entrepreneurship have faired moderately well. They prepared themselves to qualify to apply for better paying jobs which provided them with hospitalization, life insurance, retirement plans and a routine work schedule of paychecks. Others formed their own businesses and laid the foundation for the development of hair products, publications, funeral homes, insurance agencies and law and medical professions. They became examples of achievement, overcame barriers and delved deeply into qualifying themselves to be at that time what was known as "a credit to his race." Still others worked in professional capacities for white-owned firms and delivered to them the finest ideas and creativity that the Black mind could conceive. They established a system of class distinction among other Blacks, a separation based on high earnings called the upper class or well-to-do families. They felt completely removed from the problems and concerns of the less qualified Blacks they left behind. Many of them are quite surprised today to learn that so much time has passed and they have so little to show for it. Because of their imitation of success according to European prerequisites they alienated themselves and lost their identities on another level. They started to believe that they were just a person and equal to any other person — no matter what color. They took up tennis, skiing, boating, bridge and private social clubs.

2) *Joined the Civil Rights Industry*

These Blackmen soared high in the public eye for quite a while. They were portrayed as charging warriors working on the front line for desegregation of public facilities, sexual integration and social reform. They received many spotlights for their involvements and were always happy to prove their bravery during protests and took pride in announcing their arrests. They were fiery speakers, available spokespersons and delighted in outlining political strategies to reach their goals. They played on the emotionalism of the people, white and Black, and believed that if Blacks were permitted to infiltrate white owned businesses, industry, education and neighborhoods; that they would prove themselves qualified to function on every other level. They thought that the removal of the above barriers and unencumbered entrance into the gateways of white American life would allow Blacks to be accepted as equals. They sought employment and personal involvement with whites, and agreed that voting rights were the major key to Blacks' future security in the U.S.A. Today, Blackmen who fostered these ideas as a platform to become a national leader, are few in number. Many have disappeared due to death, burn-out, ego damage brought on by rejection, or their eventual failure to convince whites, either through the courts or fervor filled dialogue, that Blacks deserved special attention and favors. They aligned themselves with President John Kennedy and his brother, Bobby. But soon their scripts ran out, public attention waned and their presence became unwelcome. Many went on to organize national agencies founded on loosely related principles of the Civil Rights Movement, and these, too, ultimately faded from powerlessness and their inability to reinspire the desperate displays of emotion required to maintain their platforms. They are rarely even mentioned anymore. One or two remain as representative of the entire group. They, too, are disappointed. They grew few permanent fruits from their labors. The benefits they pleaded for are today found to be lacking in helping Blacks attain food, clothing and shelter. But they did make it possible for Blacks to spend their money in any white owned establishment they please.

3) *Joined the Military*
Back in the day joining the "service" appeared as an honorable option for many Blackmen. They were raised to be patriotic so going off to fight in a war they were told would defend their country and maintain their democratic way of life, appealed to their need to be responsible for getting a job done. It also gave them an opportunity to take training courses, prove their physical abilities and work as a team with other men. They perceived the military as a gigantic masculine club where they could compete, shoot guns, travel, meet women, earn pay, send a stipend home, gain Veteran's benefits, medical care, extra points on civil service tests, V.A. loans, college grants — and of course, the special pride of wearing their uniform to church, and walking around in their neighborhoods. It additionally provided them with a process which they had to qualify to go through, and earn recognition and respect for passing various tests in a man's domain — the war. Some protested the war in

Vietnam while others praised their involvement, and if they survived, came home bragging about their war conquests. If they had any doubts about their citizenship before they went in, by the time they came out of boot camp they were true Americans, firm in their inclusion as being useful, needed and trained. Military practice included skilled mastery of their weapons and duties which gave them confidence in their ability to fight for their country. As usual, for many Blackmen, military service further alienated them from their true nature, culture and character. They had to become unified with American ideals in order to enlist, and they had to be totally mentally committed beyond testable doubt of their allegiance to ol' Glory and all it stood for. They also saw participation in the war as a way to prove they were willing to join forces with white boys and fight for the country they all loved. Today, those who suffered near mortal injury have their aching disabilities to remind them of that involvement. Some wound up mentally ill due to shell shock or Agent Orange. Others bound by encapsulated memories of the vivid horrors of war just never recovered from the ordeal. The Blackman found that he did not have the killing nature of their Anglo-saxon comrades, and were not accustomed to destroying people who had not personally offended them. Initially they tried, as they had been trained, to view the Viet Cong as evil and a threat to their free way of life. But soon they concluded that the war was unorganized and that they were being shoved to the front lines and promptly being killed. The Blackman had never as a group ever been mad enough to fight anybody — less known a yellow man who lived on the other side of the world. And they also realized that racial prejudice, segregation and rejection based on his color was thriving strong and well in the military ranks. He became disillusioned and his disillusionment contributed to the internal strife already brewing among the negro troops and his objections, not necessarily to the Vietnam War, but to his presence in it, eventually got him expelled or dismissed accused of cowardice. His next surprise came when he got back home, and after a quick flurry of praise and center attention from his neighborhood cronies, and the rapt attention he received from his family while reciting war stories; things went back to normal. He couldn't find work, he had bad dreams of guilt and his mind kept returning to war scenes where his own fear had made him shudder, retch from bile in his throat, or lose control of his bowels. He felt angry and

29

used. Uncle Sam had let him down. He was out of sync with the times and people got tired of hearing the same stories over and over. He was disappointed. The war had taken complete control of his mind and body and would take him years to recover. Thousands lost their lives or limbs. The Vietnam War started in about 1969 and lasted approximately 15 years. President Lyndon B. Johnson inherited it from President Kennedy after he was assassinated but it remained an undeclared war. The government never wanted to admit it but America lost that war. The negative public opinion about the war from American citizens at home deprived the new veterans of any special help they might have received, and the silent majority just wanted to forget the war and the soldiers who they had heard had killed innocent women and children. All mothers of draftable age sons were furious with the government for killing their boys in a useless cause they didn't understand.

4&5) *Acceptance of Politically Affiliated Jobs in the System*
Some Blackmen took advantage of their new attention and became involved in the political systems existing in the halls of government. They believed that their political views would permit them to be instrumental in making and passing laws to help Black people. They figured out how to qualify in local, state and federal politics and invaded the White House. Politics gave them a place to vent their opinions, allowed them to be included in social affairs connected to their party, and gave them a stage to perform on. On local levels Blackmen were rumored to have been "bought" out of the grassroots or militant struggle by being offered a high-paying job or some other leadership position in one of the newly-formed agencies designed for Blacks under the Anti-Poverty Act. They accepted community posts where they operated job training programs, distributed goods and services, housing, day care, free clinics, parks, pools, school improvements, playgrounds and other outreach programs. These institutions were actually feeble post-riot attempts to be reparations of a sort to make up to Blacks for the many denials recently pointed out during the civil unrest. Having a steady paycheck proved to be a soothing balm to the wounds of racism and silenced a lot of loud mouths who cancelled on complaining to spend their new money. Some of them worked in these anti-poverty programs for years, the names of the jobs often changed depending on the administration in office. These jobs were filled

by the educated and the uneducated, conservatives, moderates and liberals — among Blackmen. As the popularity of civil disobedience waned, the effectiveness of the Blackmen leaders subsided and they unexpectedly collided with new Federal or State administrators who cancelled funding based on new studies they claimed proved that their jobs were a sham and hadn't really improved the quality of life for the people they were appointed to serve. Their clientele became ungrateful and demanding, and comfortably dependent on the free services they thought would last forever. Blackmen placed in charge of such programs had a wide variety of individual control over the operation of their sites. Many of them were not really qualified to be CEO's and their lack of expertise shortly slumped them into boredom and they began to view their jobs as just an easy way to rip off the system and earn some easy money. Others learned how to file for grants, understand line items and received budgeted sums to implement their community ideas. Later when they became embittered about being fired, they ceased any efforts to help the people entrusted to their care due to disappointment in the striving human spirit they believed existed in "the people." They found out that "the people" were lazy, ungrateful, vindictive and greedy — and the furthest thing from their minds was becoming free and independent if they had to give up their entitlements. There was much panic and scrambling for the last minute morsels of government jobs. Some of these Blackmen went on to City Hall, City Council and Mayorships, Congressional Reps and other political service oriented jobs. The Blackman had become confident in his ability to negotiate with whites. Today, the storm clouds crouching on the horizon threatens the removal or disqualification of Blackmen candidates from all high ranking posts. It is unspokenly assumed by the power structure that they (Blackmen) had their chance, their clear-cut opportunity, including special recognition and fame; and yet they did not lighten the welfare rolls, nor teach their constituents self-sufficiency, a better attitude or respect for government. Instead they had become hooked on a cycle of dependency criss-crossing two and three generations sometimes in the same household, they had no guaranteed loyalty to any particular party or candidate and were insatiable for free services and benefits. Blackmen know by now that the government is incapable of regulating laws to solve social problems such as racism. This is a hard reality.

31

They have not been able to love or legislate racism away. Being a Blackman politician, once slippery and fluid, has now frozen into a solid block of icy refusals for everything they suggest as a help-out Blacks idea. They had come from the pulpits and the schools but they are denouncing their involvement and retiring to the private sector to have some peace.

6) *Joined Ethnic Organizations*
Throngs of Blackmen filled with the new thrilling desire to be pro-Black joined or created unique organizations for *Blacks only*, so they could come together to celebrate their newly acquired acceptance. These were Blackmen who were decidedly too militant in their thinking to join what they viewed as weak, jelly roll, 'Uncle Tom' factions such as the N.A.A.C.P. or S.C.L.C. who were quite moderate by comparison. Those Blackmen sought out groups with strong masculine influence which contained activities allowing them to vent their frustration by addressing their grievances in positive action. A few signed up with the Black Panther Party, a notoriously defiant group consisting of young men who weren't afraid to retaliate against white police agitators whom they said invaded their neighborhoods harassing the residents. The Panthers were indicative of the growing impatience of the Blackman. Their terroristic threats against the U.S. government helped furnish the emotional fuel needed for white women to sign up for gun and rifle training — allegedly to protect themselves from Blackmen who might somehow invade the suburbs. The Black Panthers made military training in vigorous guerrilla warfare the main thrust of their organization. This included weaponry, self-defense, drilling, surveillance and protective services for their communities. They developed a ten-point program outlining their demands called the "Black Panther Manifesto." They claimed their members were level headed and almost drug-free, and they tested the right of citizens to bear arms by marching around openly with high-powered rifles slung over their shoulders. The Panthers fell into budget problems and were trapped into accepting some of the free flowing anti-poverty money being poured into African-American communities across the country. The raw bravery compressed in their units created large numbers of loose cannon egos eager to make their mark and prove their greatness. Their clumsy military notions and faulty logistics landed them in many confrontations with the law —

whom they called "pigs." After many internal clashes, outside conspiracies, and bloodshed from brutal police attacks, they disbanded. Prior to their end they decided to integrate their ranks to include white radical liberationists and change their policy from anti-racism to a class struggle — the poor against the rich. All of the Blackmen heading up the Panthers retired in shame or embarrassment. But the Panthers made an impressive sight in their Black tams and red and black uniforms. They provided many Blackmen with an outlet to practice leadership and obedience, gave them a home base, a place to belong and a chance to confirm their identity as strong brave warriors always ready to die for their cause. They should have been ready to live for it. Their tragedy was in using all their energies to be combative and abandoning their original precepts — they couldn't stay unified but they made awkward attempts to involve children in their activities to teach and train them for a war they were confident was being waged by their oppressor — the white power structure.

The Black college campuses were alive and bursting with student protests. Other Blackmen opted to join the Nation of Islam, a stable appearing religious organization who called themselves Black Muslims. They were most powerfully rooted in Chicago, Detroit, Philadelphia and New York. The Muslims eliminated any concepts that God was white, gave up their "slave" name and received an "X," refrained from eating pork, formed Black-owned businesses, respected Blackwomen and obeyed moral codes. They offered Blackmen a chance to be independent, said they wanted separation from whites, and taught the Blackman that his real God was Black, named Allah, and that their leader was His last messenger to the people. Charges of racial hatred directed towards whites and mumblings about Black supremacy frightened off many Blacks and kept them from joining the group. The Muslims were against social integration and strived to teach Blackmen to be independent and clean living. Other, slightly popular, but not as prominent as the aforementioned organizations were:

    The Student Non-Violent Coordinating Committee (SNCC)
    Students for a Democratic Society (SDS)
    Congress of Racial Equality (CORE)
    Uhuru Movement
    Group on Advanced Leadership (GOAL)
    Freedom Now Party (FNP)

United Black Nationalists of America (UBNA)
The New Pan-African Movement (TNPAM)
The National Urban League (NUL)
Committee on Racial and Religious Progress (CORARP)

There were many local community based organizations not listed here.

7) *The Arts*

Blackmen choosing the arts as painters, poets, actors or entertainers enjoyed a brief but fertile period of special notoriety and success. Black art became avant garde, such anger had never been expressed in any medium. Following was the African clothing, boldly colored fabrics, headwraps, kufis, flags, buttons, clenched fist items, sandals, wood carvings, statues and all kinds of cultural paraphernalia for the masses. Blackmen sported pullover shirts called "dashikis" — allegedly fashioned after African garbs but really manufactured by the Japanese. They "took" African names, some too difficult to pronounce making the titles short-lived. After a few years fashion trends changed, the dashikis faded, they got haircuts, put their shoes and socks back on and got a job someplace. Few pieces of their original art work is available today.

Many of their poetic rantings served to gain enough attention from elite white liberals to get them invited to their social affairs for readings. Many times they provided the entertainment for the evening and permitted whites to relieve themselves of some of their capitalistic guilt by sitting quietly in rapt attention while a Blackman stood on the podium blaming, cursing and insulting whites for their racist genocidal behaviors. It was a weird set but many Blackmen provided this special service to interested whites. For a while many of their poems, plays or short stories were included in African-American history classes on the university level but were restructured somewhat.

Blackmen who selected the entertainment industry got an opportunity to act on television in a few minor roles, and briefly starred in many new wave Black themed movies mostly about drugs, thugs, prostitution, pimps, illegal activities, outlandish monsters, kung-fu or sweet daddy roles. Blackwomen were the first allowed to penetrate television, and it was later that Blackmen garnered roles which portrayed them as intelligent contributing human beings in realistic viable positions. Many turned to comedy, singing and dancing. Blackmen created and named many popular dances mimicked nationwide. They wrote and performed songs and musical pieces and were featured on television on rock-n-roll shows or specials. Their tunes made the rhythm and blues charts and they enjoyed immense popularity which they were grossly underpaid for. Much of their material was stolen or purchased for only a few dollars — because they needed the money or opted to get their work published even if not owned by themselves. But they were spectacular when on stage and screen. There emerged a few major Black owned record companies who tried to control their section of the industry — Black music. They worked hard but it was the white board members of the music industry who decided who would be promoted, have their records distributed or played on the radio. Whites were in charge of exposure — marketing. Nevertheless, Blackmen sung about love, finding love, lost love, mighty love, wrong love, hot love, needed love, sunshine, bushes and birds. Anything they could rhyme and set to music. They appealed to their lovelorn listeners and melodized every aspect of heartbreak. They saw no need to sing about their African roots. But they enjoyed the success of being what Blacks referred to as "nigger rich," which is a temporary conditional period of having control of large sums of money and material possessions mostly by those who are not used to having any. Many of these now old-timers have tried to hang on clinging to their standard subjects and tunes but most have disappeared from the popular charts. Some of their music is being used as the background sound for other artists who talk poems.

8) *Drugs, Prison & Society Drop-outs*
Naturally, not all Blackmen picked sensible lifestyles grounded in legality. Some got strung out on drugs like heroin which was most popular at the time. A few dabbled in LSD, a hallucinatory drug, used speed or smoked pot (marijuana). The more elite snorted cocaine in their private sets. Everybody experimented with drugs but some got addicted and declined in productivity becoming the street animals foraging for money to get their "fix." Blackmen used heroin intravenously or snorted it, roughing out the terrible stomach pains to get to the high. The more industrious ones sold the drug itself, had big fine "hogs," elaborate wardrobes, hostels of fancy women (Black and white), and lived surrounded by other Blackmen who served as

their flunkies. They had flashy jewelry and sponsored many immoral parties. These Blackmen considered Blackmen not involved in the slick life as "square" or "green." They made little permanent progress despite all the money they handled, as they were not the least bit concerned about preserving Black culture, pride or social advancement. They lived in a gritty underground world of their own. They dragged many wayward Blackwomen into their mire of filth, yet these were the types of Blackmen portrayed as heroes or role models for younger Black males in what the critics termed as trendy "Blaxploitation" films. The pimps and drug dealing Blackmen were featured as mighty cool, sharp dressers who did whatever they wanted to do regardless of how "the man" (white police) felt. Their behavior and fashions were imitated by adult Blackmen of that time who tried to dress, walk, or talk like the drug dealing pimps on the screen.

Still others tried to get away with committing various crimes like robbery, shoplifting, thuggery, shooting or murdering people — 99% of whom were Black. Many got caught and were awarded stiff prison sentences for their errors in crime. They received jail sentences far outweighing the nature of their crimes, but their tentative guilt and absence of strong legal counsel landed them in prison for many years, many to never be heard from again. They rioted in prison to express their support of the civil rights movement on the streets, or organized against prison mismanagement of human life, mainly Black male inmates. Blackmen studied religion in prison and chose the Black Muslim doctrine because of their disappointment with the white controlled judicial system. Their absence from the community in great and large numbers prevented them from being contributing supportive workers, husbands and fathers. Prison was much worse in those days according to respondents. Their aberrant behavior helped to portray and identify Blackmen as dangerous savages who must be isolated from the working public. Their vast numbers in jail implied that they were violent law breakers and made others suspicious of the whole lot of them. Some were shot, killed or unmercifully beaten by police when caught doing wrong. There was not much interest in Blackmen in prison and many Blacks felt they got what they deserved for breaking the law. Blackmen police seemed extremely hard on Blackmen perpetrators to prove to their white co-officers their dedication to law and order — no matter what color.

9&10) *Developed a Lifestyle Rooted in Social and Sexual Integration*

These Blackmen involved themselves with seeking ways to integrate socially and be the "first" negro to accomplish certain goals. They decided that it doesn't matter what color a person is, and all they wanted was a chance to prove themselves and to be left alone to do their own thing. They became the regular hard working apolitical Joe Blow or John Doe. They got a job, got married, reared a family, went to church, enjoyed an occasional night out, went on vacation, voted, and did the best they could to be unnoticed and fit in with society as best they could. Or so they thought. They kept a ready smile for whites even if they hated them in their private circle of friends, they did their best to please their bosses and taught their children not to be prejudiced. They might support the NAACP and believed in much of Martin Luther King's program. They celebrated all holidays and were not concerned with preserving Black culture other than attending family reunions. They exerted no effort to identify themselves as anything other than colored or negro. It didn't matter in that way. They coined the saying: "the good Lord made us all." They sent their children to church to pray to a white God, bought their daughters white dolls and watched their sons play cowboys and Indians, the good guys and the bad. He hung pictures and portraits of caucasians in his home — mainly John or Bobby Kennedy. The Jesus picture on his wall seemed to have eyes that followed you around the room — no matter where you stood. If a Blackman was included it was Dr. Martin Luther King — after his death. Otherwise it was okay with him if white families appeared on his yearly calendar that hung visibly in his home 365 days year after year. And his full-color Bible contained several pages of holy white people in various settings in the holy land. Many felt at odds with the mothers of their children and were not on hand to help raise or train them. And when they did see their children they did not talk about being Black, Africa, culture or what it takes to be a good Blackman. They expressed no opposition to what their sons were being taught in school or at home. They left child rearing mostly to the mothers, the schools and the church. They felt no compulsion or obligation to reinforce old outdated unimportant Black history stories. They themselves had long since disregarded all that Black stuff. Things have not changed much.

It was during this period that Blackmen planted the idea that they (Blackmen) wanted to be judged and accepted on their individual merits, and not counted with or included with other Blackmen. They did not realize that psychologically that this mode of thinking would isolate and separate them even further from identifying with each other or acknowledging their brotherhood rooted in coming from the same background and nationality. They commenced to do everything they could to convince whites that they were "different" and not like "the rest of them." They made a public call for disavowment of each other and released all bonds, and claimed no connection or responsibility for the actions and behaviors of other Blackmen. The house negro and the field negro had come to their final parting.

On examination of the ten major choices that broadly describe the lifestyle selections made by Blackmen 30-45 years ago, it is clear that few of their choices fostered retention of Black culture nor reinforcement of African values or traditions. No guidelines were developed or substantiated from one generation to the next. It is incredulous for the Blackman to now expect his son to respect or love their Blackness, or to be conscious of what their foreparents endured — since he did not teach it to him. Deeper analogy of this crucial oversight is detailed in other chapters. This brief conspectus is only a primary dissection to demonstrate how each lifestyle choice the Blackman made 30 years ago moved him further and further away from opportunities to establish a definite positive identity for himself. And he has been floundering since that time trying to settle on a description of who he is. And everybody else is waiting to find out, too.

It is time to look at the original tactics used to manipulate him into forgetting his identity during his initial enslavement.

During a time when he was treated as a prisoner of war (without the Geneva Convention), the slavemaster used a two level process to force the Blackman into developing amnesia so he could be a tool for labor.

The first level consisted of:

1) *Physical Trauma*
A ploy implemented by long term, uncomfortable transport by ship across the ocean in cramped, overcrowded, inhumane

corridors below deck where he was stacked like sardines and left to sleep in his own excrement.

2) *Disorientation*
The ships took him to a land geographically unfamiliar to him containing foliage, wildlife and a climate he was not accustomed to. And it was far, far away, many days and nights.

3) *Hostility*
He was treated badly, disrespected, rough-handled, chained and rendered helpless — and then forced to watch the brutalization of his mother, his woman and his children.

The second level, a more devastating one, consisted of:

4) *He was prevented from speaking his own language.*
Languages are sounds used to transmit and receive information, to reflect the intensity of ideas, express history, and describe things indigenous to a particular people. Prohibiting his language stopped Blackmen from communicating with each other and broke ties.

5) *His name was changed.*
The slavemaster insisted on renaming his charges according to his own whims, ignoring their given names. It was important to impress upon the Blackman that he was no longer the same person so he was given a new identity in a new land with new status as a slave.

6) *The slavemaster abolished his religion.*
His God concept was taken from him to prevent him from receiving comfort or calling on his own Lord for help. His God was replaced with the whiteman's God — another whiteman who was more powerful and currently in charge of him. Religious authority was redistributed by changing it from Black to white.

This is not new information. Practically all Blackmen know that their ancestors were stripped of their names and religion while in slavery. But the reclaiming of these two important identifying features has never been paramount enough for him to address the issue on a national agenda. The question becomes how can he re-establish his own culture or define his own identity while still clutching the European labels forced on him during his enslavement? It is irrational thinking for the Blackman to continue to bellyache about his real identity without investigating what his real identity was before he was enslaved and returning to it.

The only part of his cultural traditions the slavemaster allowed him to keep and maintain was sport and play under the auspices of:

1) Singing and dancing
2) Games and sport competitions
3) Making jokes and playing the fool

These are the three components that are now looked upon as skills that Blackmen specialize in to a fault. They are activities for which he is best known, and most sought after for today. He is acclaimed an expert in these categories, and they gain him recognition, earn him the most money, and make him the most admired. He can be found exhibiting these attributes for a fee or for free in front of whatever audience is available. He is accustomed, in certain circles, to being called upon to do his little dance, tell his little joke, or demonstrate his physical proficiency in some sort of challenge. He takes pride in being singled out or requested to show off his special talents. He is sometimes known for being the ambassador of clowning, the chairman of laughing at his ownself, and the president of general tom-foolery. He delights in some people referring to him by saying "that nigger is crazy" or "you are so funny," or "you crazy." Sadly, when he responds, he is. He thinks that it is all in fun, but the biggest joke is on him because it keeps other adults from taking him seriously. It is futile to convince him of this. These actions proliferate a behavior he perfected during slavery to stay on his master's good side. Unfortunately, this behavior is also part of his identity today.

Currently the Blackman refuses to give up the names the slavemaster saddled their family with. So his identity remains clouded by names connected to other nationalities from all over Europe. He insists that his name is now his own. And as long as he keeps his European name he will continue to grow away from the so-called Black culture he claims he is so proud of and desires to return to.

Another unique aspect of his name problem is that Blackmen, especially those claiming to be versed and trained in psychology, have not investigated or reported on the significance of the Blackman carrying a whiteman's name, or how it affects his mental status. Black male psychologists are remiss as scientists due to their collective refusal to bring attention to the negative psychodynamics inherent in taking a man's name and religion from him. The Blackman's ego derives its energy and motivation from identifiable points of basic reference — such as by the name one is called by or answers to. They have failed to address the virtual impossibility of the Blackman reclaiming his cultural roots while maintaining and protecting the very symbols and systems used against him to control his body and mind during slavery.

The slave system was a very well planned and thought out process which contained no useless motions or insignificant techniques. So if the main possessions taken from the Blackman was his name and his religion — obviously they are the most crucial elements that have the greatest influence on a man's mentality, strength and confidence.

Blackmen use the following excuses for holding on to their European names:

1) A name is not important, it's what you do that counts.

2) It doesn't matter what they call me, just give me a chance.

3) Some are too embarrassed or ashamed to announce to their friends, family or white counterparts that they are reclaiming their own historically Black names.

4) They don't want to go through the rejection or mockery from family or friends (especially from their mothers and their women), who may refuse to refer to them by their new name and make mockery of them.

5) They think changing their names will be disrespectful to their parents who gave them the name at birth, possibly they are even named after a now deceased popular relative.

6) The idea of informing their church, club, co-workers or children and mailman of their new name is an overwhelming thought to them — they are apprehensive about the resistance they expect to encounter from all of these groups.

7) They don't want to cause a problem on their jobs by informing their white bosses or the personnel office of their new name or why they changed it.

8) They are emotionally connected to their name having been taught that it is their "Christian name."

9) They don't know how to change their name and think it will ruin their credit or cause them problems with the I.R.S.

10) They don't know any African or Arabic names.

What they don't know is that American laws do not prevent or oppose an individual from changing their name. It is relatively simple and inexpensive to do. A name change does not interfere with records on file at the credit bureau or post office or library. All one has to do is inform all of the people he does business with. Changing one's name will not cause problems with the I.R.S. because the social security number remains the same, as does the driver's license number, voter registration, or any other numerical code or symbol connected to the individual. The only change that takes place is a psychological one, inside the Blackman himself. A part of his self-pride returns as he signs and answers to the name of his forefathers. Correcting his name serves as a reminder, a bond, an attachment with his glorious pre-slavery ancestors.

Public proof of the Blackman's intentional disconnection and subsequent rejection of his Black name was internationally demonstrated when famous author Alex Haley presented his *ROOTS* book in the late 1970's. Haley, an expert writer and historian, embarked on a lifelong project of tracing his personal family tree all the way back to Africa. In 1976-77 he delivered up his findings in both book and movie form for which he gained worldwide acclaim. The movie *ROOTS* achieved the highest Black viewership in the history of television. Haley's study served to provoke other African-Americans into tracing their own family histories. All well and good. But what happened after Haley completed his research exemplifies and validates charges against the Blackman for denying his past and rejecting himself.

Mr. Haley spent all that time and energy, invested a tidy sum of money, and became consumed day and night for many years with his project to trace his family to their pre-slavery existence. He wrote vividly about his findings and then allowed them to be cinematized as a documentary starring major Black actors. One of the most moving heart rendering scenes was when Alex Haley finally meets the living proof of his lineage. He traced his source to Kunta Kinte. *Kinte* was his family's *real* name. Haley's book depicted scenarios where Kunta Kinte was forced to give up his name and religion by the slavemasters who captured him. Despite all this proof, Alex Haley returned to America as Alex Haley, and still today answers to the name of Alex Haley. How can that be? Here is the one Blackman in America who knows for an actual fact that his *real* name is Kinte and not

Haley, yet continues, after gaining full knowledge of his past, to hold on to the name he knows was forced on his family during slavery. This issue has never come up nor has he ever been questioned about it. Alex Haley set a very bad example for Black youth because he was in a prime position to demonstrate the act of reclaiming his *real* family name. It would have impacted on Black youth and Black adults all over the country, and reminded them that the names they have are not their own. But Haley did not accept his *real* name and other Blackmen did not think it odd. He blew an opportunity to set a precedence on the importance of re-embracing Black kinship for freedom. Haley has also continued to practice the Christian faith after finding out that his family's original religion was Islam. By doing all this he is a perfect example of how the Blackman, even on discovery with absolute proof of his real identity, refuses to reclaim his own. Haley's findings survive as one of the most important historical studies that Blacks have ever had access to. However, his findings have not made one iota of difference in what Blacks believe in or what they do. His documentation should have, under normal intellectual awareness, been required reading for discussion by every Black child every year that they attend school. But it is not. And *ROOTS* has all but been forgotten. And the beat goes on. Toby survived.

The Blackman has incessantly failed at establishing a sensible, dignified, respectable identity for himself because he has been trying to do this without taking into account his special history of coming to America and the fact that he was not a voluntary immigrant. He will routinely fail to recognize his Black culture as long as he keeps trying to mix slavery and freedom to establish his identity, or come up with a workable plan out of those two opposing forces. Without taking back their names and their religion they will never reconnect with the past. Any other plan will continue to be a waste of time and end in failure — as usual. He must restore his own image in his brain.

Caucasian boys grow up surrounded by and, in some cases, bombarded by the accomplishments of his ancestors. The white male child knows from a very early age that he is most important because nearly everywhere he looks he sees an image of himself. Every holiday, every celebration, every major event evolves around him and the people who look and act like him. All the history he studies throughout his entire life is about his forefathers who look like him. White parents would not ever consider raising their children completely surrounded exclusively by religious images, holidays or historical feats that featured only African-Americans, Hispanics or Asians. Never in a million years. But the Blackman has allowed his children to be reared on a steady diet of pictures, symbols and information about other nationalities. And he must be held accountable for creating the damaging climate of destruction his brethren are now experiencing due to his blindness. It is his fault that the Blackman's survival is in peril. He did not lead his tribe in the right direction and now that they are lost he wants to blame others for their bewilderment.

Another way Blackmen attempt to reclaim their culture is by joining a club or organization such as the Masons or a fraternity. These are the most popular units which Blackmen think provides them with a special identity linked to their Black past.

The Masonic Orders have a very involved set of secret signs, symbols and practices allegedly known only to the brothers in the club. These days there are no such secrets, however, the internal workings and rituals are so complicated that they will not be fully divulged here. Loosely, the Masons, Elks or Shriners are actually social type agencies which host many elite affairs and generally raise money to donate to service agencies or selected charities. They do good work and have a good time doing it. They wear identifying uniforms such as tall fezzes with tassels, have special jewelry such as rings, pendants or lapel pins imprinted with their emblems or other symbols relating to their secret union. They have intense rituals for admission, hand and finger signs that supposedly help them negotiate in court or when stranded on the highway in distress. Their premise has something to do with biblical characters like Hiram Abiff trying to get somebody up out of a grave whose body is already decomposed. They have cornerstones, temples and pyramids along with hot desert sand and swords, half-moons and rulers. They reportedly earn certain "degrees" of knowledge by submitting themselves to a few internally devised ceremonies wherein they receive bits and pieces of information at each step. They pay hefty dues, are respected for their unity and meet periodically in groups consisting of Black males only. This is a good aspect of their membership because it places Blackmen routinely alone together to talk amongst themselves.

The second most popular organization Blackmen take pride

in are fraternities which they usually join up with in college and retain their members throughout the rest of their adult lives. Fraternity means brotherhood — they say. And Blackmen who belong to a fraternity are considered prime stock. They identify themselves by using Greek language and symbols for the names of their groups, this is supposedly remotely similar to hieroglyphics of Egypt and the Nile River in Africa. Fraternities represent another attempt by Blackmen to formulate him an identity achieved by going through certain rites and rituals designed to gain him acceptance into the brotherhood of men. They call their groups, for example, Alpha Phi Alpha, Kappa Alpha Psi, Psi Beta Sigma or Omega Psi Phi. Their female counterparts have similarly sounding Greek words to identify their participation in the sorority. Fraternities have very lofty and honorable goals for their slogans, they set high standards for membership and vow to work to serve their communities and to better humanity on all fronts. They have their associated symbols which are marketed on caps, hats, t-shirts, sweaters, patches, rings, ties, etc. The items with their logos are nearly infinite. They have special colors assigned to each frat, and are exceptionally proud of their affiliation. They go through a process called pledging, during which they may be required to dress alike, overcome some daring predicament, become servants to the senior members or prove their endurance by standing in a certain spot or completing a difficult feat. Frat brothers have become a bit more brazen in modern times and they have lost some of their class and clout, but they are still considered respectable and special. They put on a good show doing their stomping routines which is a kind of dance and military drill blended together and may feature costumes or wooden canes. They compete with each other to determine who has the best audio, visual and creative stomping routine.

Part of their initiation is to prove they can survive the ceremonial rites of passage. Examples of the rites for fraternities and sororities are:

1) *Tar and Feathering*
They participate in this rite in the nude and actually get tarred and feathered a little, which is supposed to be symbolic of the slave's experience after being recaptured from running away.

2) "The Meal"

They must eat some type of slop or a dish simulated to represent foods the slave was forced to eat to survive.

3) Walking through Fire

This is supposed to be reminiscent of his walking over a hot desert to civilization someplace in Africa. Actual fire is used and the enlistees must prove their sincerity by walking through the fire, sometimes barefoot.

4) Being Lost

Sometimes new recruits are left in a strange place or unfamiliar part of town and must find their way back home with no map or directional tools.

5) Passing Food from Mouth to Mouth

This symbology is related to the slave's need to share some of the same food, often off the same plate. It may be typified by two Blackmen eating off the same bone to emulate the act of sharing – everything with a brother.

Each initiation is designed to promote each member towards self-reliance.   Many African-Egyptian references are used in these pledging ceremonies such as the Sphinx, the Crescent or the Pyramids. With charter goals like service, high moral character, sharing, building, scholarship and respect, they are an honorable clique to belong to.   Their kinship is recognized nationwide and they try to keep in contact at their annual conferences or periodic local meetings.   Fraternities have produced many confident lawyers, doctors, businessmen, politicians and leaders.   They have a clearly defined identity earned by accomplishing goals that serve as rites of passage for transformation into responsible adults.

It is unfortunate that such noble intentions are tainted by them trying to emulate the sufferings of their slavery bound ancestors, instead of their free and powerful forefathers who never arrived on American shores. What they have done is adopted a confusing blend of European, African and African-American historical events and used their conclusions to create rites based on all three stories. Perhaps one day they will explain their reasoning for this. Their rituals contain certain leaps in logic that undermine any real significance they might gain from slavery or pre-slavery existence of Blackmen of old. Blackmen fraternity brothers retain the slavemasters names and are known to be good Americans.

Chapter 3

APPEARANCE

While it is both obvious and accurate to acknowledge that the Blackman is a fine physical specimen of the masculine gender, it is a good idea to study other categories of his appearance such as his wardrobe, his jewelry, his hair styles and his external expression of himself. These factors help determine how he feels about himself, are examples of how he views himself, and contain innuendos regarding what message he is trying to convey to onlookers.

While it can be proven that he has faltered on many of his responsibilities adjacent to his home and related areas, and while it is visibly apparent that he has compromised on his needs and been systematically thwarted by others, there is one part of him that he remains in charge of. That part is his appearance. He has throughout history attempted to dress as together and finely as possible.

To start with, the marketeers and advertising firms have tricked him into being incredibly mislead on the value of fashion. If he can afford to, and if it is at all possible, he will wear the best of available garments. This includes underwear, socks, shirts, leisure tops, slacks, suits, recreational wear, hats, overcoats, sport jackets, ties, scarves, and of course his shoes. Starting with shoes, which also took on an exaggerated importance, he sanctioned the idea that one of the ways a replete man was recognized was by what he wore on his feet. Many of them wear the very best shoes that white shoemakers can design. They may range in price from $75 to $500 depending on the designer name attached to them, the type of leather used, and the level of comfort. Some have all different colors from yellow to green, some with laces or slip-ons. Shoes used to be a very necessary component of the Blackman's wardrobe. They were something he took pride in and a necessity.

As he has become more leisure oriented he has relaxed his shoe requirements. When the shoe industry noted this kind of trend they quickly responded and provided footwear to reflect the mood of a less uptight male. The growing popularity of Blackmen as basketball greats or other public sports figures, from whom many Blackmen and Black boys derive special pleasure from watching and see as heroic, gave the shoe industry an inroad to gaining their attention. So what started out as being called gym shoes are now almost strictly referred to as sneakers, running or tennis shoes. Thus arrived the acceptance of regular day-to-day wearing of gym shoes.

In a societal climate where relaxation has become the major goal, sneakers appear to be the natural foot covering for this transformation. The industry responded by supplying them in all colors, weights and ankle lengths — and attached hefty price tags ranging from $50 to $300, settling on an average of say $75 per pair. The manufacturers assigned certain catchy brand name titles to them, then developed contemporary fast track commercials to advertise them, then dropped a blockbuster whammy of an idea and started labeling the sneakers after names of basketball superstars whom Black males admire. That's all there was to it. This kind of marketing launched the now multi-billion dollar industry of sneaker sales. Practically every Blackman and Black boy owns a pair or several pair. The younger Black males, competitive in spirit, make it a fashion no-no to wear non-brand name sneakers, or to continue to wear them after they become old, worn or soiled. This makes it psychologically necessary not only to wear expensive designer sneakers, but to purchase them frequently so that they always look new. Preferably one would have several pair to match different outfits. Analyzing the sneaker craze on another level, the original design and purpose of sneakers was for exercise, playing sport games, and to ease standing or walking long distances. When the Blackman took to wearing sneakers all day every day, all week throughout all seasons, it placed him in a position to always be ready to play or exhibit informal overly playful behavior. Keeping a Blackman in sneakers ensures that on a moments notice he will be willing to play around or jump or run immaturely. They are a sure sign of recreation. A man who wears hard bottomed shoes is less apt to break into a prance or dance a jig. Hard bottom shoes require the Blackman to walk differently, stand differently, and they bring more seriousness to his motion and decorum. This is why professional businessmen are required to wear standard hard bottom shoes. They are a must requirement in all genuine business, social or religious affairs among civilized well bred adults. The Blackman needs to take off the sneakers and go back to wearing hard bottom shoes. He also needs to give up wearing shorts and running suits in public, and go back to donning slacks or regular pants preferably with a belt. The same goes for the now fashionable slogan t-shirts. Adult Blackmen should set an example of serious manly attire. Sneakers have singlehandedly reduced almost the entire Black male population to behaving like youngsters. If worn they should be used exclusively for recreational activities and then taken off. Wearing hard bottomed shoes is another way to separate the men from the boys. Currently practically all of them look like boys. Yet if anyone refers to him as a "boy" he claims it is the worst insult imaginable. If he establishes a boy's identity for himself then he should not mind being recognized as one.

The Blackman is in a unique position because he has fewer outlets to express his frustrations in than his woman. He can't very well complain of menstrual cramps once a month or get excused for his off-time erratic behavior by blaming it on PMS. He has to handle it 24-7-52 per year. One of the arenas he has used for self-expression of his feeling, his mood, his superiority or rebellion, is his personal appearance. His search for an identity, which was the prominent issue during the 60's, seemingly lead him to the notion that, in agreement with whites who were also seeking a new definition of life at that time, the major inference of consideration was one's obligation to self. He envisioned all of this to mean that he should start having a good time best expressed by his clothes, leisure activities, cars and sports. His self-perception began in his closet. He chose his outer garment body coverings as a tool to portray his self image. Image is the root word for imagination, most manifested by symbols or signs that project a certain idea or impression. Image is a voiceless message. And many of the image messages Blackmen project are visible proof of his scattered ideas and confusing thoughts.

Deeply rooted in his psyche is his pre-American history of being ornate. This is best expressed in the intricately decorated findings of the Chiefs, Queens and other members of royal Black families who decked out in arabesque outfits, and adorned flamboyant jewelry from head to toe. His being an ornamentalist has made him somewhat of a spectacle in many circles. He has a reputation for being intentionally embellished in flashy, conspicuous, high colored outfits. His choice of fancy garbs is something he takes special pride in. He delights in receiving special attention for assembling a conglomeration of pieces that attract stares or admiration from unknown by-standers. He wants to project an image of him that denotes his baroque expert taste and ability to organize a look of exceptional good taste on wardrobe selection. His use of symbols has thrived throughout his existence. As he lost contact with more and more attachment to his past he came to rely almost exclusively on outside means to convey his identity. They do believe that clothes indeed create power. No price is too high, no risk is too great and no mountain is high enough to keep him from getting and wearing a unique piece of clothing. It also gets him extra notice from women who admire such garishness. In all mammals the males who are the most fancily plumed or uniquely endowed receive the most attention from the female population. The Blackman is a natural showoff. And he does it very well. Naturally.

Those Blackmen who are not artificially competitive tend to place less importance on outer appearance. Clothes are just to cover the body to them and they are more embroiled with internal issues. Of course some of them cannot afford to dress as finely as they would prefer. However, even among that unaffected group, there are certain rules that must be followed to ensure a basic measure of acceptance from the Black public. These rules, which no one knows how they originated or who made them up, consist of standards such as:

1) He is not to wear plaids and stripes or polka dots and tweed.
2) He must not wear wide leg pants, or pants without pockets.
3) He, under no circumstances, is to wear no-name sneakers.
4) He must never put on a pair of pants that land above his ankles.

5) He cannot adorn a suit with the wrong size lapels.
6) He should not mix unsimilar shades of colors in random sequence.

These are just examples of the guidelines that are used to measure his public image. Violation of these rules earn him disdain, laughter, mockery, dislike, less consideration, and may cause him to be perceived as unintellectually endowed. It can prevent him from gaining the attention of a woman and imply that he has no style. "Style" is a word used to clarify not only a particular type of clothing but a Blackman's total demeanor. The use of clothing as a symbol to project an image is an ever changing one because the wearer must assume that the person appraising his appearance is aware of whatever the current standard is. A symbolic image is only effective if the definition of the symbol is widely known and practiced. Usually the Blackman creates new definitions for certain symbols. By doing so he subliminally dictates to the fashion industry which slant their designs should lean toward. They occasionally turn a fashion designer's effort into a new creative concept, of how to wear it, or what to wear it with. They set the standard and in many cases define what the season-to-season styles will be. The brand names they revere are routinely the names of white males or reflective of white imagery taken from white experiences.

In refining his image somewhere along the line he developed a positional stance referred to as "cool." "Cool" is explicitly defined by them as:
1) To be able to dress fine and stand absolutely still.
2) Not to become ruffled under pressure.
3) Slow walking, slow talking, low voice or quiet.
4) To proudly be the first to display some outlandish style.
5) Be impeccably dressed and color coordinated all the time.
6) To drive a slick expensive model of car and act unaffected.
7) To stand back from the crowd and not reveal what he is thinking.
8) Be by himself a lot.
9) Keep a noncommittal look on his face and show no emotion.
10) To be very conservative in his lifestyle and clothing selection.

There exists several visible cliques of Blackmen who have affiliated themselves with various religious causes which dictate they wear non-Western attire. If nothing else, they are bold since they go against the fashion grain of what Blackmen usually wear. These men dress in long white or brightly colored gowns or robe-like outfits that are patterned after Eastern fashions. The design of these garments were specifically arrived at by Easterners in warm climates because their light color reflects heat and covers the body loosely for comfort and ventilation. The Blackmen who wear these draping outfits mostly are seen in them in the summer. The fabrics are usually cotton, rayon or a polyester blend to promote coolness. These Blackmen will wear some type of matching baggy pants under their long robe-like tops or they wear regular slacks. Their fashion statement is usually not effectively seen to project their image during the winter because they either have to wear large shawls or capes or a regular western designed overcoat or jacket. This is due to the fact that since these garments are worn in warm eastern climates they do not have matching coats or winterwear for frigid seasons as they do not have any. This also makes wearing sandals in winter counterproductive to providing protection and warmth. The American climate is not really conducive to wearing African styled clothing year round. This presents somewhat of a problem which has not yet been solved by Blackmen who wear these types of clothing. Their desire is to reflect their honorable efforts to dress like their ancestors, and to identify with them by wearing a symbol of their ancient attire. Their outfits are also to project an idea of their Black consciousness and refusal to wear western styled clothing. Their sparse numbers make them a spectacle and it is falsely assumed that if a Blackman is wearing a complete outfit of African or Eastern clothes that he is culturally aware. It is a costume of escape. Many of them wear those outfits to get special attention or to just rebel against the popular norm or to make dressing simpler and more predictable. Some of them are clean and others are shabby looking or soiled.

Ornate by nature, Blackmen also like flashy oversized, attention attracting jewelry if they can obtain or afford it. Big rings, long neck chains, thick linked or bands. Some of them are so impressed with their names or their nicknames as their special identity that they have specially made diamond or gold pieces with their names emblazoned in recognizable lettering.

The standard is that every Blackman who is on top of style must have an admirable piece of jewelry on his person somewhere, and it must be verifiable "real" — meaning it must be gold, silver or contain precious stones like diamonds, rubies or emeralds. On the lower end onyx, carnelian, ivory, agate or amber is acceptable. The more unusual the design or assembly of stones, the more prized the piece is considered to be. They vie with each other to be the most different. They make it a point to not want to own anything similar or just like each other. The younger Black males often do the opposite. They make their alikeness in dress a kind of requirement for acceptance of each other. They perceive their alikeness in wardrobe to signify their unity of ideas about what is "decent' or "all that," which are examples of some of the vernacular they made up themselves to communicate covertly to each other about approved items. Their search for an identity or identifying symbols is a desperate pitiful one. Just like their father's.

The Blackman's hair has also been an accessory to try to establish his identity. Certain groups have always assumed their own haircut style, or beard shape or side-burns. A haircut is very important. Certain jobs they pursue have definite hair style requirements. The most consistent haircut and the one perceivably accepted in the majority of circles he frequents is the closely shaven one with low sides and a small amount on top with possibly a part on either side of his head. This is the conservative choice. However, they have experimented with many other styles like the "process" achieved by a lye-based chemical which straightens their hair and is then indented in rows with designs to simulate waves, possibly a few curls in a pompadour top or just slicked back. They abandoned this one, mostly worn by entertainers, because it was too hard to maintain. They also adopted the "Afro" hairstyle consisting of a wide puffed out circle of hair shaped like a globe. Chemicals and sprays were also developed to maintain this look that they wore to identify themselves as being proud of their formerly disdained nappy or kinky hair. They agreed to voluntarily no longer try to chemically force their hair into looking similar to the straight or fluffy look of white males. Variations of the Afro have survived through the years and are still somewhat accept-able as long as it is not too prominent in length. Blackmen wear braids or dreadlocks, too. Other hairstyles they chose, like the "Jheri curl," consisted of a chemical that artificially made them have curly shiny locks of varying lengths. This hairstyle requires a lot of care, a lot of accessory products to keep it shiny and moist looking, and was greasy to the touch. This look had no radical identifying overtones and just represented a trendy look inspired by hair salons and hair product manufacturers to capture the Black dollars spent on permanent waves or in regular barbershops. The "box" hairstyle, created by more youthful Black males, popped up a few years ago conceivably attached to boredom and an attempt to be different. It started out short, got higher and higher, and eventually started to look like a tall crown of sorts with the hair cut very close on the sides of the head. This no doubt gives many of them a subtle sense of royalty of the wearing of a crown of sorts. Then came many variations of this cut, different slants, angles and curves. Next came the procedure of shaving off portions of the hair in odd configurations, having several parts cut into the hair in unique designs and even to having certain symbols or names carved into the hair to advertise or identify with individual ideas or interpretations. Even adult Blackmen commenced to get several parts neatly carved into their hair. Others attach so much meaning to having a head of hair that they wear wigs on top of a bald spot or, even more modernly, they get hair weaves. While women can get away with fooling bystanders about the length or texture of her hair, a man cannot. Every Blackman who wears a hair piece or has a hair weave is spotted immediately. Some wear them like an extra hat because their presence, recognizable or not, uplifts their confidence and makes them feel equal.

They spend a great deal of money and time selecting expensive smelling after shave lotions and talcums. Their wardrobe standards require they wear a name brand fragrance. Whatever the popular or expensive brand is is the one they seek out to splash themselves with. Some of their wear more eastern fragrances found in body oils. They use many cosmetics attached to shaving. They even use liquid or pancake make-up which they also think is unnoticeable but they use it anyway to make others think they have smooth creamy looking skin. They also use the cut of their mustaches to project their individual image.

Other Blackmen decide to wear their hair long in flamboyant styles, or the jagged mop-like "dreadlock" hairstyle long or short. All of these looks are attempts to make a statement that expresses their position either about their Blackness or sophistication. It has not worked.

They have established certain looks and behaviors to designate themselves as having ideas and a culture of their own. It's interesting to note that their symbols are transferable. If a white male shows up in their circle who has studied how to look, dress, talk, walk and dress "Black," he is apt to be accepted into the group based on his identification with the symbols the Black man has established as qualifiers for inclusion. The technique of copying symbols is also used by Blacks who desire to function among whites and receive acceptance for their ability to display and mimic the symbols inherent in white life. Blackmen do not arbitrarily oust other nationalities from their groups especially if that person can fit in by being the same as them. They will even start to refer to the white male in their midst as a "brother" by virtue of his physical actions or sounds. Many of them refer to whites by the term "brother" even if they do not function as to resemble their symbols. They do this to remind white males that they are related and to remind themselves that they are the same. Blackmen answer any questions a white man may walk up to them and ask. They give all the information they know about any given subject when called upon. It's almost automatic for them to quickly respond. Dressed up or not. The latest trend among Black males is to seek out ethnic items to denote their pride in their Blackness. They are great advertisers. They delight in wearing garments advertising Reebok, Nike, Adidas, Fila, Puma or other popular names, just as much as they do in wearing a strip of kente cloth, a fez hat, a kufi, an African pendant, pan-African colors of red, black and green or an entire African costume. They are strictly dealing with symbols which they define as having identifiable meanings. Or so they think. The resurgence in African clothing and African products really only represents a change in fashion and is a profitable trend for manufacturers. T-shirts stating political or amusing statements are now popular because they let the Blackman wear a sign which supposedly announces his identity or position. Some of them wear t-shirts boldly imprinted with vulgar sentences or words or pictures. They do not see them as offensive and consider themselves brave for taking the challenge of wearing a sign. They are trying to make an identity for themselves. They already have an identity but they reject it because it requires them to change the way they think and live. They are too mentally lazy to attempt this so they continually rely on external shields they can wear and forget about.

To further the gossip regularly circulated about their mythological grandiose sexuality, many Blackmen purposely select clothes to accentuate their sexual presence. They try to formulate an identity by wearing shirts half open to the waist revealing their chests, they walk down the street in biker shorts displaying the outline of their penis, they might wear tight fitting pants to hug their thighs or buttocks or they wear skimpy swim trunks also chosen to draw attention to the imprint of their sex organ. Some just choose to walk around with no shirt on at all or in short shorts to display their bodies and hopefully their virility. Blackwomen use clothes to look better. Blackmen use them to feel better.

These days, modern surgical technology makes it possible for the Blackman to make physical cosmetic changes in his looks. He can get a nose job and change the shape or size of his beak, he can have his ears pinned back, he can have his lips trimmed and his eyes widened. He can reconstruct his entire face including his eyes with contacts, to look as much like a Black European as possible. These are vain actions that further demonstrate his dissatisfaction with himself. Few Blackmen have their nose made flatter or wider, and none desire to have their lips enlarged. The Blackman has internalized the jokes and racial slurs about his proud distinct and different African facial features. This is also obviously the attitude of Blackmen who use a tad of chemical hair straightener in his hair to create a slight curl or wave. He is still trying to emulate the looks and hair texture of the group he says are his oppressors. He does everything he can to look as much like them because he thinks it will make him more acceptable and allow him to blend in more. But he can never get very far from his actual skin color unless he is so fair skinned as to be able to pass for white. Some of them do that, too. They want to be as far removed from their Blackness as possible. While it is important to be able to speak the language used to communicate in America, the Blackman will adopt a European style of talking and tone of voice that on the telephone makes it impossible to determine whether he is white or Black. While speaking this way in itself may be considered harmless, the problem lies in the Blackman not only copying the language but mimicking the ideas, attitudes and priorities of others. The use of specialized language intonations of another race or nationality makes the Blackman take on an entire mental disguise to imitate others and become further removed from the complications of his own nationality. They use the language as a defense mechanism to deny their identity and to absorb other ones.

As a final revelation regarding Blackmen proudly wearing "namebrand" and "designer" sneakers — while walking around claiming they are trying to reclaim their "African" culture; the word *NIKE* is defined as the name of the Winged Goddess of Victory in Greek mythology. It is doubtful that any Blackman or Black teenage male in America knows that the white woman named *Nike* who they honor (and represent) by wearing sneakers, caps, sweat suits, socks and other items; is not representative of African or any other non-white culture. Much of what the Blackman says, wears, does or supports is in direct contradiction to his verbal expressions of being a true Black man, or his attempts to reconnect to his pre-slavery legacy.

The Blackman should investigate all of the labels (words) on the clothing he wears so that he will understand how confusing he appears to intelligent people. He should not wear signs or symbols which are alien to his Blackness. His clothes do not have to have a name on them at all to serve the purpose of covering the body neatly. Blackmen are drawn to wearing garments with "names" on them because it gives them an identity. He knows nothing about the companies he supports with his patronage (money).

NOTES

Chapter 4

COMMUNICATIONS

The oral communications from the Blackman are a topic of concerned study mostly involving attempts to decipher exactly what it is he is trying to say, and what is his point in saying it. Complicating this issue are charges from his women that he is not open enough about his feelings, thoughts, and ideas. Many of them, even those who are married, rarely venture out verbally to express themselves and some hardly talk at all. And if they do talk they confine their comments to detached external issues unrelated to his personal feelings or conclusions. When they do attempt to make a communicative contribution or explain how they interpret a particular subject they are met with criticism or rejection. This is based on some of their illusionary never-will-happen solutions, and their proclivity to hesitate or take the long way around to arrive at a goal. It is very difficult to convince them that one of their idealistic postures is erroneous. They will hold fast to a losing position in a debate and refuse to concede if it means admitting they are wrong. They complain they are tired of their women doing all the talking, trying to tell them what to do, and being so opinionated on issues they believe only pertain to them. It astounds them how fast women think or take action, and they are baffled when they try to explain something that is so crystal clear to them, but appears to confuse their listeners. It is obvious that Blackmen speak and interpret the language and deduce the crux of an issue in an entirely different way than their women — and nearly everyone else. This difference of approach and system of delayed consideration often prevents the Blackman from getting his ideas across to others. However, this does not necessarily mean that they are wrong, just that because of how he says it nobody's interested in listening. Methods of communication and use of the language has evolved in one way for Blackwomen and another way for Blackmen. For example, it is possible that many of the misunderstandings between couples occur because they are speaking two different dialects. Each gender has pre-established certain definitions based on their personal feelings and priorities. They are rarely adjustable between intimate parties. Feminine and masculine perceptions determine what a word means. As long as each sex insists on devising their own definitions of the language, Blackmen and Blackwomen will continue to misinterpret each other and become combative when trying to hold a sane conversation. Set definitions must be agreed upon for general topics that routinely must be discussed in a relationship. These definitions become the rules of the discussion and each party must communicate within the framework of the wording which both speakers understand. Complicated.

Words, breath sounds and musical tones are all ways to communicate to elicit a response from another person. Sound waves (even English) stimulates the nervous system to react if the brain has been trained to understand the meaning of the sounds. European musicians learned how to arrange musical notes and tones to stimulate a chill which seems to pass over the body when the music is heard or sang. This chill-bump feeling is experienced by the Blackman when he sings or hears the national anthem or *America the Beautiful* — both patriotic songs. The Blackman thinks that the chill he experiences means that the words and the music have special spiritual meaning and thus the chill feeling fills him with great emotions — which he believes is his loyalty. Many regular words have private meanings to him and he is insulted easily. When called upon they have a ready list of examples about how unfairly they are dealt with in every category of their lives. They demand the right to say anything about any topic they choose, and expound determinedly on numerous subjects in which they believe their opinions are right. They think everybody else is wrong as hell.

Communication is best facilitated by the use of oral sounds. Words are the vehicles that transport ideas derived from a particular culture basically understood by those who speak it. The previously mentioned non-verbal communications also include body language. The experts say that when a person talks only 7% of what they say is verbal, 23% is conveyed by body language, 35% by facial expression and 35% tone of voice. If this is true, then all kinds of messages are being sent between Blackmen and Blackwomen, mixed messages and fleeting thoughts. English is not considered a complete language anyway. It was meshed out of a blend of words from the British, the Italians, the Swedes, the Germans, the Irish, the Jews, the Dutch, the French and the Portuguese. More recently Spanish and Asian words have been included. No parts of the Blackman's language from Africa are included in any translation of the mother tongue English. This puts the Blackman at another disadvantage due to the total elimination of his ancestral forms of communication. Scholars report that since 1900, new English words have been added at a rate of 500 to 1000 per year. Dictionary editors say that of 300,000 words, the meanings/definitions of over 200,000 of them have been revised/changed in the past 20 years. The American dialect is not rooted in the Blackman's experience. He develops his own "slang" language to communicate with his own kind. English was difficult for him to learn so that's how he developed words like dis', dat', twas', massa', twern't, ain't, seent, duh, yessum, etc.

Out of his frustration he uses words or phrases designated as foul or curse words. The Japanese, Malayans, Polynesians and American Indians do not have curse words in their languages. The Romans had about 800 dirty words. American English has 20, plus over a thousand terms for sexual intercourse. Additionally, the English language contains sounds that do not represent actual words but are defined as having definite meanings. These sounds are included as part of the language.

Examples are:
1) Uh-huh
2) Uh-Oh
3) psssst!
4) Hummph
5) Tsk. Tsk. Tsk.
6) Mmmmmm-Huh
7) Huh?
8) ooooooo-wee
9) Aaahhhhhhhh
10) mmmmm-mmmmm-mmmmm

All of the above lip sounds have valuable meanings in any conversation. They express every emotion from agreement to disdain. These sounds are indigenous only to Americans. Nevertheless they make up a great part of the vocabulary used to give or receive information. The Blackman will periodically make up words, sayings or slogans to aid his expressions. Some of the slang words the Blackman has made up to transmit his own ideas are: hip, jive, dig, hulley-gulley, right on, done deal, fittin' to, nigger please, the crib, lay dead, cool, fly, dissing, all that, rip off, and others. Obviously this list represents only a hint at the amount or kinds of words which sometimes are only used or understood in certain cities, or even neighborhoods. Trying to talk in America is not an easy task. Especially for Blackmen.

When the Blackman does communicate, what does he say? Well, his women respond that one of the ways he is noted for communicating is by lying. They say he is routinely subject to lie about the following things:

1) How much money he makes
2) How well he can play or played a sport: basketball, football, etc.
3) What his position or job is
4) How much they paid for something
5) How many women they got
6) Their marital status
7) About how many children they have
8) About how they get along with their wife or woman
9) How much power they wield in their house
10) How fast their car can go
11) Their physical abilities
12) About what they did in the war
13) How they functioned in a physical fight
14) How many times they can climax in one night
15) How many women they quit
16) Things women have done to or for them
17) How much money they have
18) How they got somebody told
19) What a woman did to them in bed
20) Where they are going when leaving the house
21) Where they just came from
22) Their skills
23) Why they broke up with their wife or ladyfriend

24) About their childhood
25) About how much their clothes cost
26) About who he's related to
27) What he spent his money on
28) About how much he had to drink
29) About completing a task or chore
30) About being broke

And, as suspected, the list goes on and on. His lies are connected someway to his trying to earn respect, keep the peace, gain recognition or admiration. He says he gets in more trouble with the truth than he does with a lie, so he has adjusted his life to include a repugnance for absolute truth. His infamy as a habitual liar with his women has garnered him a reputation of having diabolic intent to defraud. His women say that lying is apparently a singular Black male phenomena. He mainly lies to get out of trouble and to avoid punishment or disapproval. They shudder at the thought of their women catching them in a lie. They feel completely defenseless when they get busted. Their reason for telling so many lies is to avoid the consequences of being honest. Then his guilt causes him to worry, worry gives him anxiety and anxiety leads to weariness. Thus he is tired. Lying is a negative defensive habit that creates distrust and suspicion in his relationships.

Sometimes he is able to joke himself out of getting caught in a lie, or he manages to explain it off convincingly or resort to more serious tactics depending on the seriousness of the issue, and he will cry. Real tears. Whenever he is caught in a lie he knows he has two emotions going for him: 1) the unwavering desire his women has to believe and trust him, and 2) a man crying brings out the maternal instincts of a female and she is more apt to forgive him. The crying tactic is not really that unconscionable if one considers that to the Blackman with rascal tendencies to lie, tears fall within the sphere of being a handy, distracting survival tool. Many times his woman listens to his weak explanations until he finally stumbles on one she can half-way settle with. Whether his use of lies is an innate defense mechanism or a wicked character flaw cannot easily be determined because most of the time his woman knows when he is lying anyway. The Blackman has a history of being daring, taking risks and testing himself in many areas of endeavor. It could be that lying provides him with a warped kind of challenge that requires him to be quick on his feet, always ready to meet

the moment, and wiggle out of conflict based on his own ingenuity, and when he gets away with a gigantic lie he can anoint
himself the winner. Albeit this is a strange way to achieve self-
worth, esteem or confidence, — taking responsibility to defend
the truth is more emotionally difficult and takes a much longer
time to settle. Until he works out his lying problem his
communication voids will persist. Lying has seriously damaged
the credibility of the Blackman.

So how does he react to the truth? He claims that his woman
can't handle truth very well, but the Blackman does not
assimilate with it any better than she does. He thinks that he
has never received any rewards or satisfaction for telling the
truth — from his parents, friends or his mate. So he figuratively
pats himself on the back every time he outwits an opponent with
a masterful superior lie. There are many truths that he will not
acknowledge about himself. Truths which are verifiable according to his original nature, but have become distorted and
perverted. Some of the daily issues he refuses to recognize as
true are:

1) He will not admit that Blackwomen should dress more
modestly because that position requires him to change his
immoral ideas and adulterous reactions to her nudity.

2) He won't admit that he has sacrificed the Black child's
life by not fulfilling his responsibilities as father.

3) He can't agree with a self-help platform because it
necessitates his becoming qualified to be independent using his
own steam.

4) He can't admit that the civil rights movement failed
because it's easier to have blind faith in a system than to
abandon it.

5) He can't acknowledge that Black boys need to be in a
separate school to address their special needs because he will
have to take a more active role in their educational process.

6) He won't admit that he could exert more control over the
drug influx in his neighborhood because it would demand he
take action to remove the problem.

7) He can't agree that his woman rules him or that he is
afraid of her because he prefers using her misbehavior as an
excuse to do the negative things he himself does.

8) He won't say that he dislikes seeing Blackwomen with
whitemen because it is an unpopular stand and could get him
expelled from certain circles.

9) He doesn't admit that he really does want to be in charge of his wife and family because he is afraid of failure and the blame it entails.

10) He can't admit that the real reason he's angry with the Asians who buy and operate businesses in his own neighborhoods is simply because he doesn't know how to operate a business himself.

11) He won't admit that he spends too much money outside the African-American community because he is so enthralled with the material goodies produced by the Europeans and the Japanese.

12) He can't accept the fact that white folks are never going to give him reparations, or apologize to him for how badly he has been treated after slavery because he feels like a chump.

13) He won't acknowledge that he is never really comfortable around whites as he is with his own kind because then he has to admit that the two races actually are different.

14) He can't admit that while he publicly claims to admire Nelson Mandela or Malcolm X that he's too scared to make moral judgments and stand up for what he believes in like they did.

15) He certainly can't admit that he would like to have two women because he has been convinced that it's wrong and unjustifiable.

16) He can't admit that it's wrong for Blackmen to be homosexual because he doesn't want to offend anyone, or force his values on others, plus he's not sure on what basis he thinks it's wrong.

17) He can't announce his feelings of helplessness because he thinks that he must always impress others of his massive strength even when there's no proof that it even exists.

18) He can't admit that he doesn't know how to express his Black culture other than wearing African clothes or symbols.

19) He can't admit that he has wasted a lot of time believing in and chasing rainbow colored dreams that never materialized.

20) And finally, he can't admit that he no longer has any confidence in the American political system as a solutional base for his problems because it would require him to develop independent strategies to reach his own goals.

If he decided that any of the above statements were true he would immediately start to function differently and go to work to implement some potential for real change for his grandchildren. Carrying around lies in his head is a heavy burden and makes him always keep alert to avoid situations that might show him up as a hypocrite.

Another way he gets out of being confronted with his lies is to drop out of sight for a while, just disappear completely until he thinks it's importance has blown over. He is good at ducking the truth because it condemns him and exposes his masquerade of being honest. He lives in a perpetual state of fear of being attacked.

Exactly what is he afraid of? He is afraid someone might kill him, take something from him, steal his car, take his woman, blow his credit. He's scared of being found out, of losing respect, of moving too fast, of forgetting something, of dropping dead from the pressure of having people depend on him or of getting caught. He is afraid that he will be arrested for something, he is afraid of losing his job and he is afraid that things are getting progressively worse. His fears cause him to hesitate. He complains too much instead of acting.

What does the Blackman do with his frustration and pent up rage or anger? Sociologists say that familial deprivation and lack of cultural contact leads an individual to instinctive hostility and aggression as a byproduct of these vacancies in their development. Much of the Blackman's anger is dammed up inside of him. His inability to understand or modulate processes in Western civilization, and the intimidation of racism has led him to distrust and fear — which is the basis for his anger. It is now flowing in his veins as a conditional reflex driven by every genetic drop of DNA in his body. He is outraged. His ego has been violated. Many of his hostile reactions to social conflict result from past small failures in varied situations. He often turns his anger on those closest to him. The overbearing contact of inner-city or project-dwelling Black males stuffed into cramped quarters brings about fatigue and impatience. They have not been trained to channel their anger into healthy non-violent outlets. The only harmless activity he knows of to avert some of his aggression is through sports. This no longer works as many Blackmen wind up killing or injuring each other over sport games. While they claim the threats to their survival are external to their own communities, in many cases this is where they express their disappointment and rage. When mammals of the same species become alarmed when danger is near, they press together for safety. But because Blackmen have eliminated all ties that bound them together, they turn on each other. Animals show their beastly unselfishness when it comes to the good or preservation of the community. Black males spend a lot of time plotting and planning how to kill or hurt one another. So when claims are made that Blackmen act like animals — they do not. Because animals show more love and respect for each other than Blackmen do. Animals have unity. They all live the same way, eat the same foods, maintain the same breeding techniques and care for and train their young.

The Blackman communicates his aggression sometimes randomly on innocent victims as a sort of death wish. Every mammal resorts to self-defense when cornered with no way to escape. This is what the Blackman experiences every time he fails at trying to better himself, provide for his family or get something, and is blocked from doing so by abject racism, or rules made up by people he has no control over, or when he is disqualified based on a trick or legality he wasn't told about. He does not know how to resolve these conflicts and maintain his manhood. Anger and conflict are said to be two different things. Conflict is the problem and anger is the reaction to it. So he implodes for as long as he can and then he explodes out of desperation. His lack of knowledge puts him at a constant disadvantage.

The Blackman's hostility against other Blackmen is more clearly understood when one realizes that the urge to fight is quicker to be expressed with familiar people in familiar places. The middle of a Blackman's territory is the most likely battleground for a fist war, because of the psychological advantage of his own turf—the home court. The further he travels away from home the less likely he is to voluntarily go on the warpath. This also explains why he raises the most hell in his own home, and charges so hard in his own backyard. All of his pent-up misdirected anger validates the stats claiming he has a five to seven times greater chance of being murdered than a white male. Out of every 1000 white males about 11 will die involuntarily, out of this same number over 110 Blackmen will die of violence usually at the hands of another Black male. Warning them about their likely endangerment doesn't provoke the desired reaction because they have no value for life. The life they know about is filled with disappointment and powerlessness. He's living in someone else's house and is forced to obey the house rules and restrictions because he has nowhere else to go.

There have always been and will continue to be Blackmen who claim they are so fed up with the injustices done against Blacks that they resort to violence and say they want to wage physical war with America. These Blackmen are the biggest fools of them all. Gun studies say there are more than 200 million firearms in the USA. The bulk of these are owned, assembled and distributed by white males. Let's consider the basic requirements for any nation to wage war on another government. Certain institutions have to be in place — especially to pass the first lick.

The minimal needs are:
1) A Military Budget
2) Vehicular Mobility
3) Material Suppliers
4) High Tech Weapons
5) Trained Soldiers
6) Food and Medical Care
7) A Communications System
8) Supportive Allies

The following is the Blackman's status regarding the above:

NUMBER ONE — Budget
Most Blackmen have a difficult time pulling together their rent budget. They do not own a bank and are not known to pool their dollars for major purchases because they do not trust each other with the money. Wars cost money and Blackmen will never be able to beg enough donations to finance such an extreme, destined to fail, naive idea.

NUMBER TWO — Mobility
Cadillacs, Benz's, BMWs or vans are of no value in a war zone, nor can they take the place of a tank. Blacks own no airline, have no helicopters, and few trained pilots would jeopardize their positions at major airlines to fly fighter planes for the Blackman's war against America. Guerilla warfare on concrete will be difficult.

NUMBER THREE — Supplies

Only a few Blackmen qualify as manufacturers in their businesses. They do not have a central warehouse to order ammo, equipment, clothing, helmets, shields, or any of the incidental items needed in a war. Neither do they have off-shore contacts to have stock drop-shipped in.

NUMBER FOUR — Weapons

Blackmen do not have, nor ever will be allowed to have, enough firearms or contracts to stockpile the kinds of weaponry and explosives necessary to pull off a military coup against the American government. A few 22's and 38's, shotguns and several automatic weapons are not sufficient to attack the most powerful warring nation on the globe.

NUMBER FIVE — Soldiers

Blackmen have never had but two organizations that trained them for military competence and they are no longer in existence. And when they were the majority of Blackmen disagreed with their theories about preparing themselves for self-defense. They have no sane trained Generals or necessary personnel plus they will never be able to convince Blackmen in any sizable numbers to voluntarily commit suicide for a cause.

NUMBER SIX — Food & Medicine

Blackmen do not have a hospital controlled by them to take in their injured and wounded. They do not have access to volume prescription medications either. Blacks get all their foodstuffs from European producers who are stocked by European farmers. The Blackman buys all his food at a supermarket or fast food chain. A people who cannot even feed themselves independently have no business ever considering going to war with the nation providing them with food, clothing and shelter. The U.S.A. could win the war by simply starving them to death, and blocking the doors of KFC.

NUMBER SEVEN — Communications

Blackmen use home telephones, car phones and phone booths to contact each other and most are operated and owned by AT&T. Most Blackmen do not even have a CB or walkie-talkie. If they started the war in California they would have no way to know what was happening in NYC. The only people they could communicate with would be those they could physically reach out and touch.

NUMBER EIGHT — Allies

Blackmen are not militarily affiliated with any foreign governments. As much as they say they love and support the motherland, or launch verbal campaigns against apartheid in South Africa, nobody from Africa is going to ever use a hostile invasion of America to rescue or help the Blackman. No African nation has ever expressed public outrage at how the Blackman is treated in America. Blackmen do not qualify for recognition as a nation because they are dependent upon the USA for all their needs and are not nationally organized. Nor have they African names or religions to identify them as a lost tribe worthy of defending.

So there it is, in black and white, Blackmen are not qualified or prepared to go to war, and any attempts at such will end in bloodshed and humiliation. The Blackmen who espouse this kind of pointless rhetoric have no consideration for Blackwomen and Black children or the elders. The Blackman is not divinely defenseless, but he would be delusional, psychotically so, to think he could win anything but a casket, or lengthy jail sentence, by employing this method to seek freedom.

Additionally, Blackmen tend to decide to believe in, or align themselves with the political dogma of strong Blackmen who are now dead. They claim a few ideas, or a statement from them, and try to build an entire allegiance based on a few parables or slogans. It seems the most enduring slogan, catapulted into popularity by Malcolm X during the 60's, which resurfaces periodically, as it has now, is "By Any Means Necessary." Blackmen say that "By Any Means Necessary" means that they should fight for their freedom and get it no matter what it takes. Let's consider some of the means that might become necessary:

1) It could mean that Blackmen must quit their jobs working in the system, abandon all their credit cards, and default on their car notes in order to give full attention to important issues in the struggle, like pooling their resources and energies to form independent businesses, schools and food distribution systems.

2) It could entail Blackmen to stop going to church and study their own cultural religions, give up the slavemaster's name, and work daily to figure out how to get along with each other.

3) It might mean going without the latest style of clothing, selling all their jewelry to get cash to finance their projects, or eating only one meal a day to conserve food and expenses.

4) It could mean that Blackmen have to start taking Blackwomen off the streets who are living immorally, or claiming some of the Black babies and youth who have been left in agencies, to keep them from being absorbed in cross-racial adoption.

5) It could mean going into a room with his neighbors or club members and not coming out until they came to an agreement about what must be done to salvage Black communities, and formulate an agenda and assign themselves duties to get the job done.

6) It could also mean that they have to start making their word their bond and doing what they say they are going to do. And clean up their own neighborhoods and make repairs where needed. This would include policing their own areas and making them a safe and clean place to live.

What if the above six examples are the "means necessary" to restore values and self-sufficiency in African-American communities? How many Blackmen are really willing to use "Any Means Necessary" to rebuild Black culture and Black pride by sacrificing their individual greed and personal aspirations for the benefit of the Black nation at large?

How many Blackmen are confident enough in themselves to step out on air, decide that the Black God is with them, and use their lives to be an example to young Black males of what taking responsibility looks like?

And how many Black males are serious and concerned to the point of standing up for what they think is right, and try to build something that they don't ask the white man to finance?

These are the questions. This is the call. A yea or nay response is expected to be forthcoming.

So the next time a Blackman is found, or heard elaborating on what Blacks should do to get out of their predicament and to re-establish values in the Black family, to save the children, ask him to read this chapter, take positive action, or suggest he hush and stop fooling himself. They are the only men on earth who insist on trying to talk themselves into a better condition instead of working for one.

The Blackman annoys a lot of people who identify him by his so-called sky rocketing ego. It seems that just about anything he brags he can do that is different from how things are usually done is referred to as "ego-tripping." He is charged with having an undeserving value for himself and is too self-centered, thinks he's great, does a lot of unsubstantiated tall talk and when in this trance talks like he has the whole wide world in his hands. The dimensions of his ego-libido fluctuates from big, bigger to biggest. And his ego is just as spry and sturdy as any other male mammal, and stands for his last clutch for life.

It is the European male who has always set the clearest example of having the greatest amount of king-size ego. What size of an ego did it take for European explorers to travel around the world and decide that wherever they stopped they had a right to claim the land, rename it, and put the people already residing there under their authority? And what is the depth and breadth of an ego that convinced them that they are solely in charge of distributing information, according to their own writings, to the rest of the world by claiming that they are the sacred leaders of all civilized standards? And what kind of an overblown ego tells them that while they do rank as the least number of people on the earth that they have the right to claim the supreme being/God, as a member of their sparse race? If anyone has over-exaggerated their worth, power or desires — it is the whiteman not the Blackman. And then these same self-proclaimed world leaders had the nerve during the conflict between Iraq and Kuwait to rush to Kuwait's side expressing shock and outrage at Saddam Hussein's savage disrespect for human life in order to gain control of another territory. Saddam was charged with invading Kuwait, plundering their villages, enslaving the men and raping the women, taking control of their natural resources, and staking claim to the entire area. Saddam was further lambasted for accomplishing all this by brute force, trickery and sophisticated weaponry. Ironically, Saddam's methods exactly parallel with the war tactics used by the whitemen when he claimed to have "found" America and set upon the Indians with a vengeance. It was this same cowardly, self-serving egomania that was used by the Dutch, the British and the French in Africa, Australia and multiple surrounding islands. There is absolutely no difference at all. And the whiteman has the nerve to get misty eyed and sentimental when singing the national anthem and experiences great pride at overpowering American soil and building his own civilization. This is the kind of disregard they have for all other forms of human life if it doesn't look like them. Even in territories around the globe where they number the least amount in the population, they are in charge. They are the rulers of any non-white peoples in the area. The question is who gave them the right to claim the whole earth as theirs and to be boss over everybody else on it?

NOTES

Chapter 5

EDUCATION

The education of Blackmen has changed drastically over the past several years. The definitions and responsibilities of compulsory public education has also been altered depending on the social politics regarding its value, which often changes every four years. Teachers and instructors have been required to incorporate their teaching techniques with lessons on self-control and to also function as disciplinarians. Children are now showing up for class dressed inappropriately, sleepy, carrying no utensils for participation, loud and unruly, disrespectful and combative. Teachers find beneath all these layers of personality deficiencies that Black children score low and remember little of what they learned in their previous years of school, and are indifferent to approaching new topics of learning. Teacher salaries are too low, wage increases are bleak and many have left for better paying positions in the private sector. Hall monitors are replaced with police or security guards and many teachers have been attacked by irate parents and terrorized by students. The era of schools being a happy, fun filled organized institution is over. Public schools now, especially from ninth grade on up, feel lucky if they can keep attendance at a decent level to justify their existence, and feel blessed if they can just get all of the children to stop talking at the same time, or at least long enough for them to take the roll. Fewer children take books home or complete homework, parents rarely show up at P.T.A. or other school functions, and all involved agree that public education has failed.

The overall scholastic achievement of the Black male is

reportedly at its lowest ebb since 1954 when the Supreme Court declared segregated schools and recreational facilities unconstitutional. Hard civil right and legal battles were fought yearly to secure what the Blackmen of the early 1960's perceived as equal opportunity to education. These moves signalled a new better chance to gain knowledge and skills that would prepare Blackmen for acceptance into the American work force. Many Blacks benefitted by integrating predominantly white colleges and universities, and managed to uncomfortably learn more from the more qualified teachers and professors who now headed their classes. Busing elementary Black children into white schools located in white neighborhoods was very traumatic but was doggedly accomplished. This penetration was complicated and no studies were made to determine the psychological adjustment Black children had to make to comply with their parents and school board requests of forcing them into places where they were not wanted. By 1965 Blackmen leaders, prompted by college youth and educators, demanded that Black studies be included in curriculums — especially on the college level. A frantic search for Afro-American historical data ensued which included modification of dress codes to accept Blackmen's rights to wear their hair in the then popular Afro hairstyles. Black curriculums were hastily thrown together including a few Blackmen scholars, scientists, post-slavery politicians and a few courageous slaves who accompanied remarkable feats while enslaved. This also opened up new teaching positions for Black professors hired to direct and teach these new Black study courses. Incorporated into these classes were the works of contemporary Black writers of that period such as Leroi Jones (Amiri Baraka), Don L. Lee (Haki Mahubuti), Etheridge Knight, Dudley Randall, Ralph Ellison and Frantz Fanon. Blackmen were thirsty for knowledge about themselves and were eager to learn.

The new project of studying Black history uncovered many discrepancies in what Blackmen had been taught. On the university level many of these misleading documentations were dispelled, however, on the elementary, junior and senior high levels of American public schools, few changes were made in the methodology of teaching American or world history to Black children. So while many of the adult Blackmen of that era cleared up a lot of their misunderstandings about their real achievements and potential, the oncoming younger generations did not have this information imparted to them. By 1975 faces and drawings of Afro-Americans began showing up in elementary level text books but all else remained the same. The same history was taught with Black faces added. As it turned out, the popularity of the Black pride and Black history studies began to subside, and as the fads and trends of civil unrest faded so did excitement and interest about Black history. Bored white hippies disintegrated and their communes disappeared. They grew older, became bored with their rebellion, and returned to school to eventually assume the places prepared for them by their parents and society. The debunking of the civil rights industry shortly followed. On the trail of the dwindling participation of the Vietnam War, the youthful Blackmen leaders without adult leadership representation, caused the Black pride movement to become tired and unfashionable — and finished. Gone went the African clothes, symbols and poetry, and they were replaced with bell-bottomed pants, disco lights and mini-skirts. American business as usual resumed. The more outspoken Blackmen leaders were quieted either by murder, political appointment, business ventures or jail. The existence of specialized day care centers for Black children dwindled, government funding was withdrawn and only a few unwavering Blackmen leaders continued the struggle. As an oversight, this was the only period in the Blackman's background that would have permitted him to establish his own unintegrated schools where he could teach his own Black history. This was his immediate chance to pass on to his children their real legacy by teaching them what he had learned about Black pride. But he blew it. He did not opt for single control of his own schools on the elementary level — even in his own community. He did not insist on remaining in charge of the curriculums Black children would be taught from. Blackmen leaders moved on to other political notions pertaining mostly to adults. They parlayed all of their mental energies toward voter registration and lobbying for expanded civil rights. He made no preparations for the oncoming Black generations and he formulated no new standards for Black family home life. Instead he placed his hope and faith in his dreams that the ballot and equal employment opportunities along with social integration would solve all his problems. He made no effort to redirect Black dollars into Black businesses, and he made no attempts to restructure Black traditions, holidays or celebrations for his children. He left everything intact. His educational demands consisted of better school buildings, recess materials, school lunches, immunization and health care, sport teams that included Black males, and integrated teaching staffs and classrooms. He continued to depend on the government, the state and the city to teach his children. He has always done this. Back in the day, during pre- and post-slavery periods, the Methodists, the Quakers and the Presbyterians were the first whites to establish Black schools. Their presence of authority, whether they were sympathizers or not, wedged them into position to teach and instill European histories and values, ideas, customs and religions into the minds of Black children. The white female, dedicated and prim, was in charge of serving the plates of education the Black children ate from. This was an honorable work and dictated the format for maintenance at school. There were independent Black owned and operated schools who felt compelled to maintain the standards approved and taught by whites. They were, of course, understaffed and underequipped. And they were mostly taught by women while the men worked at other locations to earn money to support their families. This pattern has just today become under closer scrutiny as many new styled Blackmen educators have started to realize that by the time they inherit a Black male in high school, after several years of being taught by white and Black women, that it is often too late to effectively teach him ideals and values he needs as a man. They are now trying to establish programs enabling them to reach Black male youth early in age, to try to make a masculine impact on their character development during their formative years. More on this later.

Part of the Blackman's problem concerning him establishing his own educational system is that he does not know how to do it independently. Certainly financing such an arrangement has its weight in the project, but next to that is his confusion regarding what to teach. What source will he use to teach the thematic sequence of Black history? And how can he teach this information and still turn out Black youth qualified to enter a European manned work force to get a job? On the tail end of this dilemma is his concern that whites may not approve of him trying to form his own school. So much had already been put into motion for progress through integration. How can he abandon all this without sending a message that might be misread as hostile or rejection of European values. If the

Blackman was able to objectively analyze Western approaches to this topic, and subjectively deduce the principles needed to establish his own standards for cultural transmission, he would be successful. This is not to suggest that the Blackman copy all the whiteman's means and methods, but there are two major reasons to do this.

Number one: accomplishments are made by using formulas that contain instructions and principles to achieve certain goals.

Number two: there is no point in spending any more time searching throughout history to replicate ancient ideas now extinct and uncompetitive in today's high-tech scholastic environment. As an example, this is how the European implanted his ideas for permanency:

I. He programmed all the people with the same information. Taught the same sequence of history, used the same names, places and dates and supplied events to document them as reality.

II. More documentation was provided in books, literature, arts, preservation of artifacts and pictures of his white male leaders.

III. He further defined his system of democracy, rules of trade, formed his monetary system, decreed laws and legal recourse, named his religion and anointed his holidays, and made moral judgments regarding home and family life.

IV. Then he appointed able bodied men to be in charge of each and every territory he claimed so that they could monitor the continued development of his ideas, to stay visible to keep the people on track, to reinforce his guidelines for setting up communities, and to evoke the rules if someone strayed from the plan. He called this politics, labeled the members of the board politicians, and hired them to govern the people.

If analyzed unemotionally, they did a magnificent job, one worthy of respect by those who use this kind of achievement as a measure of success. There is one word which best describes what the Europeans did. That one word is "agree." They agreed among themselves on the strategies to reach their goals. They acted on their commitments and followed through on the plan. And yes, some of their methods were unconscionable but their plan worked — today they own American and plot its destiny.

They designed their style of education based on the same principles they used to build their nation. They put variations of their history in their schoolbooks and continually drummed this information into the brains of every school age child in America. This is the way to educate someone into believing in something as a way of life, and to inspire them to defend and feel allegiance towards the institution giving them citizenship. It worked. So there is no way to save Black male youth from destruction by their own design, until the Blackman takes charge of dictating what it is that they will learn. Each resurgence of ideas about studying or hailing Black history produces new scholars and historians who uncover or report new information. They deserve evaluation. The first step the Blackman must make is to come together with other concerned Blackmen and determine a definite format for teaching Black history, Black culture, Black ethics and Black celebrations. He would have to decide on the wording, do the writing himself and print and distribute the books. These books would become mandatory documents from which every Black child would learn and study. Parents would be required to reinforce this information at home, and keep the ideas in the forefront of the child's everyday life — in entertainment, meals, recreation, bedtime stories, wall signs, emblems, pictures and every other symbol in the home must reflect these impressions. The teachers in the schools who accept the responsibility of tattooing the brains of Black children with this information must make it a lifetime work, and assemble written reports of each child's progress and problem areas, so that the next generation of teachers would add more pressure in the weak areas. These teachers should consist of men for the boys and women for the girls up until the youth reached their late teens. Currently Black male boys are presented with so much conflicting information about themselves and others that their little brains are overloaded.

A new plan is undeniably needed. The suggested approaches above would have to be worked out detail by detail by those appointed. Progress and monitoring are a must. Installing this system could take 30 to 50 years. This is a serious undertaking and there will be no time for sports or play. While this project sounds heavy and riddled with complications, African-Americans uniformly admit that the public and private school systems have failed. Statistic takers report that one of every five Black boys will not complete high school. And those remaining have a tendency to not pay rapt attention, get good grades or muster up enough genuine interest to appreciate the experience. Public schools have become battlegrounds for drugs, prostitution, fights, shootings, delinquency, pregnancy, diseases, extortion, murder, intimidation, distraction and promiscuity. And to top it all off, Black youth know about as much about Black history today as Black youths did in 1954. They come out of school unable to read, write or do simple math. They are categorized on the national scales as functionally illiterate or learning disabled. For the most part there is nothing unrepairably wrong with their brains when they start kindergarten, yet around 4th or 5th grade they commence to exhibit fact retention problems. Little Black girls have a similar problem that brews in their teen years. Today's generation of teenage Black girls are the most immoral, fickle, unprincipled, silly and raunchy young women on the scene. They have the most filthy mouths of any other female population ever to be produced from the African-American community. They shame any civilized adult Blackwoman because of their low class behavior and gross ignorance. The equally outrageous behaviors of young Black male teenagers is covered in another chapter.

A separate series of Black educational facilities on the elementary level is desperately needed. Many Black American citizens object to this as if the idea is blasphemous and suggestive of seceding the union. The idea of establishing an all Black school is not a new one. Booker T. Washington did his best to impress negroes that they should always maintain their own learning and training centers in the 1800's. He was rejected because negroes even back then wanted to integrate with whites educationally. The next time a major separate Black school, specifically designed to serve the unique needs of Black youth, emerged was in the early 1940's established by Elijah Muhammad under the rulership of the Nation of Islam. His idea was rejected, too — this time based on his racial politics. This is not to suggest that there have never been any attempts to establish Black owned or Black operated schools or colleges. But ALL the rest of them are fashioned after, and are functionary using the same information dispersed in the regular public school systems. The government insists on certain prerequisites that must be met in order to be considered certified or authorized to qualify for and receive federal or state funds allocated for general public education. Any school not meeting the set requirements is unable to obtain grants or research awards. So even if the school does claim to be a Black academy of sorts, none of them have figured out how to be financially independent of the system — and therefore are under the same guidelines as any other public institution — although modified cosmetically to appear solely ethnic.

Blackmen leaders in educational positions of authority, or as teachers, do not think that they are qualified to take over their own school system and have complete control over what African-American children are taught. Black history month is in February. Dr. King's birthday is celebrated in January. There's a tiny bit of recognition. The rest is gleaned from T.V., movies, record albums, sports stars, from watching the people outside their doors and the people inside their homes. Not much positive imagery can be gotten out of such tunnel vision. With no specific directions regarding interpretation of how Blackmen are portrayed in society, they may as well not receive any exposure at all. So any partially intelligent Black adult recognizes the need for Blacks to establish their own schools. Separate ones. Ones for the Black boys and ones for the Black girls. With Black male and Black female teachers.

In August of 1991 a few educators around the country created quite a media stir for suggesting that Black boys need separate educational facilities to address their special needs. There are only a few of these types of schools allowed to exist. But fearing a trend, the public outcry against them from both feminists and liberals, soon a court of law informed these few Blackmen that they could do no such thing. After a few days of protests from the sponsors of the separate Black school idea for Black boys, the issue was dropped. As usual things went back to normal. Many parents and female teachers spoke out in support of the schools but their experience and recommendation were ignored and disregarded. As they have always been.

While it may be understandable why the Public School System disagreed with this idea and slightly explainable why some Black and white females were against it, it is totally inconceivable why every Blackman in America did not stand up and demand that they be allowed to teach and train their own sons, as every other nationality on earth has the right to do. Blackmen know they got little if anything out of their public school experience or college campus life that serves or benefits them today, or helped them define their identity and purpose, or manhood. They know they were not taught anything about the role or responsibility of a Blackman. But as usual, Blackmen heard about the separate school issue and cowardly slinked out of sight and pretended that whatever else they were doing was more important. They are now using a reverse psyche on themselves as a form of denial. For example, they say they have been duped into thinking that they have special problems, but that they are just as normal as the next fellow and they are not going to go for stories and innuendo that they have unique problems indigenous only to Black males. The error in their analogy is that the newspapers, T.V. and jail houses validate every day and every night that they do indeed have some kind of a special problem. Every Blackman father or father-to-be in America should have stood up and supported the few Blackmen educators who were bold enough to stake a public claim for the minds of Black boys. They defended their positions well — to no avail. No other well-known popular Blackmen leaders came out in support of them, no sport heroes, no actors, no politicians, no civil rights activists. The same kind of handkerchief head negro man who failed to support or start separate schools for Black children 30 and 40 years ago, continue to avoid the issue today. And this time they are accompanied by their chickenhearted grown sons who also do not take part in any issue involving motions that require them to be responsible for their own children. These charges are leveled at every Blackman in America because they should have stood up and supported those few Blackmen educators who were negotiating with the government for the brains of Black boys. Certainly every Black male school teacher should have voiced their support and wrote letters. The sponsors of the separate school made a fatal mistake. The same mistake Blackmen have been making for 90 years, they keep asking the whitemen for permission to exert their own ideas. They should've endured, solicited funds from Blacks in sports and entertainment, and petitioned the umpteen million Black service organizations who claim they are working for the good of the people. If the Blackman believed that God was on his side he would have courage to execute his own ideas despite the political opposition of other races. The truth of the matter is that the Blackman has been taught so long to go against his nature that it makes him cringe when faced with making significant decisions because every decision he makes for himself requires him to reject the rules already ingrained in him by Europeans. The most important outcome of having Blackmen teach Black boys is that it hopefully will produce a better breed of Blackmen more qualified to marry, protect, and direct Blackwomen. Our Black girls also need special attention in the development of femininity, home economics, child rearing and general education skills. This is not to say that Black girls should be taught less important information than Black boys, but it does suggest that if things are going to get back to normal, then Blackmen must be trained to provide and rule, and Blackwomen must be taught how to be a wife and mother to rear a more authentic generation. Whites have always maintained separate schools for their male offspring. They maintained them under the guise of referring to them as Boarding Schools, Military Academies, the Y.M.C.A. or Boy Scouts. But they have always existed and all teach codes of behavior, honor, religion, defense, responsibility and patriotism. They boast of graduating some of America's top leaders and many successful businessmen. These units provide a male filled environment without the distraction of females, outside competition, or interference of popular social trends. The Blackman must also have these kinds of institutions for his own young males. European adult males made this decision independent of the regular public school system and needless to say, did not ask or seek permission from Blackmen. They evoked natural law which dictates that a man has a right to raise his son in any manner he chooses as long as it doesn't conflict with the rights of others. A man who wants his own seed to survive must teach him self-worth and the value of his life by dedicating his own life to transferring this information to his offspring.

The Blackmen who graduate from African-American colleges are ultimately not in any better condition than the ones who attended European ran universities. They matriculate, seek positions, preferably somewhere near the Fortune 500 or other corporate appropriate affiliation. Then launch into giving every drop of brain power they have to a European firm for as long as they permit them to. Many of the younger graduates are determined to get a better "job" than their fathers. Most of their parents sent them to college to qualify for that singular accomplishment — to get a good or better "job." Every educational aim Blackmen have had for the past years has been motivated by him trying to prepare himself to get a gig in one of the European owned existing operations. Even those who do go into business do not feel comfortable in their careers unless they are integrated as far as possible into the European equation of their selected vocation. Some even hire whites.

Due to government cutbacks in Affirmative Action stipulations many Blackmen are finding it not as easy to snuggle in the warm armpits of the European corporate body. The Blackman is the original form of human life to first surface on earth. He used to be the most peaceful and most powerful ruler on the planet. But he has dropped to his lowest level ever recorded and until he replaces the information that led him to the spot he is in today, his current endangerment will develop into his extinction.

Television is partially responsible for the miseducation of Black youth. Studies say that 9% of an American child's life is spent on education, 91% is spent watching television and playing sports or video games. Yearly this breaks down to 10% of their day spent on education and 90% spent staring at a T.V. set. Television programs teach values, standards, ethics, sexuality, ways to commit crimes, loopholes in the law, styles of dress, how to make excuses, how to get out of doing things, how to kill people, how to torture animals, how to smuggle drugs, how to rape or mug, integration, religion, and zillions of other immoral and illegal activities. The messages of violence and situation ethics are no longer considered subliminal. The easy availability of cable provides easy access to x-rated movies at any time of the day or night. Television is a teaching tool. Television also teaches envy, inadequacy and jealousy. T.V. is not a real world but a Black child who spends hours daily admiring and longing for the rich living lifestyles portrayed on television is more apt to look at his own surroundings and feel inadequate, develop resentment for people who live in luxury, and become obsessed with obtaining material possessions that he learns from the television to equate with success. The VCR machine is not much better. Movies are easily rented and many a child and adult is under the video spell, hypnotized by watching hours of motion pictures with no commercial breaks. Few children have been educated on how to watch television. First of all every program on television is designed and specifically geared to attract consumers to see commercials to sell stuff. They provide a constant review of products repeated on the average of every three to five minutes. It's easy enough to claim that Blacks always get the poorest most degrading roles on T.V. — but Black actors are not forced to take any part. So if they keep showing up in low grade roles it's because they chose to. Either for the money or raw exhibition purposes. Blackmen are back acting in movies now. Spike Lee melted the ice a few years back and since that time history is repeating itself. Back in the 60's, due to the civil rights movement, Blacks were given new opportunities to break into Hollywood and star in movies. After a few brief years of being given the chance to act out their warped fantasies on the wide screen in stories about drugs, pimps, karate heroes, sweaty slaves, gangsters, dope addicts and Black versions of monster movies, Black actors fell from grace with the theatrical world. The movies became more and more pointless, slid to being ignorant and ended up being remembered as plain silly. Today, the same thing is happening in the same insidious way. Blackmen and women are starting to show up in unrealistic, comedic or crime laden roles. The producers of these films say they present stories featuring actual Black lifestyles currently going on. If they are currently going on then African-Americans already are familiar with the plots and climaxes. If movies are going to ever be viewed as educational tools then they should write scripts showing what Black life "should" be as opposed to the confusion it's in today. The Black film makers have another unique chance while they have the attention of the public to produce creative pictures of new images and positive ideals. If they don't do this it won't be long before they are obliterated from the big show — again. Remember that movies, like television, are concocted to attract movie lovers who will spend money to go see a movie. When any particular topic or image loses its drawing power they move on to the next prevailing attraction. They should be making films about African-Americans to sell to the schools and movies featuring capitalism tricks for the Black dollar and attention. The subjects are endless. Every movie, video, television show or picture poster — teaches something and conveys a meaning.

Academicians report that Black boys respond poorly in math. Math produces analytical skills sadly missing in Blackmen. Math has rules which must be remembered throughout the solving of a problem. This is a thinking process that Blackmen do not have. When engaged in various types of encounters both positive or negative in nature they do not know the rules to call on to make value judgments or arrive peacefully at a solution each time they encounter the same type of problem. The basic tenets of math are addition, subtraction, multiplication and division. Theoretically they signal:

Addition — when to do more/or give
Subtraction — when to stop/pull
Multiply — when to join/build on
Divide — separation/elimination

Math teaches life coping skills and how to keep certain values and standards in mind when working through conflict or confusion. Like math, when these skills are known and practiced, the answer comes out right. This is an example of a way that mathematics can be used to teach Black youth the importance of learning rules and how to use them. Meanwhile, each year thousands of Blackmen graduate from college and cannot find employment to exercise their newly acquired skills. Unless the introduction of education is altered to become a more usable and tangible tool it will become extremely difficult to continue to convince Black youth of the value of getting an education, because when they get out of school, having such knowledge as they receive now, if they can't secure a job, the education proves to be a waste of time and money. They are not trained to do anything with an education but to seek employment working for you know who. Some are in debt from hefty student loans which they can't pay back because they can't find work.

Blackmen learn attitudes and information from many sources. One of the more unusual ways is through superstitious nonsense. The ones they say they are the most familiar with originate from Judeo-Christian lore. They are:

1) While Black cats were considered lucky during the times of Egyptian Pharaohs, later in Europe in the middle-ages, Black cats came to stand for evil and bad luck by being associated with witches. This myth followed the Europeans to America and Blacks grabbed hold to it and believed what they said. Black people don't like to admit it but they avoid Black cats when possible to keep it from crossing in front of them and causing them bad luck. Even if they just see a Black cat this thought comes to mind. They suggest another subliminal reason to avoid and dislike the color Black.

87

2) Friday the 13th or the number 13 as being bad luck came from the same source. Friday was allegedly the day Adam and Eve ate the forbidden fruit and got in big trouble with God. It's also said to be the day Cain killed Abel and the day Jesus got crucified. These days some hotels do not have a 13th floor because so many Americans believe this number to be bad luck. The number 13 is like a terroristic threat, and when Blacks see it they go the other way.

3) Crossing the fingers is supposed to help a person succeed at something and it stands for a special prayer done with the fingers. This stands for making the sign of the cross which is supposed to ward off evil with its magical powers.

There are equally ridiculous others such as throwing salt over his left shoulder, not stepping on a crack in the sidewalk, opening an umbrella in the house, splitting a pole, not washing clothes on New Year's, making sure that a man is the first one to walk through their door on New Year's, not letting a bird fly directly over his head and the list goes on and on. Some even insist on eating black-eyed peas, candied yams, hog jowls and rice for New Year's Day dinner because it's supposed to guarantee good luck for the rest of the year. Some carry a rabbit's foot on their key chains, are happy if they find a four leaf clover plant and hang a horse shoe over their doors. Many study astrology, numerology, witchcraft and voodoo. They become very well versed with these customs and each time they honor, submit to, remember or practice any of these traditions from European folklore they immeasurably deepen their entrenchment in a heritage which has turned them into what they are today.

The next time he completes the requirements to earn his college degree he needs to remember one other thing as he resplendently and proudly marches down the aisle dressed in his royal cap and gown outfit. This especially pertains to those matriculating in some of our dignified historically Black colleges. He should keep in mind that the headpiece he wears was originally worn by those in the academic community of Medieval Europe. They used the colors of Black, red, and purple to signify various degrees of knowledge. The transferring of the tassel signalled even higher elevation. The European Bishops in the Church of Rome continue to wear their cap with the tassel and their matching gowns today. Perhaps soon a Blackman will search and find out what kind of symbols his Black ancestors used to commemorate completion of an education and change to wearing those.

Compulsory attendance in public schools victimized the Blackman in many areas of his cultural development, and the required subjects rearranged his priorities and narrowed the possibilities of him ever getting a chance to study his own history. He does not know and is not familiar with his own languages but is offered Latin, French, Russian or Spanish as a foreign language requirement for graduation or college level pursuits. The Blackmen who attended Catholic school received the worst kind of brainwashing because even when separated from girls during their educational process, they were totally surrounded by images, pictures and rituals alien to their African heritage. He was raised on a steady daily diet of praying to white male images, honoring the blessed virgin portrayed as a white female, and worshipping saints and other religious representatives — who all happened to be Caucasian. As part of his participation in the Catholic school curriculum, which was more strict and more civilized than the standard public schools, he still lost out in the end because Catholic school made it easier for him to forget about his own people and to work to blend in with white viewpoints. He became one of "you guys" or "the fellas." And he was fiercely instructed to refer to his instructors as Father, Mother or Sister. He grew to believe he really was related to them.

And his studies consisted of daily classes on the Catholic religion with books filled with holy white men and women. Saints. He had to memorize several names of patron saints to protect him, give him strength, provide for him and take care of his family. He was taught that no matter what he needed or wanted there was a white saint who had the religious power to give it to him if he turned to them in prayer. Based on the kind of intense brainwashing that took place in the Black boy's mind in Catholic school, it was considerably worse than attending regular public school because he lost himself completely.

Catholic school also reinforced the Blackman into developing a special regard and respect for white women because of the profound love they were taught to have for the virgin Mary, due to her being the saintly mother of Jesus Christ. All of their prayers began with her name at the helm, they asked the mother to convince the son to bless them. And all the statues and pomp and circumstance during Mass was copied after European or Greek symbolism.

NOTES

Chapter 6

EMPLOYMENT

In the fall of 1991, Tony Brown, a boldly speaking Blackman journalist, revealed in one of his sizzling syndicated columns that he had found out from a recent government report that the most successful small businesses of the 1980's were operated by white males who earned on the average about $200 grand per year. Asian men came in second making a little over $100,000 per year with Hispanic men taking third place with almost $70,000 per year. Blackmen struggled in last place grossing about $50,000 annually. Brown further attested that Blacks comprise 12% of the U.S. population but that Black businesses generate less than 1% of all business receipts. We thank Tony Brown for staying on the case year after year and periodically calling our attention to economic matters that impact on Black dollars. A few years back Brown announced that Black organizations spend $16 billion dollars every year hosting their annual national conventions in white owned hotels, restaurants, airlines, and other companies connected with getting to and from the conventions. These Black organizations, numbering nearly 1000, meet to address social and financial issues. They organize and do good works for their communities, provide scholarships and distribute information. The discovery of them spending $16 billion dollars a year to come together to discuss South Africa, poverty, illiteracy, drugs and crime in the Black community is monumentally embarrassing. Especially since many of the problems on their agendas can be eliminated with money and human resource people. No one knew they were handling such big bucks, and sadly, it still has not occurred to them to consider pooling such a vast amount of money and building their own convention centers, one in each of the four corners of America to keep those dollars among themselves. They could hire many of the African-American employees currently working at the white owned hotels, who are already trained to do that kind of work. Of course none of this will ever happen because Blackmen would rather die and go to hell before they would agree to place $16 billion dollars in the possession of another Blackman for safekeeping. So the European owned convention industry is not holding its breath waiting to see what's going to happen because they already know that their convention facility calendars are already booked for use by Black organizations, reserved through the year 2000. Reservations continued to be made after Tony Brown announced how much money was leaving the Black community and flying into the wallets of white hotel owners. It doesn't seem to matter what color the flag is when it comes up to signal an important financial discovery, the flag (information) is either ignored, or ripped to shreads. Taking on big projects to create jobs for themselves (without endorsement of the whiteman) is not appealing to the Blackman. He finds it easier to work for someone else.

The U.S. Labor Bureau reports that trends predict by the year 2000 women will make up 50% of the work force. Robotics and computers have eliminated thousands of positions and promise to erase more by the turn of the century. There used to be a time when unskilled or low skilled Blackmen could pinch out a living doing slow menial work requiring only the five senses or gargantuan strength. But these leaf raking foot dusting positions have vanished, and modern technology is biting at the heels of other middle-skilled steady jobs.

White scientists seemed to have gotten so carried away with discovering ways to increase production by making manufacturing less labor intensive that they forgot to devise an alternate plan of what to do with all the workers that their new machines replaced. Blackmen and Black male youth bear the brunt of this predicament. More of them are out of work or untrained to work than the males in any other nationality inland. Many Blackmen report that they know for a fact from experience that Blackwomen are given preferential treatment in the workplace and often snatch jobs from under their feet. They imply that the women should step back and let them get at the head of the line to get work. Public outcry from Black feminist organizations absolutely reject this idea as one designed to stop the economic progress of women, or as just another excuse the Blackman makes for not finding a job. By right, the reasons of pecking order and natural law, the Blackman should receive preference for employment because he is responsible for the condition of the rest of his people — the women, the children and the senior citizens. He is the one who is in authority and his leadership for defense, protection and decision making should be supported. In 1931 the National Education Association reported that 75% of all American cities banned the employment of white women if it would take a job away from a white male trying to support his family. This was during the depression era, and represented one of those unspoken rules among white males to support maintenance of their authority, both in the home and on the job. While this appears cruel and unfair to women who justifiably have a need to earn a living and advance their careers, the male psyche demands self-preservation as a first priority. Blackmen have this same innate attitudinal instinct, because he is the original man, the maker, owner, and creator of all we see connected to life on and off the earth. History documents that when push comes to shove on survival, women and children have never been first. While this seems barbaric or ruthless, one must not forget that the first person of specific gender who appeared on earth was God, and God is a man. Thus he functions with the assumption that if humanity is threatened in any manner, he intends to be the last to concede his life. While the Blackman demonstrates by his behavior that he is not worthy or qualified to be the boss of the Black nation according to the challenges presented as the proving ground, the funda-mental essence of his being screams out to be in charge. His feeling of superiority over every other man stems from the nucleus of his being that he is the best man. This instinct is something innate, bred in his bones, even when he can't verbalize or defend it by acceptable example. This inherent superiority often earns him accusations of being conceited, arrogant, or thinking that he is better than everybody else. This superiority instinct is nearly the best kept secret Blackmen have. Both drive and instinct are natural reactions but they can be altered by training which can turn into a habit and eventu-ally considered the norm. So today Blackmen try to make it perfectly clear that they don't think they're better than anybody

else. They recite:
"I don't think I'm better than anybody else."
"I think I'm just as good as any other man."
"I'm not superior but I'm not inferior either."
"I just want to be equal."
"I'm not any different from any other man."
"I'm not trying to say that I'm better but I'm just as good."

Imagine the frustration they must feel from wanting to vocalize and act out their superiority but must stifle these claims because of his status. The only arena in which they are encouraged to demonstrate their superiority is in their ability to play sports. In practically every other encounter in their life they are provoked in one way or another, because of the standard rules pitted against them, to agree with or claim their own inferiority. The source of this pain is rooted in every aspect of his daily life and it is a pain that he doesn't think he can do anything about.

This often happens to him when applying for a job or when he is on the job. His lack of vocational skills evoked the terminology of being referred to as the "hardcore unemployed." And certainly there are Blackmen qualified in many skills who also cannot find work in the system that compensates them enough to survive. He approaches a workplace to apply for a job with understandable apprehension. He has been told, hinted to, shown or deduces on his own that as a Blackman he is going to have a hard time convincing a white personnel clerk that he can do a job and deserves to have it. He already knows that the complications of this interaction expands the further up the job rung he climbs. He knows he is talked to differently, spoken to in a different tone, given special regulations or earns a lower pay. There are no controls to manipulate the internal workings of every job site in America. And much of what he views is degrading, and he is very sensitive on this. It hits on his ego so negatively that sometimes he would rather not work at all. So when forced to choose between doing a certain kind of work or living in poverty, the job does not rise as the lesser of the two evils. This often occurs on low paying or higher paying jobs. After being inducted through this kind of ego agony, he has to compensate himself in some way. He can either find a way around the problem, give up as explained above or rationalize to himself that he didn't want the job anyway. The latter choice is often visibly manifested in his physical posture — he walks with a swanky gait. He walks like he's strutting. He walks in some exaggerated way that reminds him on taking every step that he is somebody special, either powerfully strong, beautifully handsome or daringly antagonistic. The special way of walking attributed to him is very important to his mental state of mind — especially his tender to the touch ego. As a Blackman develops confidence from achievement, acceptance or recognition his gait returns to a more normal stance and he gives little thought to the slant of his body or his foot cadence when walking. This also applies to what he does with his hands or his arms. Interesting. A motivation to work is best stimulated by a knowledge of the results. The only knowledge that most Blackmen have about the results of working is that it will help them pay their bills, dress and have a good time. The good time may just be his ability to buy any material item he desires. This is not the right incentive for him to use to go to work but the Blackman has little knowledge or familiarity with the good feeling that comes from providing goods and services for his own consumption. He has no recollection of a time when he was not dependent upon someone else in authority over him to help him provide for him. He isn't versed in being in charge of his own destiny based on being self-sufficient or able to rely on his own abilities to supply the things he needs to survive. His lack of knowledge about the thrill of independence began about 75 years ago when he determined the only way to absorb himself into white America and match their quality of life, was to pursue legal means of accountability through the courts. While involved with the failures inherent in that system, his already temperamental ego flared, his emotions jumped in and he took to trying to shame the government and inspire enough pity from the masses to give him psychological freedom and tangible donations. Remember now, at that time he was already declared physically free and although Europeans were over 300 years ahead of him in business and industry he should have began where he was and started to work for financial independence. He could have done this because studies reveal that he actually discovered much of the machinery and technology the Europeans used to speed their economy. Had he done that he would control enough goods and services to write his own ticket and eliminated calling on the whitemen every time he wanted to do something. He should have done this. Woulda, coulda and shoulda — which is as far as the Blackman gets in solving his economic burdens. It's conceivable that he was so psychologically traumatized by his recent enslavement that he was desperate for an immediate fix and the courts seemed the shortest route. He was as wrong then as he is now but his pattern of searching for legal remedy remains. The point of these comparisons between a long time ago, the 60's, and current times, is to reveal the Blackman's pattern of technique he uses to try to get what he wants. Freeing the body and freeing the mind are two completely different motions.

It's not fair to charge Blackmen across the board with being lazy and refusing to work, but he is sometimes known for evoking creative ways to avoid physical labor. The Blackman will:

1) Say that he can't find a job which pays enough to be worthwhile.

2) Pretend to be injured under Work Comp — malingering, such as a bad back, serious headaches, dizzy spells or poor vision..

3) Playing crazy — to get unlimited free drugs and sympathy.

4) Never move out of his parent's house (usually his mother) and lets her continue to support and take care of him.

5) Become a so-called professional student, stay in school or some type of training, changing his field of study — all to avoid executing a plan for day-to-day survival by working.

6) Becoming an alcoholic or drug addict to avoid dealing with reality period.

It's perfectly understandable that after the Blackman's release from slavery, the last thing he wanted to do was go back to work — again.

Another reason Blackmen have problems working on a job is that it may sometimes be difficult for him to understand what he is supposed to do. He may lapse on his ability to understand certain terminologies, experience discomfort at being directly given an order, because he realizes immediately that he doesn't know how to do it. Blackmen do not always know how to mentally separate the steps of action required to complete a task. The savaging of his intellect has already been addressed in the chapter discussing his learning disabilities. But another aspect to be considered is that his lack of self-worth and repression of his real nature causes him to feel so emasculated that he freezes mentally. This added to his unnatural inclination to not want anybody to tell him what to do makes it appear as if he is naturally hostile or slow witted. But he is a man who all his life has been told, directed or forced to obey other people. Blackmen in business say that it is extremely difficult for a Blackman to get another Blackman to work with the same attentiveness and level of energy that they smilingly deliver to a white male or white female boss. They say this is another example of how Blackmen don't respect each other, or think that a Black male is qualified or justified in being his boss or supervisor. Blackmen who say they try to hire other Blackmen, say when employed, they are tardy too much, take too long for lunch, play around on the job, lie, take off from work for invalid reasons, will steal, undermine their efforts, argue back, sleep, come to work untidy, waste materials, work slow and have an all around lackadaisical attitude. These allegations are duly documented as typical of their work on some jobs supervised or owned by whites. White and Blackmen complain of another kind of behavior he exhibits on the job. He plays the clown. He will pass notes or photos displaying gutter humor, and will stand and listen attentively at whites telling racist jokes and laugh as if they are funny. They will also laugh at any other kind of joke a white male might share with them. They still do a lot of grinning and shuffling to try to impress their white supervisors with their affability and secret flashback of being the happy slave. This is an old styled tactical move to get on the good side of the master. This is also called brown-nosing; doing something to get special approval from the boss. Their thoughts and behaviors are contradictory to how they really feel but they think that if they present their real personalities they will be viewed as a threat for attempting to overpower the boss, or make the boss uncomfortable by functioning as an equal. He has a lot to deal with. Every Blackman who is working, or has ever worked in a majority white jobsite, or has been employed as the token Black; has laughed at jokes that were not funny, not responded to incidents they viewed as racist, and allowed white males to disrespect them or insult unrelated Blackwomen in one way or another. He has swallowed all this. It has given him a permanent lump in his throat and a crack in his mirror. "BOSS" comes from an old German word "bozan" which means "to beat." These days many Blackmen say the economy is too slow to try to go into business or attempt to do anything to make money independent of the system. There are many benefits to going into business during hard times if one can manage to get products or provide a service:

A)   Large companies who streamline their operations whose business is in recession and can no longer provide special attention or customer service to the little man or little enterprise.

B)   Wholesale goods are lower priced, cheaper to acquire.

C)   Office space is cheaper because of failed tenants.

D)   Labor rates can be negotiated at a lower level.

E)   There are more opportunities to sell lower priced items.

Blacks who say they try to do business with Blackmen in business complain as usual that their prices are too high, delivery is too slow, they don't respond to calls in a timely fashion, will abscond with deposits, don't follow through on warranties, sell defective products, take too long to finish a job, or will abandon a job before completion after they are paid in full. They use these foul-ups to explain why they only spend about 7% of their incomes trying to do business with Blackmen. Every nationality in America has established clearly defined districts in which many of them have come together in the same area and opened businesses. Sometimes these areas spread over several blocks on both sides of the street or consist of mini-malls or the like. They become booming trade and cultural centers and often tourist attractions. These ethnic groups come together and agree to work together to form a business venture of some sort to display their capabilities to make a living in their own way.   China Town districts, Hispanic, Asian, Korean businessmen are all known for basically working and living close together. They maintain their ethnic individuality while still obeying the rules and regulations to operate a business in America. The Blackman has few examples nationwide of this kind of business unity. If they are in the same business in the same town or state, they do not ordinarily come together about the needs or happenings in those businesses. They do not purchase together wholesale to get a better price, they do not share information about operational advances they have discovered, and they do not back each other up if one of them falls on financial difficulty. These practices are unworkable for progress among like groups trying to earn a living off of 280 million Americans. Europeans are masters at setting agendas, moving on an idea and convincing constituents to offer support, by showing them how it will benefit them to cooperate. From the first day they came here they agreed to uphold the plan, stick to the ideas agreed on and share in the success. The educators, the businessmen, the scientists, the doctors, the lawyers, industry, politicians, common laborers, wives and mothers and the founding fathers who set the agenda — all agreed. When any small or large group of people agree to unify to achieve something — they succeed. This is not to say that they did not have debates or problems trying to absorb or reject various suggestions, but they agreed on the basic premises and worked the kinks out as they arose. And they stood steadfast together as a solid wall unified in their conclusions to install the foundation of their ideas which would preserve their culture, and aptly provide their future generations with a system of rulership. These founding white fathers agreed. They made the sacrifices, did things they didn't want to do, worked harder than they preferred, played by the rules they agreed on, duked it out on the streets if necessary, but they held fast to the goal, and taught their sons and daughters how to preserve the system — and they, too, agreed. They agreed to continue to work day and night to keep it going and to teach it to their own children right on down the line. Each new generation perpetuated the original plan, improving on it whenever they could. Obviously the above is a broad description of how they did what they did. But it certainly gives the greatest value as being agreement and unity.

Blackmen, on the other hand, take special time to point out that they are not all alike, and do not wish to be lumped in with all other Blackmen or Blacks in general. The recent most fashionable trend in their dialogue is to intellectually point out "the Black community is not monolithic." The only unique aspect of the Blackman's personality is that he and his kind are not monolithic. Every nation all over the earth when learning of the poor quality of life and injustices Blacks endure in America realize that they suffer these indignities because they are not monolithic. In fact the number one reason the Black-man has not risen to his full economic capability is because he is not monolithic. Because monolithic means stonelike and firm. The Blackman is not firm in holding on to his own ideas. His lack of lithification causes him not to be solidified on any issue concerning his own people. He has defined and redefined, adjusted and readjusted, changed and rechanged himself over and over continually trying to fit in. Repeatedly trying to mold himself into the images others have chosen for him. Each time he remakes himself it is with the hope that he will finally qualify for full acceptance, justice and respect he believes he is due as a man. He says he is disgusted with the way other Blackmen behave and think. He says he is embarrassed by their actions and savagery and he uses the worst examples of his kind to tell himself that there's no point in him trying to make a change for the better by himself. He says that most dudes are liars, jive, can't be trusted and will steal your woman if you turn your back. They always use other Blackmen as the reason that African-Americans are not "together" or making any progress. He only feels this way because all of the solutions he thinks of require him to get a law passed, convince whites to help, petition the government, locate something impossible to find, get "all" Blackmen to agree on an action, get his woman to cooperate, get a loan, get a grant, get some help, or a long list of other obstacles he thinks he must overcome before he can do anything. The last place he looks for help is to his own determination and ingenuity. He has believed the hype. He thinks that the mountain is just too high to climb — and besides, he doesn't have a rope. Or a hope that he can succeed. He is too mentally lazy to start at the bottom. He doesn't realize that he's already at the bottom. It would be better for his wounded ego if he started this very day to try to become independent in some way. It would be better if he took charge of one of the problems he sees existing in his neighborhood. It's never too late for him to learn farming, canning, poultry or beef production, how to operate a hospital, how to run a school, how to set up a first aid center, how to set up a grocery store, how to make shoes, how to build a bed, create a stove, weave a broom, turn cotton into cloth, make a light bulb or to supply any number of the thousands of daily needs and wants of African-American people. He can't do most of these things because he was not taught to think in terms of taking care of himself. In fact, he has been innuendoed into thinking that all of his needs would always be supplied by others, and that they could do it quicker, cheaper and better. Their doing it would save him time, money and worry. But that is not how it has turned out. The way it has turned out is that today he feels useless, unable to keep up, and helpless. There's so much to do and he has so little resources to do it with that he is stunned into not doing anything. Yes, there are many Blackmen who are entrepreneurs but most of them supply the optional/recreational needs of civilization. The basics, which keep him tied and restricted from exerting masculinity, are not made or controlled by him. He has no more ownership in America than the Indians. And they have none. This entire scenario comes down to education. He has never been taught the basics of survival or the psychology behind why he needs to know how. He has been mentally bullied into inaction. He has no memory of ever supplying his own needs nor of being responsible for himself. This lack of familiarity with independence has followed him home, another place where he is not adept at taking charge of his wards, because he has allowed others to set the rules and standards there too.

As during the depression of the early 1930's, when jobs and food and opportunities are scarce, men become more impatient and hostile — to each other and to the government. During the depression whitemen and their families picketed, rioted and often stormed grocery stores to get food for their families. Welfare was first given to poor whites during this era as a way to calm down the angry husbands and fathers who were not able to support their families. It was to be only a temporary measure until the economy got better. But once the government had made available welfare payments, food stamps and food rationing stamps, it became known as a "charity," a temporary governmental assistance to be given to those unable to provide for themselves at the time. There was no requirement that the white male husband or father as head of household had to leave home so that his family could qualify for welfare benefits. To the contrary, welfare was designed so that the family could stay together and maintain a household. Later these rules changed.

As the American economy becomes tighter and tighter and fewer jobs are available for white males, Blackmen will be shoved more and more out of the workplace. In the cases where this does not happen there will surface new hostilities towards them for having a job with so many white males unemployed and unable to secure their families. In the near futures there will be job wars — based on who should be employed. Men will actually start to physically fight over jobs. More women will be let go so that a man can work and more Blackmen will sink into deeper hopelessness and outrage at having nothing to do. This situation is unavoidable based on the swelling national debt, failing banking institutions and confusion in the government. All of this along with huge debts owed to America abroad that will remain uncollectible, will set the stage for mass dissatisfaction between the haves and the have-nots.

The Blackman's problem is not always that he does not have any money, but that he allocates his funds to the wrong expenditures. While big business in America complained throughout the Reagan Era that his economic gymnastics caused the quickest grand-slam redistribution of wealth ever seen during a Presidential term, this redistribution also caused a mass rearrangement in the lives of African-Americans. High paying plantations which formerly provided many Black families with dependable incomes, hospitalization, life insurance and retirement benefits all but vanished. Many who were used to working and being comfortable turned to unemployment benefits, food stamps and welfare. Blackmen were most affected. Trailing behind them, despondent Blackwomen. Those eight years were crucial. Wealth, such as it was, was redistributed from grocery stores, rent, clothes and consumer bills to the crack-cocaine drug dealers. A lot of the money low-income Blacks spent in their neighborhoods and urban shopping centers was redirected into the quicksand lifestyle of the drug culture. Never to be heard from again, and causing many smaller locally owned suppliers of goods and services to bankrupt. Closed stores and boarded up buildings pull property values down and re-route traffic to other thriving areas. Many urban areas have multiple city blocks of closed down businesses, entire shopping centers and downtown business districts that not only existed on the Blackman's money, but employed him on some level, have disappeared. The middle class Blackman slid into low, and the lower middle class Blackman landed flat on his back. There has developed the widest gap in income and lifestyle since the 30's, as there are now mainly only two classes of Americans, the rich — and the poor. The broad area in the middle is filled with those trying to hang on by sheer will. The economy is not better, jobs are not available and the recession might surprisingly slip into a depression, and despite all that is happening as a warning — might catch the Blackman by surprise. Again. Blackmen spend a lot of cash or credit on items bearing no resemblance to investments for their future survival in such a wavering unsteady economy. He is not seen readily preparing for the days of want which are predicted to descend down shortly upon the whole country. In the late 1920's installment debt was introduced (prior to the depression) and the system of $1 down and a $1 a week proliferated the start of the pre-spent income. Money received on Friday for working all week is already promised to someone for an item bought on Tuesday of the same week. Credit and credit cards are the greatest, most detrimental method of spending the Blackman has ever had access to. It gave him a way to get his hands on anything he wants by just signing on the dotted line. Heaven. There are four categories of products produced by Europeans or Japanese which the Blackman can be counted on to spend his money for. The four main categories of his major expenditures are:

1) Clothes (designer) and related accessories
2) Specialty cars, vans and fancy stereo equipment & music
3) Restaurants — including fast food takeouts
4) Sports and entertainment

Not only do they purchase these items regularly to keep up with fashion and technology advancements, but they willingly provide free advertisement by wearing or using products with the brand names boldly displayed in a conspicuous spot — like on their head, chest or back. They memorize the brand names and whatever their latest product is. They have arranged these European and Japanese made items into categories of which one is the best, the next best and the barely acceptable. To see how they dress they give the impression that they are rolling in dough. To date, it has not occurred to them to try to corner the market on the consumer goods that African-Americans use and buy the most of. His greatest thrills are derived from having the ability to afford the things he desires to compliment his image. No social reform group has ever been able to convince the Blackman to stop blowing his money on things that he could live without. He persists in financially enriching the very group of people who he claims treat him so badly. It's as if when he emotionally desires to possess and own a consumer item, he suspends those ideas until the transaction is complete. It's as if the European shopkeepers become temporarily a non-person when he goes to them to buy something and once he leaves the store his amnesia fades and he returns to his original politics that the whiteman is a capitalist. But they can't be a capitalist without a steady stream of paying customers. The Blackman is a steady paying customer. It's as if he becomes so hypnotized by an item that this suspended state prevents him from recognizing the connection. It has a masochistic theme that suggests he wishes to reward his perceived oppressors for the privilege. The advertising specialists take great care to use creatively pointed language to attract select customers to a product. The intrinsic values created penetrate the egos of Blackmen. The marketeers create such an aura of accomplishment for an individual to be able to afford and own an item in such a magnetizing way that Blackmen dashingly run to stores to make a purchase literally foaming at the wallet. The advertising contains another concept that plays on the emotions of consumers, in that they send out messages about a product suggestive that owning or wearing the product will create an improved feeling. They imply that ownership of a certain thing will make one feel better and become more powerful than a locomotive and able to leap tall buildings in a single paycheck. They do this by projecting the exclusivity of wearing designer brands, by making jewelry so divine that one simply must have some to be considered whole, or by portraying an item as a special status symbol denoting the wearer or owner as superior. Blackmen have been indoctrinated with the idea that top of the line items, no matter how much they cost, are what he needs to feel alright with himself... and guarantee the continued ballooning of his ego.

He has even been psyched into bragging about how much he spent on something. This is just another trick that psyches him into insisting on paying the ceiling price for a selected item so he can always have the satisfaction of knowing and letting others know that he owns the Rolls-Royce edition of everything he has. So they buy items that make them feel good, and items that make shopowners feel rich. Few Blackmen are willing to give up the accompanying thrill experienced when they buy something designated by advertisers and the media as "special best." He does not ever want anyone to think that he is mediocre in his tastes or unable to afford something.

This is not to say that the advertisers are wrong in the way they sell their products. The Blackman has a responsibility. A responsibility to at least attempt to supply some of his own needs and desires. And a responsibility to know when he's being gamed on. It is not the advertisers who are at fault, it's him trying to develop his character based on wardrobe fantasy and state-of-the-art equipment.

One of these days, very soon, the Blackman is going to regret not investing his hard earned pennies on more sensible needs of survival.

While the Blackman dislikes the fact that many Asian foreigners have come to America and progressed further in a shorter period of time than the Blackman has done in over 100 years, this is understandable because the Blackman is embarrassed and does not understand how they did it. The Orientals have established their own neighborhoods, they have their own churches, banks, hair salons and video stores, and a long list of other businesses they built to serve their own people's needs and the needs of others. The Koreans, Japanese, Laotists, Vietnamese and Chinese have, in a relatively short time filled with long sacrifices, imaged themselves as shrewd business dealers and unified workers. They have earned the respect of many Europeans due to their perseverance against scrutiny of their odd customs and language barriers. Nevertheless they now buy up many small and large grocery stores, laundromats, dry cleaners and the like. They purchase most of these businesses in the African-American communities. They have a different value system so it takes them a while to understand the ways of the American negro and vice-versa. But eventually the Blacks start to patronize them out of necessity — they own the only stores in the proximity of where they live. The Blackman is sometimes hostile to the Asians because he feels threatened that they are taking over their communities and treats them differently from the white shopowners who previously owned the businesses. The Orientals are usually diligent workers and keep their spot organized. The Blackman resents this intrusion into his territorial world. However, the Blackman in some cases has shopped at the neighborhood grocer for all his life and it never occurred to him to try to buy or run the business himself. Then he gets mad when somebody else, more industrious and willing to sacrifice, comes along and seizes the opportunity to advance economically. It would not be surprising if the Orientals, through their attorneys or advisors, were directed to the Black communities as fertile dependable opportunities to make money — everyday all day. It is no accident that they are slowly buying up all the business establishments available in the African-American populated areas. Everyone knows that the Blackman is a consumer. He buys from everyone else and sells to few. The Asians say that they do not understand what kind of problem the Blackman in America has. They say all they do is find a spot, stock it, open the doors and the money walks right in. They say that making money in America is the easiest money they have ever earned. They report that some Blacks come in and out of their stores several times a day, and that they pay whatever the price is to get what they want. They say Blacks eat all day long and drink alcohol just as frequently. In other words the Blackman is totally dependent on others for survival, has short term gratification goals and is easy prey to anyone who can supply his needs. The Blackman should not be angry with the Asians, instead he should try to learn from them. True, they have never been the kind of slave the Blackman has been, but many of them endured hardships to get to America. It seems that everyone feeds off of the Blackman's disunity and laziness and failure to take responsibility for his own needs. Another interesting thing about the Asians is that it is very rare to see them shopping in Kroger, A&P, Pathmark, Jewel-T or Seven-Eleven stores. It is equally odd to find them in major department stores or at the movies. The Blackman should wonder how do they get their food, buy their clothes and manage to mind their own business. They keep in contact with their homeland culture, and spend their money among themselves. They do not wear the latest styles, few name-brand sneakers, no heavy gold chains and no Oriental drunks are seen on the streets and nor does one find them living in subway stations or cardboard boxes in the park. They eat together, sleep together, shop together and plan together. If they are in downtown areas it is because they are working fruit or clothing stands. They set up early in the morning and close late in the evening. It is difficult to distinguish who is who and which tribe they belong to because they all tend to favor each other. When asked why they attach such a small mark-up on some of their products they respond that they count and save every penny they earn. If they only make a few pennies per item they are willing to do so because they are steadily stockpiling money. They have come to America against many odds to enjoy what they deem as a free enterprise system and for a better life for their families. Contrary to the negative opinions Blackmen have about them, they did not come to America just to make the Blackman look like a fool.

It seems that the Blackman is very perturbed about another nationality moving in and taking money they intended to continue spending with the whiteman. The Asians have disproved many of the Blackman's theories and excuses he uses to explain why he cannot grasp an economic foothold. Often when other Blackmen open a store comparable to their white business owner colleagues they find that Blacks will not patronize them. They blame their lack of customership on poor service, no credit policies, expensive mark-ups on products, slack business hours, inferior quality of foodstuffs and bad attitudes by cashiers or help. The Caucasians and the Asians support each other while they work the kinks out. They welcome people of their own nationality into business and offer advice, financial support for free labor to help them get on their feet.

No business is failsafe on the first day or during the first few years. Having an idea is one thing, executing an idea is another.

There are three questions that the Blackman should ask the Asians:

1) Where do they get their food from since they rarely shop in the whiteman's supermarket?

2) Where do they get their clothes from since they do not shop in the whiteman's clothing stores?

3) How and what rules do they follow that enable them to live so closely together in the same house without fighting or killing one another every Friday and Saturday night?

The answers to these questions might shed some light on some very pressing barriers that the Blackman encounters when he tries to figure out how to be independent of the whiteman. The Blackman lends credence to the premise "once a slave, always a slave." Because he does not appear either capable of acquiring the skills, or drumming up enough unity of purpose, or support from his brothers to get off the bottom rung of the ladder. So far no leader, no plan, no government support or education has been acceptable to the Blackman to inspire him to change his own condition. His refusal to do anything for himself in the way of supplying his own needs is part of the reason he has lost his woman and children because they have to go to Europeans for all their needs. This keeps the Blackman from being in a position of power and authority over his family. Because they all go to the same people to fill their needs be they food, clothing, shelter or employment. So he has no control of any sustenance he needs for life. This makes every other man appear greater and more powerful — and ultimately more respected.

The Blackman is also frustrated because of the stigma attached to receiving welfare from the government. He knows that many of his women are on the welfare and are supporting his children from it. But he feels so violated and cheated out of his birthright that he has not been able to decline reparations of any kind and begs for more. The only reparations he has received comes in the form of welfare, food stamps, medicaid health coverage, WIC, Section 8, Disability, affirmative action and workmen's compensation checks. It seems that Blackwomen and children look to the Blackman for financial solutions and he looks to the white man. This is not a secure or comfortable cycle. Welfare is just a form of economic subsidy. When major corporations receive welfare they describe it as low-interest loans, agricultural assistance, tax expenditures, accelerated depreciation, deferral of capital gains, business and property tax refunds and interest free carrying charges on public purpose state and local debt. All of these are forms of welfare subsidy. They give money to some, loan money to others and save money for the rest. So the entire American Parliamentary effort is entrenched in welfare fraud in one way or the other.

The Blackman must decide to stop rambling in the tax pockets of other races. They must learn to work among themselves based on their collective need to prove to themselves that they can. He cannot regain the amount of dignity he was stripped of 400 years ago, but if they start now to practice at conformity and cooperation with each other they could make it without welfare of any kind. Many times his lack of strength is brought on by anxiety which leaves him unable to move his physical body into action. The resulting depression entrenches him in a mentally catatonic state. He is not motivated because he is uninspired. He won't even consider this as a subject. The Blackman has had a difficult time trying to revive his fractured ego strictly by self-propulsion. He continues to search for a way or a sign that informs him that he is authentic for real.

A few decades ago if a Blackman accomplished any kind of startling or unusual advancement, he was routinely offered a left-hand compliment and told: "you're a credit to your race."

Many Blackmen were told this and took pride in being reminded that he was superior to the rest of his people and never considered that he was never told how many credits he needed to matriculate and receive validation of his self-worth. It was a subtle implication that he was lacking in something and needed credits to help him keep score of his progress towards getting it. His capabilities have always been in doubt and his massive historical accomplishments approached with suspicion by other nationalities. When European explorers pillaged through Africa in search of precious stones and glistening metals, they often uncovered spectacular artifacts such as statues, urns, jewelry, furnishings, drawings, weapons or masks. They were quite quick in suggesting that it was impossible for ancient African citizens to have created such modern beautiful items, and that obviously another European has preceded them to the area and designed such artifacts themselves. If they chose to, they could print such fraudulent information in their journals. African Blackmen always discovered progressive techniques to fill their specific needs, and specialized in skilled craftsmanship and automated manufacturing. They devised many check and balance systems as a way to stay on track of their goals. The Blackman's ancestors took enormous prestige in their business and trade practices because he knew he was born to work, and born to have many wives and sire many children. The Blackman was gyped out of receiving "credit" for many of his historic artifact contributions up until about 1910. After then it was impossible to deny it.

For several years now there has existed Blackmen who are grassroot entrepreneurs who travel around the country frequenting conventions, art shows, outdoor festivals and other densely populated areas displaying products and wares. These Blackmen are referred to as "Street Vendors" or just "Vendors." They are Blackmen who decided to forge ahead and experiment with working for themselves and being their own boss. They mostly travel in cars or vans, trucks or busses and offer body oils, incense, artwork, clothes, hats, shoes, expertly hand-crafted leather goods, designer quality handcrafted jewelry, records African flavored fabrics, t-shirts, dolls, books, tapes, records, buttons, hair products, cosmetics, foodstuffs and all sorts of ethnic goods. They have to cope with bad weather, poor sales, licensing, taxes, heavy baggage, long hours, theft and the fluctuating cost of booth space. But on the other hand they enjoy the excitement of travel, catering to an ever changing customer base, the thrill of motion, meeting new people, networking, participating in trade and commerce, making money seven days a week, the pleasure of not being confined to an hourly wage, freedom to take off when they get ready, the opportunity to learn wholesale buying and calculations of retail mark-up, the comradeship of other Blackmen vendors, the ability to provide jobs, learn investing, and gain some self-respect through ownership and recognition in the national marketplace.

Blackmen vendors complain that when Black patronize them they demand special deals and haggle about prices and try to negotiate for a lower cost. They say this started out to be interesting and similar to the marketplace excitement in the homeland; but they say now the haggling has become negative consisting of outright demands for a cheaper price or a threat to shop elsewhere. Blackmen vendors say this is unfair to them as businessmen because Blacks would not think of shopping at a major white owned and operated establishment and asking for a few dollars off the stated price. Unless there is a sale they pay the price marked and get their receipt and leave the store smiling. Blackmen vendors say this puts them in a precarious position because they are often forced to reduce their products to a no-profit price in order to do business with their own kind. They say they are trying to make a living like any other man in business and offer their wares at fair prices for their special interest consumer markets. But they can't afford to give their inventory away at wholesale prices to retail customers. They say Blacks treat them like they are trying to rip off the public or something. Blackmen vendors say they are equally disturbed that Black organizations offer them booth space at their conventions and meetings and charge them hefty fees, sometimes up to $1,000 or more, but make no plans or efforts to direct their conventioneers to their vending stands usually located in the same building or close proximity to their conferences. They charge the hosts of these conventions with allowing the hotels to offer their attendees FREE bus trips to white shopping malls or trade centers to ignore their presence. They say they believe that the organizers of these conventions are obligated to make sure they receive enough exposure in their literature and by signs and advertisement; to make sure they earn a profit on their booth space investment. The organization charges them for the space and the hotels charge them for the tables, chairs, lighting, ash trays or any other display items they may need. They also have their travel cost, food, lodging, inventory and other regular expenses attached to their roving lifestyle. So they want more accountability and cooperation from the Black organizations who solicit their money for booth space to add an extra flair of activity to their conventions. These are not unreasonable requests.

Blackmen vendors, regrettably, report they have a high occurrence of shoplifting/stealing from their display tables, mostly by other Blacks. The Blackman's overriding problem is that he has made his main challenge in life to be trying to win acceptance and approval from whites. His major goal in life is to prove to white people that he is just as good as they are and deserving of having what they have. These are harsh realities that he will deny to his dying day — which according to government statistics is not too far off if he keeps behaving like he is now. He acts like his only obstacle in life is to convince whites to accept him as an equal. And he has the delusional idea that anything he tries to do which is not sanctioned or endorsed by the government will fail miserably. He wants their blessings. He wants their jobs. And he wants their women.

Oh, he may talk freely about the natural equality of all mankind but he sees the whiteman as Mt. Everest, the biggest stumbling block he has ever known of, and he feels like a mole hill digging around at the bottom. When he works on one of their jobs, no matter how much he earns, he knows he hates having to jump to work every time the boss walks in, and he detests having to speak extra nicely to the big boss of the company every time he encounters him — or her. He deplores the fact that if his boss or supervisor shows up he has to act like he's busy even if there's nothing to do. He can't ever report that his job doesn't keep him busy enough because he is afraid he will be required to do more work for the same salary. He is trying to do as little as possible and uses up a lot of his concentration powers trying to figure out how to work slower or get out of doing certain tasks on the job. He only feels this way because it is not his job. He is a guest employee when he works on a job created, owned and operated by another nationality. When a man works for himself he is always willing to go the extra mile so he gets more done and ultimately makes more money. The Blackman acts like he has been hypnotized into being an employee instead of an employer.

Blackmen do not want to pay child support. Supplying money to pay for what they consider unnecessary needs for their children, especially if they have more than one, is not a priority to them. They take no special pride in knowing that they are supporting their own seed. In fact, if there is any way they can get out of doing anything for their children they will do so. These days the courts have new rulings to track them down, garnish their wages, take it out of their tax refunds, arrest them, put liens on their car or property to make them finance the lives of children they created with their own sperm and blood. If he and the child's mother do not have an active ongoing relationship, it is rare that he will support his baby on his own. His attitude is that the federal or state welfare or food subsidy availability lets him off the hook. He would rather see his woman on welfare, or wait and see if her new man will assume responsibility for his babies. He thinks that by paying child support that he is doing the baby's mother a favor or letting her rule him in some way. He doesn't realize that he should be ashamed to have the whiteman haul him into court because he refuses to take care of his baby. He is detached mentally from his seed and is content to let the government be the providing father for his children. Sometimes he gets with another woman and does more for her children than he does for his own. He behaves as if there is some magic wand that a Black mother can wave to provide for her children without his help. What is to happen when the welfare and food stamp budget runs out? Who is to take care of his children then? And where are all the Black fathers who sired almost 500,000 non-white children rotting in orphanages? And how can a Blackman consider himself sane and go about his daily life so happy-go-lucky, dressing in the finest clothes and driving the best cars while denying his seed time and money?

Chapter 7

RECREATION

The Blackman's brain — his entire thinking process — must be systematically decontaminated. The pointless illusions upon which his whole life is based must be dismantled and replaced with other realities pertinent to his heritage and survival. Currently he thrives on excitement to the excess, vicarious thrills, life gambles, risks and challenging physical tournaments of all sorts. Imagine what the Blackman's life would be like without sports. What would he fill that time with? What kinds of activities would he select to redirect all the energy formerly thrust into gaming? A life without sports is a terrifying thought to Blackmen.

A game can be described as a timed series of physical maneuvers using recurring sets of motions and rules that can be exploited unexpectedly to reach the goal and/or make the other player look inept. Every game is basically a challenge in dishonesty. A player must win by tricks, cunning or diversion with sneakiness being the major tool. The one who is able to execute these attributes the best is called the one with skill. Contrary to this description and definition, Blackmen have been duped into thinking that recreational sports promote development of organization, fairness, endurance, cooperation and responsibility. Sports are further defined as developing skills that will be needed throughout life in business and personal affairs. None of this is true. Additionally, sports and playing games diverts the Blackman's attention from more pressing matters and activities that he should be addressing. But sports are presented as such harmless fun. Even Blackmen who when tested would be considered a slow learner with a mild I.Q. can recite verbatim points scored in a game, goal averages, rules, shirt numbers, who got traded where, type of injuries, tournament winners, position titles, play-off dates, coaches, names and backgrounds of players, including their mascots and emblems. Discussing sports creates some of the most lively conversations Blackmen have. The topic itself exhilarates them, titillates their senses and promotes much gaiety. Sports are a way for them to show off their physical prowess. When they play at sports they get to be frisky, they can frolic, romp, whirl and twirl. They revel in being able to perform all sorts of acrobatics and contortions to outwit the other players to reach the goal. They like contests where they have to tussle, scuffle and scramble to win something. They take great pride when they win. Some of them only come to life during the sporting seasons. They will sit glued to the television or radio to see or hear a game. They will stand in long lines to get tickets or sit out in the rain or snow to see a spectator sport up close. Even if their seat is so far back or up that they can barely see — they just want to be there. They will drive long distances, take an airplane or train to attend a sports event. And it doesn't matter what the tickets cost either.

The merchandising of sports in America is an activity to itself. Hats, caps, t-shirts, sweat shirts, running suits, visors, flags, wrist and head bands, rain coats, license plates, posters, banners, and all sorts of memorabilia are made available to Blackmen to advertise their allegiance to the team of their choice. This is part of the "fun" they associate with playing sports on the spectator level. They have also been known to fall out over their different views about a certain player, sport event or team. They even kill each other over what they deem as an important point about a game. Associated with pre-game or post-game festivities is the drinking of alcoholic beverages — and cursing and yelling as part of the excitement.

Sometimes they become so enthralled with a sport that little else matters in their lives. Sports are a welcome topic just about everywhere. This distraction is started in early childhood when sports are used as a type of rite of passage. Endurance and proficiency at playing a sport, especially basketball or football, is just about a necessity for a Black boy to gain acceptance and recognition into the neighborhood group consisting of his peers. Due to their search for rites to mark crossing over, up to another level, or entrance into adulthood, they seek out activities involving feats, stunts, collision or regalement. Sports and game playing fits into the perceived requirements. Once a Black boy or adult Blackman becomes athletically inclined or worships sports as a spectator, it garners much of his attention span, including concentration and energy. Black males seek a way to distinguish themselves from younger children and embarkment on manhood. Females have menstruation as a flash point at which time they are prompted by another woman about the responsibilities, expectations and guidelines she must begin to adhere to on coming into adult womanhood. The show of blood signifies her potential to become a mother and take on even greater responsibilities in life and the world. Black males seek out a show of blood by placing themselves in a potentially dangerous combat zone — on the playing field where, if he is not adept, he may be injured. If he is able to inflict injury, all the better. Even if he experiences an injury he must shake it off, continue and survive it. The major reason for ancient African rites of passage was to extricate the son from the mother. This disengagement took on great significance and honor.   To survive such rites had a reveling and confidence building effect on the Black boy.   Sports in the Black community are a replacement for these rites of passage and the resultant feelings of achievement of getting his energy from himself, instead of his mother, to survive.

The study, learning and memorizing of the rules of sport games is ongoing throughout his life in various circles. Their involvement remains paramount on various levels until the day they die. There continues to be much discussion about whether or not sport figures are representative or qualified to be male role models to Black male youth. The aura of popularity and financial success surrounding sport figures makes playing sports a desirable job which appears to only require physical agility and a unique ability to accomplish great feats mostly involving a ball of some sort. They are supposed to represent fair play and sportsmanship which are accepted as honorable traits in the sport industry and attributes which Blackmen believe are transferrable by playing sports or watching others do so. Despite many famous sport players displaying ruthless aggression, hostility, impatience, cheating, bad language, rudeness and intolerance — they are still promoted by the media as being admirable and worthy of great respect.

115

Sports also give Blackmen something to look forward to and serves as a ventilator for some of their frustrations. Sometimes they play a game to express certain emotions be they positive or negative. The main sports or games Blackmen like to play, watch or admire are: basketball, football, baseball, golf, pool, tennis and boxing. They are the least involved with hockey. A few like fishing and hunting. Card games are also popular such as poker, bid whist, blackjack, gin rummy and bridge. Bridge is the least popular because it requires such intense concentration. The Blackmen who play chess consider themselves quite elite because it, too, requires thinking, paying attention and remembering the rules and playing by them. Chess (unlike checkers) is about a war of sorts.

Blackmen who play professional sports tend to earn huge sums of money by playing the game, doing commercials to endorse products and from personal appearances. Many make several million dollars a year. All of their money, just as with the entertainers, is on deposit in European owned banks. After they become successful at playing sports they are inducted into white social circles by virtue of their popularity. Many of them are married to white women. They become the heroes of teens and children. Many of them, after an extensive professional career, do not know when it is time to retire. They not only get hooked on earning great sums of money, but get addicted to the accolades and applause. So long after their abilities have mellowed and they have lost their speed and vitality they insist on continuing to play. They also, especially in the gladiator type sports, develop a masochistic tendency to insist on being beaten to a bloody pulp, humiliated by younger more virile players and end up looking like a fool. They become blind to any other potentials they may have. It gets so deeply entwined into their lifestyles and personalities that they do not know how to bow out gracefully and transfer their energies from sports to another vocation to live normally and earn a regular living. These Blackmen tend to mimic narcissistic trends which require them to be constantly praised or admired for being special. This narcissism, if not perpetually endorsed by others — strangers included — becomes a personality defect because they only recognize two levels of self-development; one is either champion, or inferior. Since their perceived superiority is umbilicaled to their playing of sports, when the sport playing ends, they slump into depression of days and nights spent reliving their previous sport accomplishments. This behavior is also exhibited by men who have held high business appointments as chief executives or H.N.I.C.'s , as they are commonly called fondly.

Blackmen also like to play games of chance. Gambling fits with their secret dreams of striking it rich without having to work for it. They spend money on a daily or weekly basis trying to hit "the number" or win the lottery. They go to Atlantic City and Las Vegas casinos as if making a pilgrimage. They gamble at cards, shooting dice, roulette, slot machines or bet on horses or dogs. Gambling is the Blackman's stock market of sorts, so they invest large sums of money in it hoping to propel it into big bucks. When and if they win, it often, when examined, only represents a sort of refund of the money they had already invested trying to win. Games of chance played on a local level are shooting dice or playing cards. They are seen in huddles kneeling on the ground excitedly throwing the dice, cursing, yelling and exchanging money. They attach an unrealistic opportunity value to cards and dice, and are known to shoot, stab, beat or kill each other over these games. They work tirelessly day after day trying to gain proficiency at shooting the dice to toss the winning combination of dots to win. It is considered fun. Recreation means to re-create something. So they play sports and games to re-create an activity that takes the place of working or learning skills to support themselves. Blackmen play too many games.

Europeans have always enjoyed sports, especially gladiator type bloody combats. Blackmen were used during slavery to provide them with these kinds of entertaining activities. Blackmen were featured in the old *Drum*, *Mandingo* and *Falconhurst* movies which depicted the lives of the slavemasters and the slaves in the deep south and appeared many years ago in docudrama type presentations. They showed whitemen training Blackmen to be bare-fisted boxers which they would bet huge sums of money on for the pleasure and boast of owning the most powerful and strong negro.

Blackmen have always been used to provide physical entertainment for other races because of their expert agility and bodily strength. So even if today they are compensated with high paychecks, they still being used as agile human machines capable of spectacular competitive achievements. They no longer get patted on the head for winning, now they get patted on the buttocks, hugged and clapped for. They are fine specimens of perfect anatomy, like sleek race horses, finely coordinated canines, expertly motorized vehicles — willing to show off for the highest bidder. Another example of his cultural amnesia. He thinks he only has brute force to make his way in the world.

Blackmen who play professional sports get a lot of attention from all kinds of women. They can literally write their own ticket regarding who they want to date or sleep with. They travel from city to city, including overseas, and enjoy a bevy of female admirers wherever they go. Recently they have become more aware of the dangers of practicing unrestrained unprotected random sex with multiple females. Of course, this only lasted for a short while until the discussion waned and the topic was abandoned by the media. AIDS is a very serious threat to the health of Blackmen in the sport and entertainment industry. Many are getting high to cope with the pressure and to keep up. With such a steady flow of Black earned dollars existing among Blackmen playing sports and reaping the attached benefits, the only independently owned Black bank in New York City failed to thrive in 1990 due to a financial deficit under $10 million dollars — and not one Blackman in sports or entertainment came forth to make a major deposit or organize his peers into coming up with the money for such a worthy cause. They have used little of their fortunes to aid failing Black owned or Black operated institutions other strong Blackmen struggle to maintain. They believe themselves to be so accepted and so valuable to the American public that they are safe from demise or any need to stay connected to Blacks still struggling to survive. This does not mean that they do not donate heavily to major charities. But there are no major charity organizations independently operated by Blacks except the United Negro College Fund — and that is not entirely Black operated because it exists by depending on donations or contributions from white philanthropy. So what prevents Black sport figures or high powered entertainers from supporting African-American owned and operated ventures? Answer: The Blackman is disrelated, unassociated and detached from any semblance of nationality or brotherhood with his own kind. And he is afraid that his white supporters will define any move he makes to support his own people as a sign of racism or support of Black segregation.

Many of them boast to the media that they do not consider

themselves Black or white, they are just ballplayers. They are the most nonpolitical bunch of Blackmen in America. They think they are protecting themselves from criticism or un-sportsman-like reputations. No, they do not owe other Black-men anything. Theoretically, they don't. But they owe it to themselves and their foreparents who suffered untold punish-ment to make sure future generations of Blackmen survived. He owes it to his children to maintain visible institutions of the Blackman's ability and talent to be self-sufficient and self-governing over his own destiny. And he owes it to himself to acknowledge his own culture, heritage and traditions because a man who denies his past afflictions, and rejects contact with his own kind for the purpose of social approval and financial gain, is soon erased from the memory of everyone he associates with. Just how many future generations of Blackmen will have to look at 5,000 year old pyramids and King Tut as the only proof of Blackmen in history who produced great things independent of other nationalities? Every other nationality residing in America builds monument institutions or maintain annual traditions that continually link them to their proud pasts. This is not considered racist, nor is it considered unnecessary because of integration. They are maintained for their children's benefit and to provide them with a personal foundation of ideas from which they can continue to grow and progress with the rest of the world. The Blackman is the only man who has decided that it is not necessary to stay in contact with his roots based on his presumption that men in other nationalities will frown on his efforts. This doesn't make any sense for survival. Profes-sional sport players are only another kind of an entertainer who perform for the amusement of paying customers in an arena.

When participating in recreational activities of the sports scene the Blackman may frequent dinner spots, take a trip using an airplane, stay a few days in a hotel or park his car in a private lot. When he uses any of these public facilities he is known to over-tip. Most of them are not aware of the scale or amount to be tipped and due to them identifying emotionally with the maid, the bellman, the bellhop or the waiter, they will tip excessively. They also do this to impress the hired help that they are big time spenders who can afford to pass out huge tips. Other Blackmen do not tip at all and take the attitude that they are doing enough by paying for their meal, hotel room or other basic services. Nevertheless, he devotes a lot of energy in discovering new ways to expend his leisure time. If his work is repetitive and boring requiring no real thought or concentration, his leisure time swells in importance. He tries to make up for his dull job by seeking exciting recreation.

Television opened up a new field of entertainment for the Blackman, and he watched *The Nat King Cole Show* in 1956, *I Spy* with Bill Cosby in 1956 and *Julia* starring Diahann Carroll in 1968. "Julia" was a nurse, a divorced single parent with one son. She worked for a white physician and nearly all of her and her son's life centered around her doctor employer. While this show was considered a massive social advancement by featuring a competent attractive intelligent Black female, "Julia" sent out the wrong message about Blackmen. Her situation subliminally implied that Blackmen messed up some kind of way and lost their women, who were left behind to care for their children, and that the Black father rarely, if ever, shows up to see his son. Entire segments were devoted to "Julia" trying to explain to "Corey" why he didn't have a father. Or, she was trying to fill the gap by seeking advice or aid from her doctor boss. This show set a theme by demonstrating the accomplishments of a single Blackwoman who had her own apartment and job, who was raising her son comfortably, and maintaining a fulfilled life without a Blackman in the home. The country was not ready to show scenes of the daily life of a regular Black family so this entity was treated as if it was nonexistent. Bill Cosby on *I Spy* was a sort of detective flick which requires no comment. One has to see it to believe it. Nat Cole was the first Blackman to host a T.V. variety show and he handled it with grace and dignity and he was always dressed sharp. These days the Blackman is seen on multiple T.V. shows in all kinds of roles. This, too, is considered advancement and inclusion in the show-biz industry. Blackmen used to complain that they should be included in commercials about deodorant, mouthwash, toothpaste, soap, cosmetics and other household products or machinery. However, the main commercials where Blackmen are found are for beer with high alcohol content, liquor sales, soft drinks, sneakers, telephones, or cereal.

Cable viewing is almost a norm in Black homes as is VCR usage. Other T.V. shows such as *The Cosby Show*, filled with delightful characters, portrays a nicely operating African family, including grandparents. It's a good comedy but there is never any doubt that it is the Black wife who runs the house and has the final say about what goes on. Care is taken to make sure the "Clare" periodically gets "Cliff" told. This is always turned into a joke of some sort. The Black father on the old *Good Times* series, John Amos, was a stronger male figure in the home and it was clearly understood that "James" and not "Florida" was in charge of the family and the home. He was the final authority. Then today comes *True Colors*, a sit-com with a Blackman husband/father, and a white wife and stepmother, including a white mother-in-law. This is a soft attempt to introduce interracial marriage by showing it as fun. Other Blackmen are seen in crucial or supporting roles and they are glad to be working. A few Blackmen are seen in soap operas wooing white women or pretending to be white, and there's even a Black-woman actress who appears routinely lying in bed with a white male co-actor. Theatre movies show Blackmen and white women irresistibly drawn together or vice versa. Whites have appeared on television in all kinds of romantic relationships and never saw a need to present themselves as falling in love with a Black person. Yet, as soon as Blacks infiltrate this medium practically every other role has them romantically inclined with Caucasians instead of other Black people. This is wrong.

There is one major Black operated national television station called BET out of Washington, DC and the West Coast. BET has several shows intellectually appealing to African-Americans, and they have other shows which have no redeeming social value for Blacks and are a waste of valuable air time. BET does not have a lot of leeway on programming because they count almost entirely on white advertisers to buy commercial space to offer their products to a select audience.

A reliable, apparently conceivable looking role for Blackmen actors is as a judge in a courtroom metering out justice. One of the most ridiculous parts is when Blackmen are portrayed as police chiefs. This is a role where they loudly curse out and lambast other officers — always white males. They call them on the carpet and say all kinds of insulting things to them and the white officers just take it and say "yes sir." The inferior looking white subordinates cower down, take their punishment and leave with their tails tucked neatly between their legs. Not likely. Purportedly this is supposed to demonstrate a Blackman in a supervisory position making big decisions and talking really bad to white men. It is contrived and weak. But there are all sorts of spots in law enforcement departments that let other Blackmen get off vicariously by letting off a little steam by seeing a Blackman talk to a whiteman the way they themselves have always wanted to do. The sublimatory message is absorbed greedily and Blackmen seeing this type of scene enjoy watching one of their own kind put the whiteman in check. There's an entire new crop of Blackmen actors invading Hollywood and New York accepting all kinds of crazy parts just to break into the industry. They repeatedly complain that white writers are not designing enough meaty or realistic parts for Black actors. They should just try out for parts in their own Black written and Black directed films. But every time they want to do something they seek out some white people who are already established doing it and try to squeeze in among them and benefit from what they have going.

As much as African-Americans frequent movie houses — they see every movie that hits the screen — there is only one African-American owned independent movie theatre in the entire country and it's located in California. Blackmen ought to operate a movie house in every city since Blacks go to the movies often to mentally escape their lives for an hour.

On a final note, Blackmen who participate in games of sport and play and achieve acclaim as the "winner" always thank their mothers. They rarely thank their fathers for helping them accomplish anything. In this society the mother is always referred to in honorable situations, and the father, who the Blackman is separated from, is not mentioned. After thanking his mother, they thank Jesus/God for their winnings.

Chapter 8

The Law "911"

Many Blackmen are in constant conflict with the American legal system and the parameters of its laws. Setting the stage, consider that at the 21st Century Commission on the Status of African-American Males, hosted in DC in the summer of 1991, reports were made that a Black male is three times more likely as a white male to die from a gun-related death, eleven times more likely to be killed by a gun, five times more likely to be arrested, seven times more likely to be convicted and eleven times more likely to be executed. Furthermore, in 1991, 50% of all homicide victims were a Black male. This represents a 10% increase since 1981. Squeezing in between this depressing data is a government report stating that the average life span of Black males is at its lowest in 12 years. African-Americans are churning out millions in funeral and graveyard expenses to bury their male relatives prematurely. An ACLU study compiled from a report called "Americans Behind Bars" reveals that there are always fewer people imprisoned in non-white countries than in Caucasian ones. Blackmen in America are imprisoned at a rate of four times more than Blackmen in South Africa. In America, for every 100,000 Black males, over 3,000 are incarcerated. In South Africa, out of that same number only a little over 700 are jailed. The ACLU Sentencing Project includes in their demands government investigations of the following:

1)   They seek government funding to reduce the high rate of imprisonment of Black males.

2)   They wish to establish a national commission to examine the high rate of incarceration of African-American men.

The American Civil Liberties Union (ACLU) works for the rights of citizens. This is much needed information valuably crucial to the futures of millions of Black children since over one-half million Black males are in jail and out of that number 70% are fathers. Whew!

The question becomes why didn't a Blackman allegate these charges and pose these questions? Blackmen have hundreds of organizations, clubs, frats, support groups and political platforms and they contribute heavily to many causes. Many of them have done their best to support the Free South Africa efforts to end apartheid, and numerous other global pressing issues. But not one of them have publicly come forward to organize an agenda to find out why so many Blackmen are in jail. It's as if they don't care, or don't even want to know. They are too busy addressing the concerns of their own needs and goals to give as much support to Blackmen imprisoned in America as they try to give those in South Africa, which we have learned are not as bad off as the Blackman in America regarding prison. Blackmen have a concensus of opinion about Blackmen not receiving justice in American courts of law. They say they know that a Blackman cannot get justice in any court, and they say they know for a fact that Blackmen get sentences often outweighing their crimes. But they have become so disconnected as members of the same ethnic heritage and like backgrounds, that they give no thought to trying to free or rehabilitate their own kind.

This is not to suggest all Blackmen in prison do not need to be there. Many Blackmen require being locked up, not always so much for their crime, but because of their warped mental conditions which propel them to act out their rage of violence against innocent people. They get busted for homicide, robbery, assault, burglary, larceny, car theft, fraud, rape, sex offences, bootlegging, etc., etc. This is not appropriate behavior for a civilized person to engage in and there must be some kind of a method of doing something to them to protect everyone else. But as the saying goes, everybody in jail ain't guilty and everybody free ain't innocent. For whatever comfort it brings, Blackmen are rarely recorded in history as being serial killers or mass murderers. They don't chop up people or take heads. A mass murderer kills strangers without motive cause or remorse. A serial killer murders periodically with time or space in between. These types of crimes are categorically only committed by white males or white females. Blackmen don't have the heart or nature to kill in this way. Blackmen kill trying to rob somebody or while under emotional stress — most likely connected to a domestic involvement. As already discussed, many times the emotional stress they attach to a situation far outweighs the overall importance or value of the issue they are involved in. As an example, in the drug culture or among gangs, they have their own sets of rules and regulations mostly pertaining to violations of their masculinity. Cultural variations of masculinity definitions are different among every nationality. The only part of masculinity the Blackman recognizes as expression of his maleness is aggression, more often than not, misplaced. Daring to try to look at some of the reasons Blackmen are so violent brings forth the issue of fear. Blackmen, especially those who are uneducated in ways to rechannel their fear or remove themselves from a negative environment, are so unsure of his own safety that he makes attack the best weapon. Psychologists say that a violent person seeks to project his rage onto others to make somebody know what it feels like. Television is guilty of legitimizing violence by referring to it as self-defense. The connection between taking drugs and violence has not yet been discovered. However, it must be pointed out that the drugs that Blackmen used 30 years ago tended to slow them down. The drugs Blackmen consume today speed them up. Drug acceleration of an already fragile personality creates irritability, bad temper, sulking, verbal attacks, assaults or murder. Drugs make a person live in a world of fantasy with distorted thought patterns. Anything can happen. And usually does. Alcohol can be included in this category. It actually is the number one drug.

Next, Blackmen who steal or rob are jealous, envious, greedy and lazy. No matter what financial need they use as a motive, they are parasitically trying to feed on the success of others. Stealing is also a perverted way for a deprived Blackman to achieve. He can feel good about accomplishing a goal under strenuous circumstances. They may pick someone at random who they think has something, either money or a material possession, they wish to own. A Blackman who is a thief is of the lowest caliber of man there is, because he seeks to take from those who have things he does not know how to acquire. He desires the easy way out. And he delights in the warped thrill of overpowering someone by force. Many Blackmen steal as a profession. There are many other types of criminals in jail and on the street who rape women, molest children, abuse elders and beat women — or men. A great number of them who are confined have done or perpetrate these atrocities on other Black people. This is real wrong.

Once in prison, after a period of adjustment, the personal crisis of coming to grips with being confined, the Blackman must find something to do with his time. Whatever his former status was on the streets is of little value in his new environment. Status stripping is a major process in American prison. No unique identifying objects are allowed. This is part of the reason for uniforms. This is particularly difficult for Blackmen because on the street his clothes are used to distinguish him from everybody else. After initially giving in to depression, hostility, fear or breakdown, then they are ready to use their time confined as best they know how. Some take GED courses, read a lot of books, lift weights, take up a vocational trade, become involved in sports, study criminal law or they become politically astute or get religion. As soon as he recognizes that by no power of his own can he get out of jail — he gets religion. Then he turns to God for help and mostly mercy. He studies the Bible, memorizes the Quran and if possible, becomes a Born-Again Christian. This is often his last resort. He becomes known for his strict religious code of behavior and impresses his family and friends on the outside with his new knowledge of God. Had they turned to God while they were free it would have prevented them from doing the dastardly deed that landed them in prison. To get out of jail they are willing to promise to do anything. They develop a slight brown-nosing technique with the guards to persuade them for better treatment or minute special privileges. Some of them go further into themselves and continue with their violent psychotic episodes which sometimes end in self-mutilation or suicide. Blackmen in prison acknowledge that illegal substances (drugs) are just as readily available in jail almost as much as they are on the street. Psychiatrists say that drug addiction is a compulsive chase of a mood change regardless of the negative aftermath. Since Blackmen are prone to senseless searches of external means to feel better, drugs become the nerve soother of choice. They say it can be difficult but they can maintain their habits in jail. They write long winding letters and try to hold on to their family or woman while locked up. It is not an easy maneuver especially since some of them receive sentences extending from five to ten years until the 12th of never. Some of them have no idea when they are going to get out because they earn extra time for bad behavior of some sort. They say living without female sex is the worst experience they have ever known. They say jail is not so bad as compared to not being able to have a woman. They participate in what they term "jail only" sexual behavior. They keep secret about it even to each other after they are released. But if any Blackmen claims to have been in prison for umpteen years and never participated in prison sex, they are lying. Many Blackmen in jail become so institutionalized that they go in and out as if in a revolving door. For some of them it represents the only choice they think they have to survive — three hots and a cot. They get free food, clothing, medicine, shelter, and a bit of recreation. The only stipulation is that they have to stay inside to benefit. Prison life is an entire indoor community with guidelines and regulations established among the men separate and apart from those imposed on them from the County, State or Federal Government. They learn to live by these rules if they want to survive. And they do. A Blackman is more pressed to exert his real masculinity when he is in prison than at any other juncture of his life. Prison forces him to follow rules of honor among men that he does not practice on the street. The rules of prison require that a Blackman form allegiance with his own kind, his word becomes his bond. If he says he is going to do a thing he has to do it, he has to have a religious affiliation, and he better not steal anything from another inmate, and most important of all, he better not snitch to the man on anyone. While this is the worst place for a Blackman to be, manhood rules are clearly defined and expected of him. These are some of the values and a kind of honor system the Blackman should practice when he is free. But this is considered only a life provoked because of his confinement. There are a lot of other exaggerated regulations only known to them, many of which conceivably are not right and do not make any sense anyplace other than in prison. But they have a societal structure as any other segregated community and a jailhouse version of practically everything. Fighting and sex become the testing ground for racial power and masculinity inclusion. He has a multiple choice test in prison. He learns to defend his position and space, become a punk, or flees. The boundaries are strategically outlined for him. The path he chooses socially determines how well he survives the experience and how well he does when released back into society where the rules are drastically different.

American prisons restrain and contain some of the bravest and boldest Blackmen ever born. Some have resided in the seclusion of prison life for upwards of 50 years. They are resigned to their restricted lives and are called "old heads" by other younger inmates. In 1975 Federal prisons abandoned any goals entertained about rehabilitations or social reform of incarcerated individuals. They continue to offer skill and educational programs but they spend no time in trying to decipher the minds of criminals. State and county prisons have done likewise and, other than access to a chaplain or group rap sessions, there are no funds to supply psychiatrists or psychologists to delve into the dark shadows of the criminal mind. Overcrowding has demanded that housing and transport of violators is the major task. The number of Blackmen in prison is now projected to be over 700,000 by the year 2000 — this number includes all non-whites (Latinos and Asians). No nation as small the the African-American population can survive with almost a million able-bodied marrying age men incarcerated — separated from their parents, children and women. Especially since they are not being properly prepared to re-enter society cured of their confusions.

After release they are admitted to half-way houses where they are monitored, herded and restricted and treated like immature children. Sadly, by that time, many of them are incapable of functioning independently as responsible adults. A man who has not been required to work consistently, pay living expenses and organize his own time is little able to hit the streets and explode into success. Then there are drugs. Blackmen with addictive personalities find it difficult to live without this artificial stimulation. Blackmen on drugs will never give up the desire for drugs permanently by finding Jesus, step programs, or being shut away in rehab centers maintained on medication. They go through these programs over and over and the programs are costly. Blackmen will only kick drugs when they take on a new idea about self.

The best idea would be for them to return to their own religion and names, and the real aims and purpose of their lives. Only by complete rejection of their previous life and activities will they overcome, but after abandoning their former crime-ridden lifestyles they must be offered something else to replace it with. An entire program for daily living and daily thinking. They must be given reasons and ways to monitor themselves without the great white father peering over their shoulder. They have to be motivated from within due to gaining a new value for their existence and a new purpose for their survival. Only one group has ever been able to rehabilitate Blackmen off drugs and provide them with a successful, productive, masculine existence. This was done by giving them some new information and training them in a value for self. The constant availability of cheap sources and odd mixtures of mind altering drugs available to the Blackman, right outside his door, creates a serious problem for the Black community and the Black family. The HIV and AIDS threat has shoved the crack-cocaine, heroin, ice and amphetamine problem to the back burner. But Blackmen in increasing numbers are opting for the quick-fix, the easy thrill of consuming or selling drugs. Crack is such a low grade desperate high that wears off so fast that it keeps the user involved in perpetual activity to replenish the supply. Blackmen give up every civilized standard and value when they sink into the brutal cavern of crack-cocaine. A cheap low-class short lived high. It is an accelerated artificial chemical dependency that remains uncontrollable and unreachable by rehab or detox. There is no methadone type substitute for crack. The rehab fail rate continues to be higher for crack than any other drug stimulant. Drug officials recognize the futility of trying to get users off of crack based on mounds of disappointing case studies. No solution has been found regarding what to do with crack addicts. Interest has dwindled.

Blackwomen complain that when their man gets out of jail or prison after doing a couple of years or more, they seem to want to talk about what happened while incarcerated for several months after their release. Apparently this is part of the disengagement, the come down, a subsiding of the pressure inherent in confinement. They must talk themselves out of the experience, like confession, to relieve themselves. They should be open and talk about anything that pains them. A bleak period of depression follows their release, and others, more accustomed to being institutionalized, speak of prison somewhat longingly. Overcrowding in prisons prevent any real rehab from occurring, and budgets are directed towards bunks and food. Blackmen are reduced to a near animal level if held in segregation or solitary confinement too long. The longer he is in prison the longer it takes for him to readjust to lightly monitored freedom. There is really no way for them to keep up socially, politically, or academically in prison. They are in a vacuum. But prison can be a place of reflection for a Blackman, and if he does not have to constantly be on guard against physical attack from other inmates, it is a period in his life when he can no longer deny his failure to cope with daily living. They are remorseful or vindictive, swearing to walk a chalk line when released, or concentrate on how to improve their illegal activities. They often develop lifelong friendships with other Blackmen who did time with them, and although discouraged from further association with other ex-offenders, they seek out contact when possible. The rules regarding disassociation are unreasonable, but enforced.

They say they are victimized by police harassment, unwarranted shake downs, brutality, agitation and disrespect for their manhood by police officers on the street. They say they are roughed up or beaten and terrorized just for sometimes walking the streets. They say the police are against all Blackmen and enjoy picking on them to stir a reaction so they will be justified in beating or killing them. He goes against the legal system full force but as soon as he gets busted he then calls upon that same system for compassion while trying to find a loophole in the rules to exonerate himself. When this fails — he screams racism! If he succeeds at his crime he says nothing and continues. But racism is his catch-all. In many parts of Africa, the laws broken in America that earn separation from society by jail would generate an immediate death sentence — especially if the crime involved breaking the peace of another tribal member by violation of his God given right to exist. Instant death as punishment for crime was a major deterrent. Of course this was only done if the person was proven guilty on all counts undeniably. Swift death is merciful but it is not profitable. Maintenance of prisons is. Even the death sentence has not proven to be a deterrent to crime — and there are always more Blackmen on death row than any other nationality. A death for a death among African-American men would only serve to remove more able-bodied men because if 50,000 were killed then 50,000 others would have to die. Areas in the far west (California) resemble Beirut war zones — disaster areas where Blackmen individually or in gangs stalk each other day and night. Yes, the Blackman feels powerless and helpless to do anything but talk about the racism inherent in such occurrences. And he feels so helpless because he is waiting on some outside entity (other than himself) to produce a remedy for these situations. He keeps pleading with the government to do something about it, to intervene on his behalf and solve the problems the Blackman says they created. But it hasn't happened, and it's not going to happen. What now? Does he just watch all this go down, or does he get on the case? Throwing a fit in the form of a half-baked revolution against American society will not help. But the natives are getting restless again. War clouds are brewing and rumblings can be heard penetrating the atmosphere of urban areas.

NOTES

Chapter 9

RELIGION

The Blackman is a very spiritual human being. Not necessarily attached to a church or specific faith, but he does believe himself to be connected to a/the supreme being, whom they now refer to as the creator. The first Black church is recorded to have been erected in 1787. Prior to that time Blackmen preached and worshipped outdoors and called it the invisible church. At these church services there was always much mourning and crying for the bad times and much singing and praising for the relief they expected to receive after they died. The American religion that the slavemaster gave to the Blackman to replace his own is called Christianity. The major thrust of this religion was to teach love of your enemies and servitude to your master, to keep the slave as submissive as possible to the master. The slant of the teachings given to the Blackman were mostly taken out of the New Testament which allowed the slave master to quote from the lord Jesus' word directly. Jesus, the star of the Holy Bible, was the God the slave was instructed to believe in. He was also the God used to put intense supernatural fear in him, because for a long while he was invisible and there were no pictures of him distributed to the slaves. So Jesus' word had to be translated to the slave using fire and brimstone to force him to believe. The Bible used was the King James version set forth in 1611 — several hundred years after Jesus' death. This text does not profess to be a religious teaching but certain aspects of the Blackman's involvement in religion in America must be addressed to partially explain how he got off track from his own roots.

He had practiced many kinds of religious expression in his homeland. He had been brought from a very large continent that took up 25% of all the land on earth. He did now know how small America was or that Africa was over four times as large as the U.S.A. At that time he did not know his homeland by the name of Africa. At that time he called it Asia, as he called all the lands on the entire earth. The now African continent was named after a European warrior, Alexander Africanus of Greece. Some of our Black male scholars should research this information and find out if there are any other names used for this continent before a European renamed it. Nevertheless, the original slaves were put through a battery of tests to ensure that his oncoming generations would have no memory of their former religion. Religion is taken from a Latin word called *religio*, which means linking back. That is the purpose of a religion in all nationalities, to link them back to their ancestors of like heritage. Violent steps were taken to make sure that the Blackman was prevented from linking himself back to anything in his past. He held out as long as he could in secret, but as the language disappeared, so did his references to his own God. In 1801 the first hymnal for slaves about their condition was endorsed. These hymnals stretched to contain such songs as: "Nobode no's de truble I's seen, nobode no's but Jeezus."

This was certifying that none of their relatives back home knew what they had gone through and were experiencing but Jesus. Jesus was the name of one of the ships they had arrived on as slave cargo.

"Go down Moses, way down in Egypt Land — let my people go." Also about calling on another Blackman with a history of freeing captives in Egypt and a plea for freedom. They sang of "rest beyond the river" which is what some of them thought the ocean represented — a big river, which was 9,000 miles from their homes and where they knew they would receive rest. "You can have this whole wide world, just give me my Jesus," again, calling for the ship Jesus to take them back home. Others like "Swing Low Sweet Chariot — coming for to carry me home" in which they called on fast horses to take them back to Africa — home. All the songs were sad, contained great longing for their friends and family where they would receive rest on the other side of the ocean in Africa.

Other songs with words like: "Gimme dat ole time relijun, it's good enuf fo' me," meaning that they wanted their own religion back because to them it was the best one they knew, but it had been taken from them a long time ago before they knew all the words of the English language. America had 350,000 slaveowners and all of them gave their slaves Christianity as a comfort. Even today most religious institutions in Africa are operated by Christian missionaries, mostly from America. One-half of the schools in Africa are also operated by Christian missionaries. Spreading Christianity throughout the world has always, and continues to be, a measure by which the whiteman determines if a people are civilized or not. The Christian Bible was used as a tool to convince the Blackman that God himself had decreed that the Blackman was and must continue to be a slave to the whiteman. They used the following biblical passages to burn this message into their hearts and brains:

New Testament: Ephesians Chapter 6, Verse 5: "Servants, be obedient to them that are your masters according to the flesh, with fear and trembling, in singleness of your heart, as unto Christ."

The slavemaster compared being obedient to him as being obedient to Christ — Jesus. He could have just as easily referred the slaves to Galatians Chapter 6, Verses 4 and 5: "But let every man prove his own work, and then shall he have rejoicing in himself alone and not in another. For every man shall bear his own burden." This was located on the previous page of the Ephesians selection. The Ephesians verse was used to teach the slave to be a hardworking good slave because God said so, and to suggest to him that Jesus was also a slavemaster and had included holy instructions even for the servants. He was overwhelmed with a white God so superior to him that it was impossible for him to withhold his devotion. And each slave was made to learn the Lord's Prayer by rote, along with other Bible passages.

So the slave commenced to praying to Jesus, that big white slavemaster up in the sky, and sang of their miseries in code. They had to sing in code about the little bit of knowledge they secretly retained of their former religion, because they were not permitted to even mention it. They used their secret code of singing gospel music to send messages back and forth to each other. Even today gospel music is traced to the African call and response chants. This indoctrination into the whiteman's religion of Christianity represented the little beginning of the Blackman's biggest downfall. He began on a path of seeking out

135

something or someone supernatural to answer his prayers and fulfill his needs by magic. It's interesting to note that Blackmen think that the European slave masters lied to them about everything except religion. Even down to today he thinks that the only lie told was that Jesus was white instead of Black. No further investigations have been made to check out the validity of the rest of Christian teachings in the Bible. Once the modern day Blackman found out that "Jesus' hair was like lambswool and his skin like copper," they were satisfied and started to demand that all ethnic images be removed from religious worship. They have made little progress in this demand except for a few pictures of Black Jesus' in a few churches, on a few calendars or pictures. They still have not insisted that all Bibles in Black churches at least portray pictures of all Black people. When they do try to do this they put in pictures of Black, white, Hispanic and Oriental characters. The Blackman does not really want a Bible or a religion that features only African-Americans because he thinks it tarnishes the image of God. He has taken the same charismatic events popularized by European Christianity and painted all the characters Black. Like the "Last Supper" painting which features a group of brothers surrounding a bearded Black Jesus. They now have Black angels with wings on their backs, a Black Jesus on the cross, in a manger, at the door and ascending to heaven. This is a feeble attempt to integrate themselves into the whiteman's religion to make it appear more real to them and to make God be on his side. Throughout history God has always been on the side of the downtrodden so this gave the Blackman some extra courage to try to accomplish things because there's no doubt that he represents the downtrodden, the rejected and the despised of the world. Part of his problem is that he does not understand the purpose of religion. He thinks it is to merely worship God in religious service... using prayer, singing and music. They see themselves as making "a joyful noise unto the Lord." Choosing and believing in a religion is to make a political statement because all religions dictate behavior and positions on every aspect of life. A religion gives clear repeated instructions on:

1) How to pray (worship)
2) What to eat (diet)
3) How to relate to others and function in a family
4) Societal and community responsibility

5) How to handle trouble and pain
6) Values, standards, ethics, humanity
7) Money management including charity
8) Who to love and who to hate
9) Rules of peace and war

All religions give directives in their holy books regarding a way of life. Religions are a way of life. A way designated by a supreme being presented as divine revelations from His own mouth. Any discussion of religion involves comparison of the political positions involved. This is a very delicate topic because followers of certain religions find it extremely difficult to analyze it using contemporary examination techniques. It is considered taboo in most circles to bring up the subject of religion for debate purposes. It is difficult for the Blackman to accept that the religion of Christianity is not right for them because it was the one programmed into him during slavery, with rules that go against his very nature. The Christian God is very hard on the Blackman because it requires him to be too passive. This started with the slavemaster using the following Biblical directives to control him:

St. Matthew, Chapter 5, Verses 3-11:
Blessed are the poor in spirit: for theirs is the kingdom of heaven.
Blessed are they that mourn: for they shall be comforted.
Blessed are the meek: for they shall inherit the earth.
Blessed are they which do hunger and thirst after righteous ness: for they shall be filled.
Blessed are the merciful: for they shall obtain mercy.
Blessed are the pure in heart: for they shall see God.
Blessed are the peacemakers: for they shall be called the children of God.
Blessed are they which are persecuted for righteousness sake: for theirs is the kingdom of heaven.
Blessed are ye, when men shall revile you, and persecute you, and shall say all manner of evil against you falsely, for my name sake.

St. Matthew's goes on further to instruct in Verses 39-42 in that same Chapter:

But I say unto you, That ye resist not evil, but whosoever
   shall smite thee on thy right cheek, turn to him the other
   also. And if any man will sue thee at the law, and take
   away the coat, let him have thy cloak also.
And whosoever shall compel thee to go a mile, go with him
   twain.
Give to him that asketh thee, and from him that would
   borrow of thee, turn not thou away.
Ye have heard that it hath been said, Thou shalt love thy
   neighbor, and hate thine enemy.
But I say unto you, Love your enemies, bless them that
   curse you, do good to them that hate you, and pray for
   them which despitefully use you, and persecute you.
That you may be the children of your father which is in
   heaven.

And if introducing these warped instructions were not
enough, the slavemaster went even further so there would be
doubt in what God wanted the slaves to do:

Romans, Chapter 12, Verses 14, 17, 19-21:
Bless them which persecute you: bless, and curse not.
Recompense to no man evil for evil. Provide things honest
   in the sight of all men.
Dearly beloved, avenge not yourselves, but rather give place
   unto wrath: for it is written, vengeance is mind; I will
   repay, saith the Lord.
Therefore if thine enemy hunger, feed him; if he thirst, give
   him drink: for in doing so thou shalt heap coals of fire
   on his head.
Be not overcome of evil, but overcome evil with good.

Of course, there are many other verses but these are the
main ones used, and still used today. All of the above verses
cover every aspect of reaction the Blackman might turn to to not
only defend himself but to stop working for or helping his
master. His new religion locked him in, if his master ever got
tired from beating him he was taught to go get him a drink of
water. If the master showed him hatred or disrespected his
woman, he was taught to forgive him and pray for his salvation.
Of course, this may be an oversimplification, but these verses
explain how the Blackman developed such defective logic as to

love and forgive others and no matter what happens accept them as their brother. They think they are obeying God. They think they are being Godly in insisting on ignoring wrong treatment. This also led them to the both ridiculous and impossible position of saying: I love everybody.

The Christian religion mainly forbade him from identifying his open enemy and functioning accordingly. He thought and continues to think that taking this position of passivity makes him closer to following the rules of God, thereby making him closer to God and more religious. The more he became involved in Christianity the less business and political minded he became. He was thoroughly vaccinated with the idea that all he had to do was to love everybody, do good and pray; and God would answer automatically the rest of his needs. He has always been plagued with spirits, ghosts, spooks and haunts, entities which might jump out unexpectedly and get him. A special boogeyman was created for him to frighten him in the dark. The boogeyman was some kind of fiend, a ghoul, a devilthing. They even grew to use the boogeyman to scare their own children into obedience. The point is, the European, who neither obeyed nor believed any of the mumbo-jumbo he taught to his slaves, continued in his inequitable lifestyle to commit any kind of vicious or corrupt wickedness he desired — mostly against the Blackman. These practices of terrorizing the Blackman with the Bible and the boogeyman continues throughout the ages. He can still usually be brought into line by evoking the name of Jesus or some of his words. The Christian religion does not give the Blackman any justification from God to defend himself, become self-sufficient, change his religion or dislike people who offend him. They are very quick to respond, no matter what happens, "I don't hate anybody." His religious upbringing teaches him to pray for those who despitefully use him, etc.

But if the perceived offender is Black, he doesn't even think about prayer, love or forgiveness, he reacts instinctively to fight, maybe even to kill. It is not right to psychologically prevent a man from discerning his enemies from his friends. No nation can survive in that way. The Blackman has had an indeligible imprint of the face of God as being white branded into his brain. If on his own he tries to move from this position, he loses sight completely of what God's face looks like, because he has not been given anything to replace the white image with. The faces he has been given have been rejected by him as either fake, unqualified or unacceptable. Because of his low opinion of himself he definitely can't visualize God as being Black like him. Especially since God/Jesus has been presented to him as having great supernatural powers, being able to do magic and rise from the dead. The teachings to him about Jesus rising from the dead, even after rigor mortis had set in, and teachings that one day all the dead will rise and be judged by God, convince him to delay his gratifications in life. The promise made to him in his Bible descriptively assure him that there is a better life waiting for him after he dies. So his hopes are put on hold. The Bible is written in such a way that no matter what he wants to do in a way of freedom, there are instructions from God to do the contrary. And mostly to wait, be patient and believe. So he is more apt to "put it in the hands of the Lord" than to put it in his own hands and do something about his condition. If the whiteman followed the same religious doctrines he taught and still teaches to the Blackman, there would be no America today. Because the Bible immobilizes a person who believes in its teachings. It promotes suffering as a thing to do to identify with Jesus. And it promotes self-denial as a way to be closer to God. Christianity's early hold in Africa was in Egypt and Ethiopia. So far the Blackman has not investigated any other areas to find out the religions practiced in Africa before the white missionaries came in with their Christianity. Christianity is not necessarily a bad religious program if the whiteman himself practiced it in more than Sunday rituals. The Blackman's need to be grounded in a connection to his maker makes religion more important to him. He is a spiritual being. Becoming a preacher, being called by the Lord or receiving a divine calling in a dream is tantamount to Blackmen as being contacted personally by God. The Black church has always been a place held in special regard to Black people. A place to go once or twice a week to let some of the pressure off, to be in the presence of a group of people all calling on God at once and to be respectful. There are choirs, deacon boards, usher boards, executive committees, Sunday school classes, recitals, prayer meetings, dinners, social functions and fund raisers. Becoming a preacher gives the Blackman an opportunity to serve God, interpret the Bible, express his leadership abilities, be in charge of a group of people, be idolized, be revered, meet women and be taken care of. His holiness in person. Blackmen can preach. They can take one paragraph out of the Bible and build a whole issue around it. They can perform in the pulpit — they can prance around, pant, wail and do the hoochekoochee on their podiums. They have a captive audience which usually edges them on and they get the word out. Their churches run from services being conducted in an outdoor tent to the finest most modern places of worship. There are crosses all over the place to remind them that Jesus was crucified on a cross, and that the place is holy. There are many different kinds of religions believed in and practiced by the Blackman but they all have a common thread; they are all various interpretations of the Holy Bible. Which means the principles of the faith are the same. All of them use Jesus or Mary as the focal figures, all of them involve going to heaven and Jesus rising from the dead.

The Black church has also been a place to introduce a new idea or political stand to the people. Blackmen know how to organize activities in a church. Other Blackmen know how to have unity and cooperate in a church. They do this because they believe they are working for the Lord. They raise thousands of dollars, sometimes for years, to erect big beautiful structures for their services. The finest and cleanest buildings in the African-American community are the churches. Some of them have day care programs, schools, nursing homes, thrift shops, or provide free dinners for the homeless, the sick and the shut-in. They do a lot of charity work, and raise money untirelessly to buy their pastor a special gift, send him on a special trip or buy him a new car to show their appreciation for his leadership in guiding them to God. Blackmen cooperate voluntarily more in church than any other place. It's unfortunate they have not learned to transfer that unity and fundraising to other types of business ventures to improve their condition. In these churches, which are now sometimes headed by ordained Blackwomen, there may be drums, horns, bells, keyboards, pianos, guitars, tambourines or bongos. They provide musical accompaniment for the pastor's sermon and the choirs. And they can rock a house. This noise is tolerated in most venues because it is defined as worship. There's singing, shouting, clapping and an all-around agreement that they are having a good time. The pastor also presides over baptism and communion. Baptism, symbolic of washing away one's sins, is an overwhelming event. The baptismees wear white, the pastor stands in a mini-pool usually under the pulpit, or if the minister is more dramatic, they go to a local pond of sorts, and there they wade in the water and baptize their believers. The pastor puts one hand on the person's head and one hand on their back and quickly dunks them in the water while there is prayer and singing going on. It is a very spiritual event signifying a person washing away their sins. Some of the upperclass Blacks attend churches where only a sprinkle of water on the forehead suffices baptism. Communion is supposedly symbolic of the body and blood of Jesus. The body is represented by a small soda cracker or chip of unleavened bread and the blood is represented by a tiny cup of wine or grape juice. While in any other situation the idea of eating a human's body or drinking their blood is repulsive, in the religion given to the Blackman to replace his own, this is considered an honored ritual to consume the religion totally. This is also symbolic of the European's history of having a cannibal complex of sorts. Many of their Gods, giants and heroes of Greek folklore legends are portrayed as cannibalistic. This was a ritual used as a vile degenerate satisfaction of revenge on an enemy. Cannibalism is also purported to have been practiced during European famines in the dark ages. Human flesh is described as resembling pork in taste. Mankind has always killed for alchemical purposes such as voodoo rituals, witchcraft and demon possession. Lepers in Western Europe believed that their only cure was the eating of human flesh, drinking the blood and eating the intestines. Consuming the blood and the body. While primitive tribes in Africa are portrayed in movies or rumored in studies to have been cannibals by boiling a person in a big pot or shrinking their heads, it was Rudyard Kipling who referred to cannibalism as "The Whiteman's Burden." European Norsemen or Vikings developed war skills they referred to as "blood thirsty or bloodsucking." Later tales developed about vampires, were-wolves, even involving children in stories of Little Red Riding Hood and Hansel and Gretel — both fairy tales about a human being trying to capture and eat another human being. It is from the theories surrounding these histories that the ritual of communion was established. Eating the body and drinking the blood of someone whom you wanted to possess the traits of — strength, knowledge or great power.

There are biblical passages about bloodletting in the Old Testament of the Bible. There are also stories about sacrificial offerings scattered throughout the Bible involving shedding the blood of animals as a ritual of contacting God and proving to him that the believer is serious. It is also recorded that during period of starvation such as in the siege of Leningrad during World War II the Caucasians ate human flesh. Some prophets have said that all nationalities of time of famine will be forced to eat other human beings to survive if they are not prepared for days of want. Hunger is a great motivator. Then, at other places in the Bible it is noted that Believers are warned against the eating or drinking of blood—human or animal. Humans are noted to feel comfortable in sucking their own blood if they get a small cut in their finger or hand. This kind of bloodsucking is obviously permissible. Many Blackmen brag a bit about eating their steaks rare — blood red, with the steak swimming in a pool of it. This is also not considered abnormal behavior although it should be. Blackmen who kill others are rarely if ever noted as dismembering human bodies, scaling bones or freezing the parts or savoring dead flesh in any manner. It has nothing to do with obeying God or anything similar. He does not have that kind of gory nature. He is repulsed by this sort of decadence. Thank God. He also does not use prolonged physical torture as a way to kill or instigate a massacre. If he kills it is fast, quick, and he abandons the body. Blackmen also do not do well at funerals. They have a holdover fear of dead bodies from spooky stories told to them in their youth about evil spirits rising from the dead, ghosts of dead folks coming back to haunt a house or a room. So they don't fool around or linger around dead bodies if they can help it. Christian teachings introduced the idea of the dead coming back to life but Blackmen are not particularly attracted to the idea. Even if someone showed up and said he was Jesus back from the dead it is unlikely that Blackmen would believe him.

Since the Holy Bible was presented to the Blackman during his enslavement as the word of God the savior, and the God was portrayed to him as being a whiteman surrounded by other great whitemen; this book sapped pride and confidence from him. Every major hero or religious character in the Bible was described as white — Daniel in the Lions Den, Job in the stomach of a whale, Samson and his strength, Noah and his ark, Lot in Sodom and Gomorrah and David who slew a giant. Not one figure in the Bible has ever been described as a powerful Blackman who was ordained or specially supported by God.

Since the Blackman thinks that no matter what else the

143

whiteman is guilty of, he would not be low down enough to lie about Jesus or God, he is prone to cling to the religion of Christianity no matter what else he rejects in Western culture. He thinks that religion has nothing to do with his state of mind, his confidence or his understanding of world problems. He is willing to defend to the death his right to accept Jesus as his Lord and savior. It was good enough for his mother, and it was good enough for his grandparents, so it must be good enough for him, too. And he is appalled at anyone who would attack his holy Jesus and His mighty word. He doesn't understand that Christianity is just another slavery time teaching used to control his brain and keep him subservient to a system that holds him down. He has been told all his life that he will suffer if he rejects Jesus and all he stood for. So he goes to church on Sunday, sings loudly in the choir and claps his hands joyously thinking he is making contact with God. He has such a good time being entertained in church and the music makes him feel so good he is convinced that his religion must be real. He doesn't know that he makes his own blessings depending on what he does and how he lives. He does not know that as long as he prays with the image of a whiteman in his head that he will continue to feel inadequate.

Jesus as a Man — The prophet Jesus lived over 2,000 years ago and while Blackmen believe in his existence and powers, they actually know little about him. He was born in a stable, came from a two-parent household, was educated, single, and died violently at the young age of 33. His adult career as a teacher of divinity lasted approximately three years. He was born in Bethlehem which is about six miles from Jerusalem in Palestine. He never traveled more than three miles from home (remember he was riding a donkey or walking on foot), and was labeled a radical politician. All of the words that Jesus allegedly spoke as recorded in the New Testament of the Holy Bible can be repeated in a couple of hours — like a one-time lecture. None of this is uniquely impressive until the superhuman aspects are added — such as he was born of a woman who did not have sex to conceive him, the immaculate conception. He walked barefoot on water, resurrected a dead man, healed the sick by touch, changed water to wine, died after being nailed to a cross, then came back to life three days later and ascended (floated up) into heaven — the clouds — promising to return and judge the world. When this side of his story is added it makes Jesus sound like the Terminator. Capable of all kinds of remarkable feats and possessor of extraordinary powers.

Christianity, the religion he is attributed to stand for, is a historical based account, not grounded in regular universal principles, but definite time spanning events — recorded, interpreted, bound and distributed by white males. This historical religion can always be debated and speculated about because it is not based on scientific proof which is not built on culture or nationality, but incontestable and independent truth. The Blackman does not have any proof that the information given to him about Jesus is true, or for that matter, that any of the events recorded in the Bible actually happened. Trying to disprove the idea that Jesus still lives and is coming back to save the righteous and punish the sinners is a difficult undertaking. This difficulty is often mistaken as evidence that he's really on the way. The Blackman's fear of God steers him away from challenging the worth of Jesus or the Holy Bible because he is afraid of committing blasphemy. And the very last person he wants to tick off is God. Because he believes in God he just doesn't know who his own God is. He should investigate this seriously so he can worship his own savior. Western opinion dictates that if one does not believe in Christianity then the religion is considered pagan or uncivilized. Other non-white nations abroad consider Christianity as a sort of plague that the whiteman brought to their shores and eventually used it to rule them the same way it is used to rule the Blackman.

The Blackman thinks that since slavery happened so long ago to a group of his people who he does not know or have any memory of, that he should just forget about it and go on with his life. But the only way he can forget about it is to give up everything in his life that entered the brains and hearts of his ancestors. This is the only real way that he can be sure that his actions are not contaminated with western culture and their religious foundation. He does not realize that the torture, desperation and confusion his forefathers felt still flows in his veins. The Holy Bible was used to brainwash him and while he dislikes the fact that his forefathers were slaves and feels a slight kinship to them because they were Black, he has not studied the impact on his behavior this sad history produced in the ongoing generations — of which he is a part. He has not been debriefed and all prisoners of war must be debriefed so that they are able to determine which parts of their lives were taken from them during the brainwashing — this includes religion.

He sees nothing wrong with allowing his children to be taught that Jesus/God is white. He can always claim, "well, nobody knows what color God is" or "God has no color" or "nobody has ever looked upon the face of God" or finally, "it doesn't matter if He's Black, white, green, purple or covered with polka dots, He's still God." He refers to Jesus daily in his routine activities. He may say: "Thank you, Jesus," "Oh Jesus," or "Please Jesus," or "Jesus help me," or "Jesus Christ," "the Lord Jesus," or "Oh God help me," or "God damn," or "God damn it or you." Many of them, even those practicing the most degenerate behavior, wear a cross around their necks. They wear a tiny or large gold cross strung from a gold chain highly visible. They consider this a statement of their religious recognition. They also consider it as a kind of charm to ward off undue evil. It seems that if they wanted to wear something connected to Jesus they would wear the shape of a manger like the one he was said to have been born in, or perhaps a sandal like the one he wore, or a little tool since he was a carpenter or anything else positive associated with his life. But to wear the cross, the one he was murdered on, seems negative since it represents his death not life. Who else but Americans would consider it holy to hang a symbol of a man dying around their necks? And one which Christians themselves refer to as "an emblem of suffering and shame."

Many still have crosses hanging in their homes or cars. They respect the symbol of the cross and consider it something very dear to them. Their Jesus did not write his own Bible. Neither did he interpret it so any Black preacher has the option of interpreting it to his flock in any way he chooses. It is possible to take a passage out of the Bible and put ten Black preachers in a room and tell them to write down what it means to them. Undoubtedly there would emerge ten separate different definitions of what the passage means. Jesus did not want confusion.

The average Blackman is not concerned with which religion the majority of African-Americans believe in. They refer to God modernly as "the Creator" and believe that it doesn't matter what a person believes about who God is or what they call Him because it all means the same thing because there's only one

God. There is. But he doesn't know which one it is. He thinks that religious choice is an individual one that has no bearing on the unity of a people. Taking a look at the other American nationalities and some of their reputations, they list as:

1) Italian men are known for loyal friendships and organ izational skills.
2) Japanese men exhibit honor and firmness in their dealings.
3) The Jews have determination and unity of cause.
4) The Puerto-Ricans are territorial and claim each other.
5) The Koreans have stamina and group cooperation.
6) The Indians maintain their culture and are a proud people.
7) The Europeans have agreement and systems to control and rule others.

There is one commonality that all of these nationalities have in preserving their cultures and heritage; the one link that joins them is: THEY ALL HAVE THE SAME RELIGION AND NAMES. Including the traditions and ceremonies attached to their roots. Their alikeness unifies them in accomplishing many goals that are far out of reach of the Blackman who believes almost strictly in the European religion of Christianity in one form or another. He also uses names that are extracted from all of the other nationalities or some he makes up himself which have no meanings at all — neither do they associate him with being Black. It is impossible for him to erase the picture drilled into his skull as Jesus — the blue-eyes, slender, hippy looking white male with a beard and long hair — without having another definite face and body to replace it with. He keeps trying to seek help and direction from a God that has no face that he can recognize. It keeps him worshipping whitemen.

The slavemaster knew that by making Jesus wield superhuman powers greater than a normal man he was able to attract the Blackman's allegiance to him because Jesus was described as even greater than the slavemaster himself. That was the only kind of God the Blackman would accept, one who was greater and stronger than his master. One who will make everything alright in the great hereafter — his post-existence. Despite the Blackman's overriding belief in Jesus, he is afraid to make moral judgments about some of today's immorality because he thinks that he has no right to censure others, and he doesn't want to be accused or moralizing or being overly critical of the personal actions of others. Everybody has a right to do whatever they want to do. Right? Wrong. All morals are grounded in religion so the immediate question gets to be which religion is to be chosen to represent the "right" morals? These morals conceivably must be God's selection — so next a specific God has to be recognized. Once this is done Armageddon rears it venomous head because Armageddon is the final show down between right and wrong. Blackmen are content to wage conversational Armageddon by agreeing that nothing is absolutely right and nothing is absolutely wrong, it just depends on the person and the situation. That is how they accept immoral behavior as the norm. Even the God of the European religion that he has adopted is no longer considered qualified to denounce wrongdoing, and his guidelines eliminated to pave way for modern interpretation. Religion or recognition of a supreme being is now considered an option. It always has been and there's no compulsion in it.

So the Blackman timidly defers making judgment calls and this temperament trails him in all areas of his life. He is hesitant.

He certainly is not comfortable taking an opposing position or stand on an unpopular subject publicly. He knows it will cause him despair in the form of rejection, being ostracized or demands to prove his position. He has little or nothing left to defend his positions with because he has been stripped of all his moral turpitude due to all decisions in life having been reduced to an individual choice or a personal preference. Do your own thing. Live and let live. Chill out. When the whiteman made up his ideas and rituals and called them holy he referred to it as a religion. Whenever the Blackman makes him up a religion the whiteman calls it a cult. There have been several brave Blackmen who attempted to make up a new religion for the Blackman. They desired to change the Christian guidelines around to accommodate ideas more suited to their nature. Their dogmas, all but one based on modified Christianity, failed to unite the people under one religious umbrella that would specifically cater to their needs. They were Nobel Drew Ali, Daddy Grace, Prophet Cherry, Father Divine and the Honorable Elijah Muhammad. Briefly, their platforms were as follows:

Noble Drew Ali — He wrote his own religious text called *The Koran* (not the same as the Islamic *Holy Quran*). He wanted the Negro to know their origin as Asiatics, and did not seek religious integration with whites. He began his organization in Newark. Drew founded his sect in 1913 and when he died he vowed to be reincarnated (come back to life after death). Old records say he was a Muslim at heart but respected the American flag and loyalty to the U.S.A. They celebrate their Christmas on January 5, the anniversary of the day Noble Drew was reincarnated. He titled his group the Moorish Science Temple, Moorish Americans or Moors.

Daddy Grace — Organized his own Christian sect based on holiness and conversion and being sanctified into the holy spirit. Services consisted of regular Christian church behaviors such as intense prayer services and speaking in tongues. He believed in masters and servants. His group was open to Blacks and whites, and they used the regular Bible. His program was based loosely on the format of Father Divine's except he looked and dress more like a sugar daddy with long hair.

Prophet Cherry — called his people the Black Jews of the Church of God. He used the Yiddish and Hebrew Bibles. He suggested that his Jewish God was Black. He taught his followers of three heavens — one on earth, and a second in the trees and a third in the sky. He attracted a modest following and his program, too, was a variation of Father Divine's and Daddy Grace's. Opinion was that he was an opportunist.

Father Divine — He had a humongous ego and didn't beat around the bush and informed his followers outright that he was their God — the new Jesus. He endeared himself to his flock by instructing them to refer to him as "daddy." As their "daddy" he told them to turn over all their worldly goods and house deeds to him and he would take care of all their personal needs. He developed several commercial products, a publication, and weekly hosted huge banquets which he charged only a few cents for or fed his people free. He was 4'6" tall and told his membership that they would live forever. He also told them that sexual relations in marriage were unnecessary and forbade married couples from sleeping together. He claimed that his followers did not need doctors because he would heal them. His religious meetings were loud and rowdy with singing, stomping, shouting and speaking in tongues. He required parents to absolve themselves of motherhood and fatherhood, and turn their children over to him to live in the "kingdom." His church was open to all races and he married a whitewoman who continues to carry on his work today as "Mother Lorraine." He acquired several real estate investments like hotels and a roomy castle-like dwelling. If his followers pleased him he crowned them Kings, Queens, Princes and Princesses with much pomp and royal costumes. He operated his "kingdom" for about 15 years, until he was arrested on trumped up charges of creating a nuisance.

The Honorable Elijah Muhammad — Declared he was missioned by God/Allah, in the person of Master Fard Muhammad, to become a messenger of truth to his people. He was the first Blackman since slavery to introduce the Blackman to a religion completely different and opposed to the Christian teachings given to them from the slavemaster. He identified their God as Black, showed them a picture of Him, told them the whiteman was a devil and their natural enemy and called their religion Islam. He told them that before coming to America that they were Muslims and that they should not eat pork and must learn to be self-sufficient. He told the Blackman that he was a part of God/Allah, the supreme being, and should start preparing themselves to rule the world. For over 40 years the Nation of Islam labored as the largest, most unified and successful example of the Blackman's real strength and true nature in American history.

Despite the aforementioned options, all existing in the early and mid-1900's, the masses of Blackmen opted not to join either group and clung to regular Christianity. His problem is that he seeks a God who is best experienced by an emotional feeling. He wants a religion which permits him to do anything he chooses and will still accept him as a practicing member. Christianity, including Catholicism, are the only religions that allow him to do this. If he makes up another religion he makes it a form of Christianity but calls it something else to make himself believe that he is worshipping a new idea. Today there are many popular Blackmen T.V. or radio evangelists spewing all kinds of varied interpretations of Christianity. They sell prayer cloths, hot numbers, crosses that glow, holy paper and other trinkets they swear will bring the owner good luck and special blessings. They have huge followings and exhibit no shame at ripping the people off in the name of Jesus.

The Blackman thinks that the rules or bylaws of a religion are designed to make his life miserable. He has picked up many bad habits that rob him of life longevity and good health. Yet when it is suggested to him, for his own benefit, that he stop such vices as smoking, using drugs, drinking alcohol, eating pork, carrying weapons or promiscuity, he thinks these regulations restrict him from having a good time. He has become so far removed from high moral standards and healthy living that he perceives giving up his vices as depriving him from consuming things that make him happy. He is eternally in search of artificial stimulants to make himself feel better and becomes addicted to substances and tastes that slightly delay the true reality of his days and nights. When his forefathers were brought to America they were not using intoxicants, chemicals or nicotine or caffeine. These are bad habits he has picked up since his original demise. The Blackman does not think that he can live without these unrighteous practices even though to stop them would lengthen his life, save him money and return him to his undefiled state of consciousness. Resuscitation is painful to him because wrongdoing is presented as justifiable and convenient. A sensible person in full charge of his mental capacities would embrace any program that eliminates the need for stimulants and immoral behavior. The Blackman rejects any program that requires him to clean himself up. He does not know that he must be clean internally in order to think clearly. He seeks a lifestyle that permits him to practice his vices and still authenticates his sincerity of purpose. No such program exists. And they mock the Blackmen who do try to live a vice-free life and label them squares or fanatics. Righteousness is not admired or sought. It is sad that he allows his vices to keep him separated from his God, because no God will accept him while he practices his unholy alliances.

The information and descriptions on the previous pages are not presented to insult or make fun of European religions or holidays. Europeans have every right to believe in their own religion and to celebrate any way they please. However, the Blackman has not been afforded this privilege, and has instead become the victim of a very cruel and long-lasting hoax. He was raised to ignore his own presence. He was forced into this predicament a long time ago due to being fed repeated gulps of positive information about another race which intentionally excluded his existence. His brain became muddled trying to digest the disinformation he was given, while frantically trying to sneak in a little information about himself. He got indigestion. This disease has already been linked to the slavery process endured by his ancestors to preserve his life. To vaccinate him with this slavery, everything that was real to him and verified his life was dissected out of his daily lifestyle. The psycho-emotional damage is immeasurable. As yet only partially calculable.

Every iota of seemingly unrelated misinformation he was given must be analyzed and removed one step at a time. This chapter attempts to outline selected data objectively by listing examples of how the Blackman was vilified by European Western precepts. He has negated to consider the overall effect of living a lie. Repression is a safety mechanism for him because his ego is unable to bear the gigantic pain of this 500-year-old sham, and weakened by such a waste of time, he doesn't know how to rearrange his beliefs to be grounded in truth. The truths that pertain to his life and history on earth.

He should not only feel any guilt about disregarding the European's religion because they share no remorse about ignoring his.

He most certainly should consider that white scholars and theologians write and re-write the Bible at will. There are now several "versions" available, all claiming to be authentic interpretations. Blackmen preachers are at fault here for continuing to represent the slavemasters religion to Black people attending church searching for salvation. They tell their church members that they are *praying for them* but they are really *preying on them* for personal elevation and financial gain. This chapter will inspire a lot of debate because the Blackman has never been openly challenged on his religious beliefs — factually. The Blackman does not realize that being a Christian does not just mean that he attends church, Christianity is a frame of mind, a way of thinking and acting — a type of behavior resulting from Christian teachings embedded in him when he was a baby boy.

Chapter 10

SEXUALITY & RELATIONSHIPS

The social status of Blackmen in American society is neither a new issue nor one that is fully settled. The Blackman's ideas, goals, worth and sexual practices are subjects studied or presented with the least objectivity. These days they finish last in every socioeconomic scale from child abuse to life expectancy. The generally worsening quality of intimate life of Blackmen has detrimentally affected their mental capacities. The Blackman needs a woman to be happy. The female presence completes his life cycle. The Blackman is not created without aim and purpose. He has three major accomplishments he should be about the business of acquiring. They are:

1) A knowledge of himself, his history and his God.
2) An ability to do something for himself — employment.
3) To be a good son, brother, husband and father.

Today most of them are very, very far from attaining these goals. Over the years much has happened to influence his attitudes and behavior. All studies show that of the top ten causes of death among African-Americans, every affliction kills more Blackmen than Blackwomen. This is interesting and is considered to be attributed to what Blackmen do and how they act. Despite the fact that Blackwomen complain of more ailments and say they feel bad much of the time, Blackmen die quicker. They are used to plunging themselves into daring and dangerous plots. It hasn't mattered as they live in a society where the death of Blackwomen is perceived as more horrifying and important than the death of Blackmen. Thus, rarely are

Blackmen seen as innocent in any situation. He is generally thought of as the perpetrator due to his demeaned image as being unscrupulous and exploitive — mostly of Blackwomen. This is not to say that *all* Blackmen conduct themselves in a negative way with females, but they have grown quite used to blaming women for their overall conditions. It has become a habit for him to complain "the white man won't let me because I'm Black." It has become simple with this kind of defective logic for him to blame his unacceptable behavior on uncontrollable urges brought on by racism. This call relieves him of any moral obligation to exercise self-discipline, restraint or explanation for his actions. He has all sorts of charges leveled against him by Blackwomen; he's too slow, he's too fast, he's undependable, he lies too much, he is guilty of multiple sexual infidelities, he beats his women and his children unwarranted, he won't work, he blows all his money, stays out too late, forgets things, won't admit when he's wrong... and the charges go on and on. It is fair to say that most of the time when a Blackwoman makes a charge against a Blackman he is surprised. Blackmen and Black-women decidedly have some pretty serious long-term disagree-ments and studies prove that their value system is different on different topics. It never ceases to amaze him how he can be going along his merry way thinking everything's fine and then his woman lowers the boom and lets him know that something is drastically wrong — and he should have known it. Additional to his abstract attitude about many things in his intimate relationship, he is charged with having poor impulse control — he'll have sex with anything that moves. And, he keeps going for the okeydoke from women. Whereas his grandfather had five options regarding how he decided to deal with his woman, his father had maybe ten, but today he has possibly fifty. It has become an overwhelming process these days — in trying to select, date, marry and live with a Blackwoman. Being a sportsman he has taken to ducking and dodging as the best way to wade through the murky waters surrounding Blackwomen of the nineties. It's safe to say that he doesn't know quite what to do to be accepted or confident in his dealings with females. The pressure of this predicament leads him to deception and irresponsibility in his personal affairs.

A lot of his confusion today resulted from his choices in the 60's. At that time, starting at about 1957, white Americans participated voluntarily in changing their lifestyles, in the home with their mates, on the job and in the world at large. The Blackman, filled with the fervor of desegregation and social integration, tried to emulate them except he was not in the same stage or status as whites. The 60's produced the idea of self-fulfillment and individual choice. To the previously denied Blackman this meant acquiring material goods, following his impulses now unrestricted and expanding his appetites on every level. The Women's Liberation Movement of the 60's allowed both males and females to experience more freedom of choice in all aspects of their lives. The Women's Lib Movement gave Blackwomen the right to deregulate the home, permitted promiscuity with white men, gave them a more aggressive mouth and more freedom of motion. The Blackman made similar changes in his lifestyle mostly as a predator. He was free to hunt down every and anything he wanted to satisfy his emotional needs. These needs were undirected, unrestrained and random. He thought he was free. He could now accept or reject the idea of marrying a woman he got pregnant, he could enlist or object to going to war, he could pursue the white woman, he could frequent any restaurant, nightclub, department store, emergency room or personnel office he chose. He had never had it so good. This so-called period of sexual revolution also allowed him to openly flirt with any homosexual tendencies he had. Blackwomen were plentiful, politicians were rapping and the music was good. He was in and out of love at will and no one could stop him. His love life was definitely one area of his existence that he could have complete control of. The whiteman, he thought, could not go into the bedroom with him, and this was a place where he was the boss — completely in charge and he perfected it. It was the one area he could excel in that was uninterrupted by outside entities. He went in and out of personal relationships with women at any speed he chose. He sired children and sometimes never looked back. He was in a time and place of discovery. As the national options for morality expanded, family and home systems broke down further and further, and by the time the balloon was completely deflated, so was his ego. All the trappings he counted on to support his freedom of choice disappeared. He found himself on a new path, one that was paved in hostility. His time was up. And he had not done what he was supposed to do as a son, a brother, a husband or father. As the American world returned to a hostile place filled with poor nutrition, inadequate health care, substandard living conditions, unemployment and poor education; he felt trapped and confused. In 1977, more Blackmen died in homicidal incidents than during the entire ten years of the Vietnam War. A new variable emerged — he had begun to kill himself off. None of this was good news to his woman who often bore the brunt of his societal and community rejection. He had tried many things — drugs, pimping, working in the system, the military, college, religion — and all of them had proven themselves either not to be lasting, or unsatisfactory. In his trying to settle down and have a wife and family he found that he didn't know how to do so. He was unsure of what to insist on and what to allow to go on in his home — especially with his children, so he left that up to his wife. But those who worked hard to provide for their families were determined not to give up their children to female-headed households and to the welfare department and all of its associated negatives about him as father and man. In the cases when he did marry he tried to "square up" to meet the occasion and handled it for as long as he could. Blackmen have quicker physical reactions and Blackwomen have quicker emotional ones, and by the time they both came through the 60's and 70's, the cards had been completely reshuffled and neither one knew what the new deal was. The game changed.

The Double Standard Fallacy

Blackmen have heard much about the so-called "double standard" — about him being able to do things, go more places, date women, stay out late and have premarital sex; more than Blackwomen. True, Black mothers have always tried to persuade their daughters from giving up their virginity at a young age, not getting pregnant or staying out late; it has been to no avail because when Blackmen are out late fooling around doing anything they shouldn't be doing, they are with Black females. So if the women are available to them while they are receiving more social benefits in the world, then there is no effective double standard. Men and women have always had access to each other. Even if the female is told not to have sex, and the male is urged on to do, they manage to get together anyway. Perhaps Black males have had more options regarding the results of their behavior. Since they do not get pregnant themselves, they are able to move ahead with their lives relatively unaffected unless irate parents insist on marriage or child support. So obviously the same number of Black females who obey house rules and don't have premarital sex is equalled out by the Black females who place themselves in spots to do just that. The male mammal has always had more freedom to roam and investigate out of doors than the female. As a boy child the Black male experiences his first sexual encounter at about the ages of 11-12. If he is in a poor urbanized environment he does so at about the age of 8 or 9. So Black daughters are available throughout their entire lives. If there is such a double standard in existence it's that the African-American community likes to delude itself into thinking that the boys have more freedom than the girls although this is disproven by Black girls caught up in the teen pregnancy mistake. The stats on this predicament are overwhelming from coast to coast in all income levels and family makeups.Blackmen's attitudes about sex are favorable. Most of them reach a climax 99% of the times they have sex, while Blackwomen reach an orgasm only about 2% of the time — vaginally. Other ways about 50% of the time. When a Blackman has sexual intercourse he knows exactly how it's going to end and if he is experienced can almost predict the exact moment. Many of them find themselves in an odd predicament. If he is a good lover it is because he has a great deal of experience having sex, manipulating women's bodies, trying out different moves, testing certain responses, and experimenting with pressure and technique. The only way he can get this training and learning is by doing it — having sex with various women. This experimentation can become addictive — some for the confidence it brings, some for the conquest and reassurance of his abilities. It would be rare to find a Blackman who is expert in bed who only has one woman. Of course there exist Blackmen who become a little uncomfortable in bed, even if they want to do it, and therefore give little thought to whether or not the female partner is enjoying the act. The Blackman is sometimes irresistibly drawn to Blackwomen who project themselves as being weak, mild mannered, soft spoken, shy or withdrawn. They see these women as needing to be taken care of. They see a chance to protect someone and to not worry about her getting out of hand. By the time he learns her meekness is really passive-aggressive behavior, he's usually already in much deeper, sometimes even married, than he desires to be. This puts him on the prowl again. Many Blackmen consistently choose the same kind of woman over and over. They are looking for something, usually something that doesn't exist in real human nature, but they look on regardless of this fact. Sometimes they are in a situation where they are so emotionally brutalized that they give up on their manhood and allow themselves to be manipulated, directed, told what to do, give up all their money, and obey all orders from the wife no matter how distasteful to him it is. His inability to be honest with his woman or with himself leaves him spent and impotent. This unnatural fear he has of women is derived out of his fear of being rejected, insulted, verbally attacked or ostracized. In mammals, the animal who is solely responsible for feeding and taking care of the offspring is more viciously threatening. The Blackman bears the brunt of this situation somewhat with Blackwomen. Having to root for food and shelter requires a female to take on survival skills ordinarily left to males of every species. His inability to articulate his grievances with his woman is another reason for his quietness. He has been fooled by the women's lib cries for equality. He has psychologically bought into ideas that now prevent him from speaking out. He has convinced himself that matters of great essence concerning his manhood are not important and that it is unfair for him to force his value judgments on his mate. He trembles at the blow up he knows she's going to have if he mentions certain things. Sometimes he is afraid that the woman will leave him and demand huge sums for child support, will take the house he has been paying for and living in for long years, will divorce him and get everything — including his car — or that his mate will just leave him and go find another man to satisfy her. He also is afraid of rumors that women in his circle may classify him as macho and demanding. He feels that as long as he doesn't rock the boat he can keep on sailing and express his frustration in other ways in other places. Sometimes involving another woman and sometimes not. He knows that the Blackwoman has the whiteman and his institutions on her side and whenever he backs her up against the wall too far, she can always cry out for help — and that it'll come. He is relegated to a place of only slight importance to her if it comes down to who is going to have their way. If he wants a traditional home and family life, his woman rebels and doesn't let up the pressure until he gives up his old fashioned ideas and ideals and gets with modern times. Some Blackmen have opted to stay home, keep house, raise children, cook and be Brother mom because their women are very aggressively opinionated, constantly vies with him to be the boss, and if he's out of work she convinces him it's the least he can do to help out. More and more magazines and publications are portraying the Blackman home in the kitchen cooking and his wife out working carrying her briefcase. Many Blackmen don't work for one reason or the other and do not keep house either. Many also just give up the running of the house to the woman because he sees her as a better man than he is. So let her handle it. Some of them are so accustomed to having to sit or lay and listen at their women complain or fuss that they are excessively loud when outside the home to make up for the indoor restrictions on the sound of their voices. Blackmen who go along with these kinds of behaviors are considered henpecked. Blackwomen do not like these kind of men even if they are married to one. They brag that they keep him "in line" — at the back of the line. These Blackmen get home at breakneck speed after work so their women won't be suspicious of their whereabouts. They turn over their complete check to their woman so she'll know what happens to every penny of his money. They learn how to skim off a few dollars here and there so they can have a night out or afford a drink. They are totally restricted at home from expressing their manhood in any way, shape or form. Sometimes they roam the clubs, bars or streets and even though married, behave as if they are love starved and sexually deprived. The beg women and jump at the slightest chance they think they might have to get a strange woman in bed. Most of the time when a Blackwoman contracts a venereal disease it is from a man whom she considers her steady sex partner, a man whom she thinks is not sleeping with anyone else. The biggest disappointment a Blackwoman has when a Blackman gives her a venereal disease is that she expects him to at least be careful about the women he is dealing with. Venereal diseases are still wrongly considered a result of filth or generated only in dirty people. While this may be true in some cases, doctors claim that the bacterias causing sexual infections routinely originate just from the normal mixing of body fluids between two people with different diets, hormone levels, straining during coitus and not urinating after sexual intercourse. He is very much embarrassed about contacting a venereal disease and is more apt to get more angry than anyone else. Which ever partner gets it first thinks that the other partner knew they had it and didn't tell them. To keep quiet about their infections Blackmen developed underground means to obtain penicillin, tetracycline and other prescription drugs so that they do not have to go to a physician and have a record made of it. Few Blackmen go home and tell their wives or their women right away that they have an STD infection. Admitting this kind of guilt is out of the question. Whenever they do advise their regular mates, hell for days is surely to follow. It is a very embarrassing ordeal for all concerned.

Blackmen do not like women who criticize their principles (if he has any on a particular topic), or personally attack him. He does not like accusations or being presented with proof of his inadequacy about something, and he does not like being called a liar (whether he did or didn't). Some Blackmen never admit telling a lie or misleading a woman even if he is directly caught in one. He rarely admits to it. By not admitting that he lied about something it keeps him from having to explain why he did. By not admitting the lie he keeps his woman from inflicting punishment on him for doing so. It keeps the issue at a standoff. He figures if he never admits it he can keep the upper hand. Blackmen report that at some time in their relationship they did admit to a lie, and their women never forgot it. They say living with a woman who heard you say you told a lie is the worst hell of all. By not admitting an obvious lie he takes on an aura of rascability and soon the lie is either forgotten, turned into a joke or never done again.

Blackwomen still consider sexual intercourse as their trump card, and after it's played they have no other cards in the deck to use to win his commitment or secure his respect. This is not necessarily true to Blackmen. They separate the act of sex from the mental commitment or expression of non-physical love. Since they know that having sex will not be the major determinant as to whether the relationship survives, they do not put as much emphasis of importance on it as do Blackwomen. It's possible that sex is just another level of kissing for them and unless they are emotionally involved with the woman it doesn't have near the value to them as it does to their main woman. They hide it and lie about it or sneak around only because of the value their woman puts on it. No Blackwoman is going to ever know how many times her Blackman has had sex with another woman. They are adept at working it in at the oddest times or most remote opportunities. This further convinces them that if their woman doesn't know it doesn't hurt her. It is a separate life he lives that he considers has nothing to do with his regular day-to-day life as a committed man to one woman. He often does it just for the conquest, certainly if there are problems at home and he is on punishment or experiencing sexual rejection, he is more apt to seek out another feminine outlet for his desires. If any woman is living with a man and thinks that by denying him sex she is getting back at him she is sorely mistaken because 9 1/2 times out of 10 he is getting his sex somewhere else. He does not let anyone or anything get in the way of his sex life. He definitely enjoys it if his main woman switches up a bit in the bedroom, sets a new scenario, changes the routine or wears something special. But any Blackwoman who thinks that doing all of these extra goodies is going to prevent a Blackman from being with another woman, she is mistaken again. Blackwomen make too many unstated assumptions in her relationship with her man. And then when she finds out something to the contrary she is emotionally crushed. One major misunderstanding the Blackman has about Blackwomen that causes him many problems in his relationship with them is that the Blackwoman believes anything a Blackman says if it is of a love or romantic nature. Love is one category where the Blackwoman not only believes in a Blackman, but expects him to follow through on his promises or dedication. Blackmen discount this belief. They say things they don't mean, make promises they have no intention of keeping and make agreements they can't fulfill. So when a Blackman says "I'll call you tomorrow," or "I'll see you later," or "I'll be right back," or "I love you," or "I'd like to take you out sometime," or "I'll buy you that," or "I'll pick you up at 7 Friday night — whatever he says, and obviously some of the promises are more intense than the samples, the Blackwoman not only expects, but looks forward to him doing what he says, and she expects him to keep his word regarding sustaining their personal relationship. With him it's another matter. Some of the words he uses are just passing salutations or goodbyes. He eases out as gracefully as possible if the encounter was temporary or of no real value to him. He sees this as being merciful, plus once outside and away from the woman he resumes his normal activities and does not have a photographic memory nor does he keep his word very well. He is easily distracted and if something he deems as important comes up he quickly forgets whatever he has told someone else. He is not intentionally trying to disappoint others. When and if he breaks up with a woman he says it's because of communications breakdown, infidelity, constant fighting, emotional abuse, falling out of love, boring sex, no money, physical abuse or just a desire for another life. He goes far before he gives up on a relationship.

The Blackman is distrustful of women. The more experience he has with women the more distrustful he is. He is constantly on guard to discover any infidelities she may be participating in, any inconsistencies or any unusual behavior on her part. He wants to make sure that he is aware of any change in her attitude or love for him. His jealousy is best attributed to his masculine insecurity. Some Blackmen are overly jealous. Jealousy and rivalry are learned traits. Anyone or anything perceived as a threat to his standing with his woman is seen as a danger to his well-being and one he sometimes cannot handle. He can become outraged to the point of physical violence if he thinks or knows his woman is unfaithful to him in word or deed. Some are so insecure that they keep track of their women like wardens and insist she live the life of a prisoner. He learns mistrust based on abuse, neglect or deprivation of love. Psychologists say this goes all the way back to pressure possibly applied by parents to get him to give up something or share. Sometimes this disorder manifests in a child if his introduction to the world is hostile or frustrating. If a Blackman falls in love with a girl at a very young age and she disappoints him he may use that immature incident to measure every relationship he has in his adult life. They remember all emotional pain connected to love. They are most vulnerable when they are in love. Blackmen love just as hard as women and hurt twice as badly because they connect rejection to their manhood. Rejection by a woman makes them feel powerless and represents a loss of control of their destiny. Often his rampant emotions lead him to terrorize or harass a woman who has rebuffed him. It may even lead him to go insane and kill the woman or her new man. Or both of them. Blackmen are often more deeply emotionally dependent upon a woman and the relationship than they let on. They have never been taught how to channel their frustrations or solve out problems with their women before they reach the crisis stage. Part of their frustration is that the Blackwoman is emotionally undependable so he has a difficult time understanding her or trying to calculate if she is serious when she says or does something. Her being consistently inconsistent makes him wary and suspicious of her real motives because every time he starts to believe she is one way, she turns out to be another. They are more dependable and steady in their behaviors, even if wrong, it can be assumed that he is being for real and not putting on an act. It is said that women mature much faster than men. This difference in level and speed of development accounts for many of the disagreements in his personal affairs. Plus, Blackwomen tend to read more and will adjust their attitudes or beliefs according to latest feminist trends or an idea she got from a movie or T.V. It is no wonder Blackmen are so confused about where they stand with women and how they should deal with them. Blackmen say Blackwomen close in too fast, get serious too quickly, are over anxious, start making plans, get too possessive or entrap them by pregnancy. He is not always trying to form an intimate relationship when he turns to a woman for conversation, advice or psychological comfort. Blackmen naturally turn to Blackwomen for understanding, so do other Blackwomen. Women talk about personal issues, advise and comfort each other easily. Blackmen, because they have been trained to not show certain kinds of emotional vulnerability, tend to only speak in detached statements about their personal involvements, when speaking to other Blackmen. None of them want the other man to know that they are strung out in love with a woman or in a situation they don't know how to handle. This, they think, means they are weak in some way. Unless he consults another Blackman ten to twenty years older than him he is apt to get the wrong advice anyway. Youth and experience do not coexist. This is why a man comes into his real understanding of women at age 45 and above. He is most attractive over 45. He is more steady, sure of himself and, more importantly, sure of Blackwomen. At his peak he is most attractive to Blackwomen of any age. First of all, he has made it to age 40 and that in itself is an accomplishment.

Blackmen do not cry very often. Humans are the only species to cry tears based on emotions. If a Blackman does cry it's because of anger, some of them cry when they get really mad. They are also known to cry under frustration or stress, failure, death or under pressure to get sympathy. They do not cry at movies or about T.V. shows when they are successful or just feeling good. These kinds of emotional tears are almost strictly feminine — at least they think so.

The Blackman who says he wants an independent woman is lying. If he says this, what he means is that he wants a woman who is financially independent so that she does not count on him for money. Blackmen are not making a lot of money these days so if he has a woman with her own separate source of money this relieves him of a lot of pressure. If he is disappointed in himself or depressed about his prospects for the future, the woman's independence is felt as threatening. He lives in a society where money is the measure and means to advance in society so if he doesn't have any money, or enough money, he knows that his value diminishes in the sight of a Blackwoman. This independent thing has gone much too far. There is no relationship that is not co-dependent along with mutual obligation. Independence is seen by some to mean the right to be selfish and work only on self-interests. This does not work. Part of the gratification of a personal relationship is the opportunity to share — on all levels. It takes a very special and secure Blackman to maintain a relationship with a woman who outearns him. Not because of the amount necessarily, but because of society's interpretation of what it means and the privileges that come along with it... such as power.

Fatherhood

The Blackman is not as excited as he should be about fatherhood. It has never been described or projected to him as a wonderful spot to be in. The major reason for this is that it is usually a surprise to him. Even if he has been counting on the good fairy to take care of birth control for him, when his woman becomes pregnant he is surprised. All sorts of images fly up in front of his face and none of them are happy and all of them are expensive. He sees fatherhood as a big responsibility. Certainly many Blackmen dream of having a son and experience a twinge of temporary disappointment when they sire a daughter. This quickly fades and other than their apprehension in wondering about how they will protect her, they love their sons and daughters equally. If circumstances permit they will spend time with the child and are proud of what they made. When circumstances do not permit them to raise their children because of falling out with the mother, the mother moving away, or if the child is the only thing he and the woman have in common, he has a more difficult time relating to fatherhood.

Many of them did not have fathers when they grew up so it is not entirely clear to them what the role of a father is. They love babies if ample opportunity is provided for them to get to know it and quickly learn to feed, change, bathe and dress a baby. Other times he must move on because of the failed relationship between he and the mother. He hates paying outrageous sums of child support and will often express his dissatisfaction with the mother by withholding the money. If they are apart this is his only means of causing her irritation or getting her attention. He does not equate it with denying the child even though it does in many cases. If he does not bond with the child at an early age it is easier for him to walk away from it and never look back. Blackmen have sons and daughters scattered all over the country. Some of them they have not seen since birth. Some of their whereabouts are not even known. It is not that he is cold or unfeeling but that he has been conditioned to believe that the baby belongs totally to the mother and he doesn't know how to maintain a relationship with a child whom he does not live with. Some of them are learning how to do this now but it generally is with those whom they did live with at some time. Since the baby does not grow and come out of their bodies they have to bond with it by touching and holding it and spending enough time with the child to know it and make the child aware of their existence. There is no greater joy than for him to be recognized and loved by a child — especially if it's his child. Modern Blackmen do not like children. They see them as a hassle. The real problem is that they do not know what to teach a child and they are frightened at the prospect of having the responsibility of the daily training of another human being. They can look at other older children and realize how difficult the job is. He does not want to fail and having no role model, he's unsure of his capabilities. Fathering is a very important job. Psychologists report that children with fathers are seen to be outgoing, adaptable, accept challenge, do better in school, get along with peers, have better self-esteem and less problems with drugs or alcohol. Contemporary and very secure Blackmen are now taking to adopting Black boys in an effort to save Black children and redeem themselves from rumors of failed parents. Although Blacks make up less than 12% of the American population, more than half the available children for adoption are Black. There are currently 500,000 children now available for adoption. Statisticians project that by 1995 almost one million children will be available for adoption and over 40% of these will be Black or Hispanic. Adoption agencies report that 95% of the Black families who apply for adoption through the standard systems are turned down. The main reasons they are turned down by the Federal or State agencies is 1) their mutual refusal or inability to pay the fees often between $9,000 to $25,000 — cash (for medical expenses, foster care and administrative costs), or 2) they do not have a Christian home. Having a Christian home is of paramount importance to governmental agencies to ensure that the Black baby will be taught the same information as its ancestral slave relatives. The agencies say white children are often placed within ten days. Trans-racial adoptions are becoming popular because the government says there are too few Black qualified adults to absorb the high numbers of Black babies and children waiting to be adopted. Their false premise is that it's better for a Black child to grow up in a white home than to rot in foster care. Both are horrible choices for the survival of the Black nation. Blackmen politicians have not addressed this crisis of abandoned Black babies. As usual, they do not address the issues most pressing to the survival of African-Americans.

The Blackman's Sex Organ
The Blackman's legendary mythological penis is discussed in many secret conversations. He has lived a life whereby the public refers to his penis and its great size or power over women. This kind of gossip has transcended history and followed him from slavery. The stereotypical gossip is about his unrestrained sexual desire based on his animal-sized organ. Many of them say, along with their women, that they have been rumored and judged unfairly and as far as they can tell their sexual anatomy is just not qualified to be the weapon it is claimed to be. The simplest way to explain the Blackman's feelings of either superiority or inferiority about the size of his penis is to equate it to a female's attitude and concern over the size of her breasts. Each tries to make the best of what they have, no matter what size — hence developed, "It's not the size that counts, it's what you do with it." Obviously like breasts, also fleshy appendages, they come in all lengths, widths and shapes.

The whiteman's liberation movement has forced him to address some of the issues discussed because Blackwomen keep up with social changes in behavior of whites and customarily bring these same topics or issues to the attention of the Blackman. While the Blackman is more than happy to get out from under the pressures of being considered the major bread winner, they are repulsed by suggestions that they must incorporate more femininity into their motions. He's really not interested in learning to act more like a woman in order to date or marry one in peace. His frigid boasting gives the impression of a man on the verge of bursting with pride about his own existence. Outwardly he tries to present himself as the exact prototype of a confident, take-charge, masculine bombshell. The inward man, however, bears little resemblance to the overweening vanity he projects on the outside. He has learned through painful lessons with women that intense desire and insatiable sexual passion can drive a man insane. He does not know his own mind, what he wants in a woman, or what type of woman to pursue. Yet, against hope, against reason and against all evidence, these strange creatures approach series of Blackwomen trying to impress them with their fortitude by flashing big bucks, slick dressing, irrational bragging, laid back confidence and willingness to negotiate to pave a way to the bedroom. And in all of these matters he is slow, halting, wobbly, unsure of himself and pathetically aware of his own weaknesses which he tries harder and harder to conceal. His relationships with women camouflage his cries of despair, utter misery and often continued loneliness — even when he has a woman, because he can never really be honest by introducing his real personality. Being with several women or trying to "go with" several at a time represents another one of his vain mysterious ways to seek out the purpose of his real life. He is so helplessly attracted to beautiful women.

When the Blackman admires a woman on the street he will whistle, yelp, or hoot out a yell. This may be "hey baby," or "hey mama, you sho' look good," or "hey miss lady", or "you sho' is fine," or "God——," or "Sh——," or some other catchy type phrase to get the Blackwoman's attention. If she smiles kindly and keeps walking he will usually just go on back to whatever he was doing. If she makes a mean face or ignores him, he may have a negative reaction from being rejected when he thought he was paying the woman a compliment. When this happens he might yell out a curse word, or tell her "oh you can't speak?" or "you ain't fine anyway," or "well go 'head on B——" or "F—you then" or some other hostile remark to either embarrass the woman, put her down or show off in front of his friends. Sometimes a Blackman who is raggedy, nasty looking or using crude language to approach a woman will be ignored. It's always amazing to Blackwomen that some of the most vile looking men will attempt to hit on her or get the attention of a very attractive sophisticated looking lady. Blackwomen think that he must know that he doesn't have a snowball chance in hell of getting an upgrade woman's attention — for anything.

But this tells something about the ever present ego of Blackmen. They don't care how they're dressed, how they talk or what they look like, they expect a pretty woman to respond to them. Some get so frustrated that they follow the woman down the street still yelling unsavory remarks at her to try to embarrass her for having the nerve to ignore him. The Blackman, even those with honorable intentions, who whistle at women, don't know that whistling is a habit derived from savage male animals who make burly noises to attract a female animal. They use vocal signals to express their interest in a female. Baboons using lip smacking sounds to attract their mates — just like Blackmen who smack their lips or make hissing sounds to flirt with a woman. Some of them stick out their tongues as a way to insinuate an idea of what's on their minds. Sticking out the tongue is never a decent facial motion in any society. It is done to resemble an erect penis. It is also used by some animals to their opponents to signify hostility or aggression. So all that sticking out the tongue, or running the tongue around the lips, is not a good way to attract someone. Most Blackwomen think that this means that a man is hinting that he wants to have oral sex with her and this is the way he offers it.

Saying hello or goodbye has taken on a new language. Many of the brothers now use what they think is a peace sign. They raise the forefinger and the middle finger in a "V" sign and say: Peace! this sign was originally used in old England as an insult to imply a double penis or phallic symbol. Further back it was used to signal the horns of the devil. Its meaning changed when Nixon used it in the 60's and the Vietnam War protestors picked it up to mean peace as opposed to war.

The neck tie the Blackman so proudly wears when he dresses up or has a high powered job in an office or corporate world was originally designed by the French Court in 17th century Europe. It was a badge of social elevation, phallic in design, and implied a psychosexual power of conformity among white males. In more civilized societies, the men wear bow ties or draping shawls to keep from participating in this masculine tradition of dressing up.

Blackmen over the years have become obese both from eating more junk foods and from eating better foods more often as a result of having money to do so. Those who work insist on eating three meals a day — breakfast, lunch and dinner — because Americans have been raised to believe in those three meals as a complete diet, and the only way to be nourished properly. In the middle ages the Europeans only ate two meals a day, by the 17th century they had moved to three meals per day — attached to the three parts of the Trinity — the Father, the Son and the Holy Ghost. In ancient African cultures the Blackman ate one good meal per day with possibly fruit added during the day or late night.

On the birth of a baby, if the Blackman is the proud father, he will pass out cigars to announce the new addition to his family. Passing out cigars is not a Blackman's custom throughout the earth. It is a pagan activity suggesting a burnt offering for the father's part in the birth. It is also a phallic symbol to brag about what he used to make the new baby. Europeans have always used phallic symbols to brag on their superiority. The Washington Monument in D.C. is suggestive of a phallic symbol because George Washington was their first President and therefore was very powerful in what he did. Although kissing is enjoyed by many Blackmen and they have perfected it to an art, kissing actually is a method of personal familiarity started by the Romans in Rome. Other non-white peoples usually touched cheeks or rubbed noses or hugged as a way to express love for their mates. Even today though, some Blackmen do not like to kiss and many others have never learned the knack of it. Being romantic as representing good love or high desire is also a term picked up from Rome. The Romans used this word to express their particular kind of love expression most exemplified during their orgies. The point here is that Blackmen practice a lot of traditions and follow a lot of standards and practices which they do not know the origin of. The Blackman has not taken it upon himself to find out what his own ancient traditions are so that he can announce them and adopt them in a modified way of some sort here in America. On researching many of the practices that are now acceptable habits to them, one finds that they are not from the Blackman's culture nor representative of his ideas.

The Blackman's relationship with his mother is an interesting one. He is often torn between his love and hate for her. He loves her because she fed and clothed him, looked out for him and did her best to raise him. He hates her because she restrained him, rebuffed him, tried to turn him into a daughter, and did not provide him with a father. He has been taught all his life to honor his mother and he loves her in the best way he knows how. He tolerates her and tries to get her to understand his points of view. He fakes respect for her ideals even if he has learned that she is way off base in her recommendations to him. If he was taught against his father as a child, he now understands from living with his mother, some of the reasons his father probably left her, and that his father may not be so bad after all — at least he's a man. In most cases he does know that his mother loves him and is proud of his maleness. Every mother wants to love and admire her son. His bond with her is a special one if they get along. If they do not get along he is plagued with unsuccessful relationships with women throughout his life, because his first introduction to femalehood ended in emotional tragedy.

The Blackman's relationship with his daughters is one of protection, futile protection, because he knows deep within him that there is nothing he can do to prevent her from becoming interested in boys and ultimately having sex with them. He is ill-equipped to deal with her growing rebellion as she ages and usually pulls back lets her have her way. He feels almost as powerless to direct his daughter as he feels in trying to direct her mother. If he is close to his daughter he enjoys the relationship of being the daddy to a baby girl totally dependent upon him and impressed with his abilities. The girl baby gives many Blackmen the only unabridged female acceptance they ever know. His little girl wants to please him and he works hard to please her. While he may look forward to his son growing up and being able to respond physically to some of their joint activities, he is saddened when his baby girl grows up and they lose their commonality as she draws away from him to explore the world of women. A world he wishes he could prevent her from entering because he knows what's going to happen. It has not occurred to him that he could design an alternative plan to the current process of raising girls. He doesn't know how to replace the old plan with a more controlled and moral one, because he is doubtful that he could convince her mother to cooperate. He avoids confrontation with women over his ideas on homemaking or childrearing as opposed to hers. He is afraid of being rejected and he is scared of being put on punishment of some sort for rocking the boat. So he pulls back, washes his hands of the whole matter, and lets his woman, the girl's mother, do her job. The outrage he feels when his daughter is violated is unexplainable. He is torn between his emotional love connection to her and his need to protect her for as long as he can, and knowledge of his own memories and what he used to do with females when he was young. So to condemn her completely requires that he condemn his ownself and his own corrupt morals. This personal information about his own practices keeps him quiet and prompts him to withdraw from the entire process of making judgments about other family members' behaviors. All of this is a part of his acceptance of the idea that men and women are equal, and that women have just as many rights as he does, and they can do whatever they want to do just like he does whatever he wants to do. This mode of thinking has for years further deteriorated his family and his relationships with Blackwomen. Those ideas made him mushy, weak willed and malleable, when he should be firm, insistent and authoritative. In nature when only one parent cares for the brood, it tends to become more mean or aggressive than the other parent. Single mothers manifest this.

The Other Woman
The Blackman's life with his other woman is more often than not built on falsehood. The falsehood results from his lack of knowledge of how to maintain a truthful relationship with two or more women at the same time. He thinks that in order to be qualified or justified to be with another woman outside of the wife or woman he already has, is to lie about the conditions at home. He thinks he has to put himself in a needy or sympathetic position for another woman to want him or risk becoming involved with him since he is already committed to sharing living quarters, children, financial and family responsibilities with another woman. He explains and convinces the other woman that he is being horribly misused and abused at home. He may even tell her that he and his wife do not have sex, sleep in separate rooms or barely speak. He often looks outside his

home for needs that he has that are not met at home, this does not necessarily mean that what he is saying is true. He gets another woman if things are unhappy at home, but he is just as likely to get one of things are what he may consider boringly happy. He is unpredictable in these instances. His requirements for the other woman is that she must be constantly delightful to be with in order to transcend him out of the gloomy life he has at home. She must adorn him with special attention in his food, bath, clothes or skin, or any other way she can soothe his pain of living with a woman whom he swears he doesn't want. He is dishonest and so is his other woman, not because they are sneaking around behind his wife's back, but because their relationship is predicated on fantasy and unreality. They show each other only their best side. There are no other responsibilities to each other therefore routine, or occasional conflict, does not penetrate their little world of total happiness and satisfaction. The relationship with the other woman consumes his spare time and interest. Her place becomes his sanctuary. He can always go there and be welcomed. He can soothe her for the sacrifices she makes for him in not being able to go certain places or do certain things. But as long as they can be together and share intense mind-blowing uninhibited sex, they are both satisfied and believe they have something of value to hang on to. If he has any money to spare he helps his other woman when he can. He gets to know her children if she has any and all the rest of her friends and relatives. The deep seated longing to be together plus the fact that no matter what he goes through at home, he knows he will eventually break free to go to a place where he is valued and nearly worshipped, help him make it through the days and nights in between seeing his other woman. He is careful about phone calls. If he misses a date or special holiday he makes up with some get-down sex worthy of being carved into the Hall of Fame. Since the relationship is not based on truth he must continue to devise horror stories of the monster wife. He may even tell the other woman that when the children grow up, his wife finds a job, he makes more money, when the bills are paid, his baby gets well, or when the cow jumps over the moon that he is going to leave home. Preferably to marry the other woman and live happily ever after.

Fat chance. When this does not happen, even at intervals the other woman thinks would be the perfect chance for him to

172

make his break, the second level of this clandestine relationship goes into effect. This is the level where small quarrels break out between the man and the woman because of two things: 1) The woman starts to suspect the obvious, that he has no intention of leaving his primary family and 2) she starts to think that he's a fool for staying in a situation he claims is so bad.

The other woman starts to know too much about his personal life and starts to think that he's a fraud and possibly deserves to be treated bad by the wife at home. She may start to put more strident demands on him requesting items, deadlines or activities she knows he can't possibly meet in the situation he's in. She starts to try to force him into a position where he has to make a choice. The Blackman sees all of this happening and takes it as his cue to possibly pull out for a while or take a chance and do something special for her like spend the night or take her away for a weekend to reaffirm his unwavering love, and negotiate for more time. This works for him several times until the other woman concludes that this Blackman is just running a game on her. It can get really ugly after this point depending on how vindictive the other woman is. All of this is avoided when the man comes straight with the truth — that he is not leaving his wife and family, explains how much time he has to spare for a second relationship and does not tell very much about his wife or home life. These kinds of Blackmen are rare. Indeed. Many of them like the suspense, mystery and intrigue of sneaking. It's a challenge to them to try to juggle both sides of the universe. He's under extra pressure at home during this time because he has to be on constant guard not to do, wear, say or mention anything not pertaining to his home affairs.

Blackmen can carry on a lengthy affair like this for years. Some of them can only pull it off for a few months. Whenever his wife at home becomes overly suspicious he lays dead for a while until her calm returns. Many times if he thinks his wife suspects he has another woman he will make love to her right before going out which is supposed to transmit a message that I'm having sex with you to get this over with so you'll know I'm not going to have sex anyplace else. This is a lie. A different situation and different woman can inspire him to readiness all over again — even in the same night. But he sees this as reassuring to his wife at home and offers it to her as a comfort. Or he'll do the opposite. After coming in late he'll make love to

173

his wife so she won't think he's been out having sex with another woman. He has to keep up his routine at home no matter what. Truth of the matter is that he usually has a regular on-going love life with his wife and takes care of her needs before embarking on any others so as not to disrupt his home life. Blackmen who are married also will hire the random services of a prostitute for a few moments of detached sex. These days he says he uses condoms more but they say they don't like them because they interfere with the real feeling he wants of flesh next to flesh.

When a Blackman has another woman and moves into her life as her man and husband it is a different situation. He is the maintainer of the woman and provides her with guidance, security, gratification and helps her raise her children. He may even have some there of his own. In this kind of situation both his women in both homes know about the existence of the other one. He'll bring his children together if he can, and do his best to deal fairly in each location. The most interesting thing to note about his intimate relationships with women is that women are interchangeable to him. He seeks out a good woman, one who is decent, responsive to him, respectful of him, raises his children well, is moderately attractive, doesn't hassle him, cooks well, keeps house, is fairly neat, is honest fidelity wise and has a personality that is pleasing to him. The ironic part is that other than satisfying certain needs she doesn't have to have any special qualifications as far as looks, size or shape is concerned. He just wants whatever he deems as a good woman. Certainly if possible he would like her to be exceedingly attractive, but since that possibility is usually a little remote, he accepts the woman who accepts him. In other words, if the woman has her basic act together one woman is just as good as the next to him. If she appeals to his masculine nature and proves to be sincere he'll settle down with her and try to make a life with her.

Of course the hi-tech Blackman wants a Blackwoman who is exceptionally good looking, has special legs or shape or hair length. She possibly must have some kind of college degree, belong to an organization, be from a good family, or have an important job. This kind of Blackman sees the Blackwoman as a stallion, a special breed of female that he desires to be seen with as her owner. His woman is his showhorse. He wants to provoke envy or jealousy in other Blackmen who see him with her. This kind of Blackman is shallow in nature and weak in sincerity. These relationships don't last very long, especially if the woman gains or loses any of her beauty marks. He needs her to boost his confidence.

If a Blackman is in a relationship where he has been faking confidence or being dishonest about his real motivations and is close to being found out, or if he is under pressure to make a major decision or to do something he is secretly afraid to do, he will often just punk-out completely and disappear from the scene. His fear gets the best of him and he wilts at the thought of an honest confrontation wherein he may be forced to reveal his true feelings or fears — so he takes flight. He just disappears seemingly off the face of the earth. He splits. He might leave everything he owned and it might happen at an unexpected time when nothing disruptive is happening in the relationship. This kind of Blackman has to break free to be his real self. The self he manufactured to be with a certain kind of woman can no longer be upheld. So he breaks. He goes someplace else and pretends that the relationship never happened or existed. He runs to someplace less pressured to him, a place where he is not known and where he can slip into anonymity and never have to explain himself. This Blackman is sad. He is sad because he has to live with his failure to thrive in a situation that he obviously lost control of and allowed to control him. He is never the same after each of these exits. He has to make up a new lie to tell himself.

Blackmen Who Date or Marry White Women

Up until 1967 Blackmen couldn't marry white women in the south. It was against the law. As physical institutions became less threatening due to desegregation rulings, the social institutions also crumbled and Blackmen began to stalk the white woman in droves in an attempt to:

1) Finally get their hands on the one female they had been denied.

2) Be different and to prove to whites that he was serious about integration, and to improve his status in the world.

The release of Spike Lee's movie *Jungle Fever* reopened this issue about whether or not Blackmen should sexually integrate with white woman. The recent census discovery that over 60% of Black females are single, widowed, separated and divorced confirms both the shortage of Blackmen and their absence from the home. The University of Chicago released their own deadly stats from a private study. The problems of the Blackman in America are known all over the world, and they are ignored for the most part. The Black family is shattered, Blackmen and boys continue to die, mostly at the whims of each other, and neither the sisters or the brothers have collectively confronted these tragic happenings. Blackmen, who historically have exerted special strength in times of national conflict, are unusually quiet, disinterested appearing. Blackwomen, distracted by the looming responsibilities of trying to be both mother and father, also have abandoned ship preoccupied with their own survival. Thousands of Blackmen have given up on Blackwomen and seek out interracial personal relationships with white women. Some of them consider it a novelty, something to brag about, a way to gain notoriety and go against the norm. Intermingling socially with whites has gained more acceptance by placing Blackmen and white women in product advertisements on television, in magazines and on billboard ads. Television sit-coms and dramatic series have also made it seem more natural looking. White men thrust into fictional situations where they are irresistibly drawn to Blackwomen for sexual encounters. Blackmen are portrayed in roles where they are matched with white females as a natural occurrence. They are even seen kissing white women and wallowing in the bed with them.

Black youth are drawn into it at social functions in their schools or colleges, and visual messages suggesting interracial interest is premiered in many of their rap music videos shown on cable around the clock. It is seemingly all around us, unavoidable at last and a natural evolution of the growing betterment and cohesion between Blacks and whites. Some see it as the cure-all for race relation problems. Many Blackmen do not seem to care what kind of white woman they mate with. She can be ugly, bloated, destitute and look like the shaggy dog, but it seems as long as she is white skinned he is happy. The higher classed Blackman attempts to indoctrinate his white female prize into Blackness by teaching her to dress, talk and dance Black. Others of them do not carry any part of their Blackness into the interracial relationship and instead try to pretend that they are a regular all-American white boy in Black face costume. Contemporary opinions suggest that love conquers all and that mate selection is a private individual choice, and racial separation is an old fashioned, outdated idea that can't survive in modern times.

Interracial love, the mixing of various breeds through sexual intercourse, is first of all against all the laws of nature which supports self preservation of every life form whereby each is only attracted to its own kind. Nature's system of reproduction and survival in mammals, and all human life are mammals, is maintained by this separation of life forms. The rule is like is attracted and mates with like. The lion and the common house cat are both in the feline family but they do no mate, nor do they even get along. Neither does the dog and the wolf, the horse and the zebra, or the chicken and the turkey. The comparisons can go on and on to demonstrate how all other life forms mate within the framework of their own breeds. This process of reproduction does not vary in nature. On the cultural level of this issue, race mixing is a form of ethnic genocide. When a person loves themself they are only attracted to an image as much like themselves as possible. Social integration for the Blackman indicates his frustration and rejection of his own image.

No religion upholds interracial marriage. All holy books teach against it. God himself is against it. Separation of tribes is inherent to all historical teachings all over the globe. Blackmen who are entertainers and sport performers have set a bad example of self-love because over 50% of Blackmen popular stars, as soon as they become rich and famous, immediately cross over and marry into the white race in hope that it will gain them more benefits, recognition, and complete acceptance into the European community. They take their fame, financial gain, political clout and energy over to the people who continue to repress the rest of their kind. This gives them a chance to be different and special which is what Blackmen want to be. Negro publications like *Ebony*, *Jet* and *Chocolate Singles* all promote interracial relationships with ignorant pride as if they consider it an accomplishment. Among these Blackmen are James Earl Jones, Bobby McFerrin, Joe Morton, Charles Barkley, Julian Bond, Amiri Baraka, Kareem Jabbar, Gregory Hines, Quincy Jones, Richard Pryor, James Brown, Herbie Hancock, Berry Gordy, Earl Klugh, Al Jerreau, Herschel Walker, Melvin Van Pebbles, Chubby Checker, Billy Dee Williams, George Sanford Brown, Sidney Poitier, Rick James, Miles Davis, Dorian Harewood, Jack Johnson, Redd Foxx, Sammy Davis, Jr., Jim Brown, Lionel Richie, Richard Roundtree, Lynn Swann, Billy Daniels, Clarence Thomas, Bill Lee and unknown others.

177

Regrettably each new generation of Blacks become progressively disassociated with each other. Selective amnesia takes over and they part with their pasts and consider social integration a way to pave a place for themselves in the future. The purpose of racial segregation is not based on hostility or hate, it is grounded in the principles that ensure self-preservation and love of one's own kind. White males know that social integration will dismantle the Caucasian race because Black blood changes the color, features, hair and body shape of a nationality, and if race mixing in the bedroom continues, soon the melting pot will be brimming with sewage and confusion of identity. Whenever this topic comes up both whites and Blacks profess their agreement with sexual integration as a way to mesh the races.

These Blackwomen, refusing to be outdone, are Iman, Sade, Grace Jones, Tookie Smith, Josephine Baker, Eartha Kitt, Diana Ross, Madge Sinclair, Alfre Woodard, Lisa Bonet, Whoopi Goldberg, Diahann Carroll, Lynn Whitfield, Tina Turner, Donna Summer, Rae Dawn Chong, Shari Belafonte, Lena Horne, Pearl Bailey, Leslie Uggams, Lorraine Hansberry, Roxie Roker, Nell Carter, Ann Marie Johnson, Cleo Laine, Barbara McNair, Mary Wilson, LaToya Jackson, and Debi Thomas. These two lists, of Blackmen and Blackwomen, who have sexually integrated into the white race, represent nearly all of our public, successful or famous Blacks. While the Black public embraces their success by virtue of kinship, they themselves absolve their lifestyles of anything remotely connecting them to being African-American. A mate is the closest confidant, the most trusted, the most loved and valuable. It is difficult to imagine how these Blackmen and women have hypnotized themselves into believing that they are happy and perfectly at ease living with whites nearly around the clock. It is strange indeed. This trend is growing and the people who stand for traditional values and maintenance of family culture and heritage are mocked and rejected.

When Michael Jackson appears in public with a female it is with Elizabeth Taylor, Brooke Shields, Sophia Loren or Madonna. Michael is a prime example of unidentifying himself with his Blackness. He is an aging teeny bopper now approaching middle age. He continues to don his bogus wardrobe, Cover Girl made up face, and slicked back Jheri Curl. Blacks know little of Jackson's real personality but there is no doubt that he has no idea who he is or that he is

Black.

When questioned, these race-mixing Blackmen claim that they just fell in love and that there's no difference in loving a white woman than a Black one. Love is the most confusing word in the Black dialect. Love is not self-propelled. It is not an uncontrollable disease of attraction which one has no power over. Love is a decision. It is a choice. Because the Blackman has such a low opinion of himself and does not consider himself or anything resembling him as worthy, they want to escape their heritage. They think the solution is to marry up with whites, deliver his heart, soul and attention over to them and pretend that they are just like them with no connections to their roots. Some even try to exert a kind of fractured sense of their Blackness in their white relationships by hanging Black art in their homes, attending Black political conferences or acknowledging support for Martin Luther King, Jr. There is no recognizable list of white males who become rich and successful and then reach back and marry a Blackwoman. It doesn't happen and it's not supposed to. The Blackman's abnormal curiosity about sex with white women makes him think he is overcoming the final racial taboo — and it also keeps him from the racial harmony he hypocritically says he desires. Sexual integration is just another trick the Blackman is playing on himself because he thinks that intermarriage will solve the problems of racism. Just like he thought eating at their lunch counters, going to school with them, or working next to them, or living next door would. That all failed, too.

Michael Jackson is the most prominent Blackman who disavows himself from other Black people. Michael knows that he wouldn't last ten good minutes among the brothers if he showed up in that prissy looking gear he wears, with his white socks and eyeliner make-up. This Blackman is so confused about who he is that he has gone through the surgical torture of having skin peelings and pigment bleaching done so as to scrape off his black skinned cocoon and emerge as a white butterfly. He used to have a Black shaped nose until he got enough money to have it chiseled down to a beak-like point. Michael doesn't appear on talk shows, does not attend Black events unless they are frequented and sponsored by whites, and has never been seen in public hosting a Blackwoman since his rise to mega stardom. Currently he has a new flashy video out where he prances around flinging his hair and twirling in circles singing something about "it doesn't matter if you're Black or white." Everybody in America who knows anything about Michael Jackson knows that he does not believe what he is singing about. It is difficult to conceive that a Blackman who would go through as many changes as Jackson has undergone to give up looking Black, now believes that it doesn't matter. It matters so much to him that he now looks like an artificial mannequin — a wind-up toy. He is a very sad example of a Blackman whose masterful talents removed him from reality. He is afraid of his own kind.

Blackmen who are excessively jealous, another warped category of misdevelopment, behave very badly when under the influence of the jealousy emotion. They have been known to go to many extremes to punish a woman whom they are jealous of. They unmercifully beat her, check on her whereabouts day and night, follow her around, call every hour, terrorize her, show up on her job acting a fool, embarrass her in public, shoot her, stab her and make her life a living hell.

Sexual Perversion
Many Blackmen are first introduced to sexual perversion if they are dealing in drugs or crime. Entertainment and show business are also fertile fields for him to witness or participate in sexual perversion. It is commonly agreed that any sexual behavior that occurs between two consenting adults is permissible. Blackman have a blight history of instigating group sex or orgies during the sexual revolution of the 60's and 70's. They are not ordinarily interested in wife-swapping because their egos tell them that they can have another man's woman without sharing their own. Most of them are drawn to or like the idea of having two women in bed with them but most don't know how to arrange this between any two women he loves, so experimentation on this level usually comes from women-for-hire, i.e., prostitutes. They enjoy watching two women make love to each other and most enjoy a porno movie if they have access to them. The Blackman is not interested in watching another man make love to his woman through a keyhole, neither does he want to be tied down or tie his woman down to beat her. He has no record of ever wanting to be urinated or defecated on to achieve sexual pleasure. As a rule they are not interested in sex with animals, nor do they openly display interest in having sex with children. He may perform some magnificent feats in one-on-

one sex, or dream up creative ways or places, but other than that, public proof of any oddball sexual perversions are not routinely known. Of course these days there are random cases of incest, child molestation, Oeidipal Complexes and bisexuality among some of them who are mentally disturbed. Blackmen do not participate in bloody rites, devil worship or beastiality to enjoy sex. The ones who say they derive sexual excitement out of spanking women on their buttocks are rare. Unfortunately, some Blackmen are starting to experiment with vile forms of sexual perversions unmentionable.

Homosexuality Among Blackmen — the gay way

Interviews and evaluations done with homosexual Blackmen revealed some startling information. Overall, gay Blackmen say that they became homosexual as a result of confusing sexual orientation and unsuccessful relationships with other females when they were young. They say pursuing sensual gratification from men of their same-sex is not as important as being able to have a standing relationship with an individual who accepts, and does not remind them of the disapproval he experiences with women. Accordingly, when they reject manhood they still need a sexual outlet, plus get an opportunity to rebel against societal norm. They further say that homosexuality is a protection against the rejection that causes them to fear contact with women. It is easier to avoid having intimate contact with women if he is a woman himself. He couldn't win with them so he joined them to avoid criticism. The majority of them reported that they had grown up in households overwhelmingly made up of several women, young and old. These men are ages 18 to 54. Ninety-five percent of them were from homes with no father, or where the father was overruled by the mother. There were routine accounts of how they dressed up in feminine clothes when they were children, or experienced a special thrill when dressing up like a woman on Halloween, or told to function like a man while not knowing what a man was supposed to do. The female life looks easier. They describe it as a feeling that comes over them which they discover is inappropriate, they say they believe homosexuality is their destiny. He says the affection he receives from men outweighs the frustration expressed by family, friends or society.

Gay Blackmen say that when they "come out of the closet" they are inducted into the homosexual ranks by older gay

Blackmen who teach them the ropes. Surprisingly, they say they are advised the same way women say they are advised by their mothers; they are told "don't let no man use you," or "don't be out there running the streets," "act like a lady," "take care of yourself," and "don't be no fool."

Every Black male gay interrogated said that every man they date or have sexual relations with is straight as an arrow. They say all of their men, which they have regular or periodic sex with, are straight appearing Blackmen — with wives — and children. They say it is now impossible to discern a gay male from a straight one unless he displays visible effeminate ways. The worst news is that they say the pool of available heterosexual looking Blackmen has expanded and that there are throngs of Blackmen masquerading as straight but are as crooked as lightening.

The first conclusion from this is that if homosexual Blackmen are almost strictly dealing with straight married Blackmen, this certainly would explain the higher numbers of Blackwomen infected with HIV and AIDS. The medical profession now advises us that AIDS among heterosexual men and women is growing, but the question becomes what is the root of this growth? If hoards of Blackmen are sneaking around having illicit sex with homos without being recognized in the community, their mates are at an unfair disadvantage because of this lack of knowledge. In plain view, in major cities gay Blackmen are picked up by other Blackmen dressed in suits and ties. There is daily proof that this is actually happening and that an inordinate number of Blackmen are moving towards bisexuality. Gays say to watch out for Blackmen who are over zealous in expressing their hate or disdain for homosexuals. They say homo-hate is not proof that a Blackman is not bisexual and they protest loudly to cover their tracks. Even if they swear on a stack of Bibles.

These Blackmen are what they call "in the closet" homophobic. No interviews are available from this invisible population. But they exist according to reports and eye-witness accounts.

Social scientists have become more liberal in their conclusions and now tout that homosexuality is biological, physical. They say it depends on the genes, the chromosomes and hormonal make-up of each individual as to whether or not they will have gay tendencies. By making this an explainable or justifiable option they ignore the illegal, moral and ethic violations inherent in the gay lifestyle, that for the Blackman, represents a deathstyle. And a further reduction of available Blackmen.

When inquiries were made as to why a gay Blackman would be appealing to a "straight" Blackman, they responded: "because I treat them like a man," or "'cause I'm a good woman to him," or "don't nobody know what a man does behind closed doors," or "because I'm nice to him." They say movies depict them as promiscuous and weird, but they say they only want to settle down in a regular stable relationship like everyone else, but the complications of their gender transformation makes this difficult.

It seems that parents impress a gender upon a child at birth. This impression becomes firmly established during the first few years of life. A mother teaches her child to be a girl or a boy by her tone, the choice of words she uses when communicating with it, the games, selection of clothes and toys, and a clearly defined set of standards of what they are praised or rebuffed for, and punished or rewarded for. Before about seven or eight years old, boys are purportedly made aware of the differences between sexes — and they incorporate this knowledge into their toys, the colors of their clothes, hair styles and recreational activities. His sexuality is slowly developed into his nature. On the other hand, if he lives and grows in an environment with mostly women he learns that women seem to have life a little easier — adults are more patient with them, they can cry loudly for hours, if they fall down they get more concern, they don't have to work as hard, they get prettier flashier clothes, they have hair they can play with or fix differently, they get hugged more often, they don't get spanked with the same fury, they huddle a lot whispering their private conversations and they readily accept each other with little complication. The Black boy's reaction to all this, deciphered in his immature brain, arrives at the conclusion that girls have it better, and his malehood is rejected by them, possibly by the adult female in his home.

As he grows, if the boy is not systematically separated from the influence of his caregiving female, he builds doubt resulting from not having any formal rules or rites to induct him into manhood. If he has no credible teacher from whom to inherit his masculinity by learning to get his ideas and energy from himself — separate and apart from the women — he may carry this doubt into his teenage years and ultimately to adulthood. Blackmen, normally, go through a stage of self-doubt about their masculinity. They are not sure at that time if they have any feminine traits or not, so they work hard to convince the world by their physical actions that they are male — and not female. They study themselves and may even check with another person or validate themselves by having premature sex. If he is sexually abused or a victim of incest, the accompanying guilt may imply to them that they brought the attack on because they are "sissy" or too softly natured. This also can happen to a Blackman who experiences rape while in prison. Many do not survive these attacks and decide to be gay because they were never relieved of the emotional pain that comes with being violated. They think they are marked and prevented from ever being a man again.

There are always a few gay Blackmen who have perfected the art of manufacturing themselves into a female entity. These are not the ones with the "hard ankles" or "bulging shoulders" or "big feet" or "hairy chests" or "beard and mustache." Gay Blackmen have now become a formidable political group when demonstrating for gay rights. Blackmen politicians who give in to gay-right pressure and include them as part of the normal behaving public are setting a bad example for younger Black males who may be in the doubt stage regarding their sexuality. Blackmen on the borderline are further confused regarding the right or wrong of homosexuality when major magazines like *Essence*—which claims to be for intelligent, educated, progressive Blackwomen — publish at least three or four issues per year containing stories abut Blackwomen who are lesbians. *Essence* defames the Black family and insults civilized Blackwomen by arranging their lesbian stories in such a way as to make it an attractive, viable alternative lifestyle for Black females. This is wrong and can promote the idea that they support practicing sexual deviance. This is not the way to preserve the African-American family and home. Blackmen and youth read this publication and many take direction from it and view it as an authority of Black social trends.

The penis in the rectum of the gay Blackman is his final submission to his pseudo female identity. Offering up his rectum for penetration, pain and sexual gratification can lead to other ailments other than AIDS. Many have to go in and out of hospital emergency rooms for perforated rectums. Their

rectum is packed with medication and gauze, and they sometimes have to have stitches or a blood transfusion. They say
they have oral sex with their "men" and will do anything they
want them to do. They say they don't mind kissing someone
with a mustache and beard as thick as their own. For those who
like to dress up like women — dresses, make-up and all — they
say it takes them a while to get it together but eventually they
learn to dress and walk in high heels like a woman. They feel
no special connection or responsibility to other Blacks, they are
some of the most liberal minded integrationists around. They
say they have been beat or attacked by "real" straight Blackmen
if during their encounter he finds out by surprise that he is gay.
They are also known to attack their competition and fight
viciously. They can cook, sew, bake and are determined to be
a better woman than all the women they know. And they say
their men like it. The most painful discovery for a Blackwoman
is to find out that her man is gay. African-American couples
routinely break up over this.

The gay Blackman does not understand that homosexuality
is a decision. It is an idea, which is why gay Blackmen —
without the aid of hormones or other body altering drugs —
start walking differently, their flesh relaxes becoming more soft
and pliable and they take on certain facial poses or physical
stances. The brain is a follower, it is not a leader and it obeys
the ego explicitly. When the Blackman makes the decision that
he is gay, his entire body and mind kick in to support the choice,
make it real, make it happen. This could be loosely referred to
as the will. He can will himself into anything he desires in his
mind. No matter what the obstacles, he can reshape anything
to suit his desire, even his body and personality.

Blackmen should not be homosexuals. Surveys suggest
that the majority of gays describe themselves as Democrats.
Other Blackmen leaders refuse, because of fear of losing
political clout, to announce that gay Blackmen are out of order.
Blackmen already know that they disagree with each other. So
what next? They can either stay at a stand-off claiming "I
respect your right to disagree," or they can come together and
stumble around until they uncover something that they can
agree on and start to build from there. It is a scientific fact that
everything is not correct and everybody cannot be right. The
Blackman denies the existence of any pure right or wrong
because he does not want to make a moral decision. He has

been brainwashed into thinking that there is no right or wrong. He is afraid to take a position against public adversity and stand up for what is right. Even the whiteman has what he calls "natural law" — what God intended, and what the greater nation/community must have in order to survive as a civilized enduring society. He does not accept any information as sterling truth, he has been taught to question everything and then make a personal emotional decision about whether or not he will accept it as truth. His decision has little to do with the actual facts involved in a situation. He has put his true spirit and enthusiasm about his existence aside and opted to believe "to each his own." He is separated from his brothers so he sees himself as a freewheeling individual available to make choices which he thinks does not impact on the rest of his group. He is wrong again. Blackmen gays say they share "karezza," a special communion between males as described by Walt Whitman. Homosexual Blackmen are embroiled in an out-of-body experience like a hypnotic trance. They play pretense with their brains. They are very strong willed and refuse to help to alleviate their condition. They think they have a right to abandon their Black manhood and to pretend that they are women, think like women and act like women. This is a sickness that must not be accepted as normal by Blackmen leaders.

Gay Blackmen, by mainly participating in rectal and oral copulation, are in the high risk sexual behavior group for contacting AIDS. National figures show that more than 80% of AIDS cases are prone to minority communities. Other sexually transmitted diseases like herpes, gonorrhea, yeast infections and syphilis continue to grow in the Black male population at large. A 1987 study showed that Blackmen were 25 times more likely to catch syphilis than white men. Latino men came in second. Other studies done in Africa and America claim there is a definite relationship between sexually transmitted diseases and AIDS. Some Blackmen catch what used to be termed as "the claps" several times. The new viral strains are not as easily controlled by penicillin as they used to be. And to top all of it off, the Blackman says he thinks AIDS in the African-American community is a germ-warfare attempt to kill him.

The World Health Organization announced in 1991 that 24% of U.S. women who have HIV or full-blown AIDS caught it from having sex with an infected male — an alleged heterosexual male — who claims he is straight and does not use intravenous drugs. There is something wrong with this since contacting AIDS, in other studies, report that less than 3% of homosexuals contact AIDS from each other. No stats were available regarding what percentage of this 24% is shared by African-Americans, but they are included in the total. Black females are said to be leading the case studies. WHO predicts that by the year 2000, 20 to 40 million Americans will have AIDS or the HIV virus.

The Blackman must address and control any sources of contamination in the African-American community and uncover potential bacteria carriers in order to protect his women and children. About 5,000 people per day are being infected with this plague-like ailment and Blacks and Latinos share a disproportionate number of fatal cases of this dreaded disease.

NOTES

Chapter 11

TEENAGE BLACK MALES

Our Black teenage sons. Our Black male boys. What is to become of them? This text provides much of the background history to partly reveal the circumstances that led up to producing nearly two generations of young Black males who are disinterested, ill-mannered, obnoxious, scholastically ignorant and foul mouthed, culturally unaware, lethargic, irresponsible, bored, ill-motivated and lazy. They are the perfect example of a reason the Blackman ought to insist on resegregation. Fewer Black males graduate from high school or college today than before desegregation or affirmative action. Many of them are emotionally dangerous, this is undeniable and frightening. They are socially alienated and have little economic ambition. They live in very small worlds existing only in their own little minds. Because their parents did not get along, instead of their homes providing sanctuary against the horrors outside on the streets, the household increased the strain of pressures to be a man. Due to being raised in single parent or extended relative homes, headed by Blackwomen who had to work outside the home to earn money, usually with no financial help from the missing father, they were raised by a color T.V. set.

Television stunted their abilities to think logically because the pictures on television change every 3-4 seconds creating blurry scenes with changing colors that present too many subjects in a rapid flicker. They learned to stare at the pictures rather than investigate the rest of the world. This prevented them from developing an understanding of the logical sequence of activities and sensible thinking patterns. T.V. shows a scene of the morning, and possibly ten seconds later shows night. Everything is speeded up and magically altered to fit within 30 minutes or one hour time frames — including commercials. From T.V. they learned rivalry, death and jealousy. T.V. inhibited their growth skills as they watched 30 or 40 hours of television programs per week, mainly dominated by white males and showing their ideas and values.

Also because their mothers were tired or distracted, for many of them the first word they learned to recognize, one repeated to them over and over by the age of three, was "STOP." Instructions like "hush" or "be quiet" or "shut up" or "go sit down" or "quit" or "you bad" or "you make me sick" have consequently made them turn out predictably unwell. Stop means to desist, end it, be still, pause and be dull. They have absorbed this instruction on many higher levels. Coming along during a time of such mental unrest of both their parents has made them have little value for either. They were reared during a time of exhaustion of the two parent household, then came the one parent household. With the onslaught of the crack drug, many come from the no parent household. Some have literally raised themselves and often had to fend for younger siblings, too. Little 4-5-6-7 and 8 year old boys are seen routinely around the country out on the streets at all hours of the night, dirty, ill-fed, hostile and afraid. There is no one waiting, no one cares whether they come in at night or stay out 'til dawn. Their parents, the schools, the government and society at large have let them down. Dissed them. The old rules and instructions, delivered mainly by females, is rejected by them. Certainly each oncoming generation expresses their own rebellion against the forbearers in many different ways. The Black male youth of today did not choose their own rebellion — they learned it from T.V., music, movies and advertisers. It has made them self-centered and thoughtless. They have no cause, they have no reason and they have no respect. And it is not their fault that they are in this condition. They are the children of the Blackmen who disbelieved in the warners sent to them to remedy their condition. They are the children of the Blackmen who chose the European way of life and did not instill in their sons (or their daughters) their history, expectations or value. They are mentally deformed mutations reeking of the confusion in the brain and sperm of their fathers. It was impossible for them to turn out sane or responsible. A child must have knowledge of their home citizenship and learn that the rewards of family membership come from positive contribution and work. They do not have any of these values. Their fathers did not have the strength or singleness of purpose to wade through the muck and the mire surrounding their cribs and insist upon rearing their sons. For a Blackman, nothing rivals the birth of a son. How special they are to them. But they went for society's hype about special formations for a proper family. They wilted under the strain of financial pressure and abandoned the ship that steered their sons away from them in a cloud of uncertainty. And they allowed frustrated females to dictate to them which of their children they were allowed to love. If it were not something they could carry in a bag they didn't think they had anything to give their sons. They let the government and its charity system take over. They wallowed in self-pity and became comatose, and slept through the growth of their sons. The loud wails of anger, and gnashing of teeth as their sons wade helplessly in their own blood has awakened these Black fathers from their self-imposed trance, and they are surprised. They reject the evolutionary biologists who explain to them that their deviant sons are the result of absent fathers — no matter what the excuse was. Their grotesque outcome was unavoidable. They are the sons of doom, the Blackman's fatal error in not preparing for his future. His sons are a final sign that he has no future based on his past disaction and unless he does something to resuscitate his seed — his sons will be the end of him.

Those sons have nothing to gain — or to lose. And they are not the least bit concerned about their futures. And while they appear to be living only for today... they know nothing about today either. Drugs are often at the root of their orphaned situation. Crack has managed to do something in the Black community that no other vice ever achieved — it has separated the baby from its mother, and produced a climate where babies have no special value and receive no special treatment because of its helplessness. This predicament is a baffling one because it is a new behavioral reaction to the entity which worldwide is generally recognized, protected and provided for if at all humanly possible. The parental-cub relationship has always been a dependable one throughout nature in mammals, but the mental manipulation produced by a crack-cocaine's dominant addiction has severed these ties and left Black babies to root out food and defend themselves — as adults.

While many of the cherished few receive abundant love, support, protection, attention, food, clothing and shelter, these are not the boys who represent the problem. It is the ones who were left out, the ones who make up the majority of our youth — who are now rejected and despised because of their objectionable behavior and attitude. The conditions of our Black boys is a result of the condition of the Blackman. They are different degrees of the same problems, frustration repeated visibly in each new generation of Black males to its lowest expressive form.

Scientists claim the human body contains between six and 40,000 genes with thousands of codes telling the body how to grow and develop. These codes are passed down from each generation from mother and father. Studies in eugenics conclude that every birth is directly impacted on by what a newborn is fed, the climate, the home environment, the neighborhood and other psychodymanics. These external factors determine what the newborn's five senses will observe, and supplies stimulation for certain emotional reactions. They also establish memories, habits and opinions. Any hodge-podge mixture of these factors can positively speed up or delay the development of the baby. Any deprivation of what the baby sees, hears, touches, tastes or smells can cause the baby to be distrustful and confused and possibly hallucinate straight through adult life. So the Blackman's son does not just look like him physically, but they have inherited the moral characteristics of his darkest ideas. This coupled with his woman's hypocritical ideas about manhood, has delivered up his worst nightmares — disobedient, disrespectful and simple-minded sons. The failure of a son to thrive is a serious constant pain, an ache that never goes away like an unhealed sore. An ever-present infection that eats at the core of the heart.

And there is no point in the Blackman trying to disown his seed. They look just like him because he made them. Hoards of Black boys bear witness to his failure daily. In 1990, African-American boys were teen fathers triple the rate of white boys. 230 Black boys are teen fathers as compared to 49 white ones in each time frame studied. They are impregnating Black girls from age 9 to 16 at an alarming rate. Of course they are not qualified to be fathers or mentors to a baby so the cycle continues — they, too, are now failing their sons. Ditto.

Blackmen say they already know that all of their cultural traditions have been extinguished since his forced arrival in America in 1555 as a slave. Having this information has been of no benefit to them. They should have worked extra hard to train their sons into knowledge and responsibility, and imparted values and standards to ensure that they grew into civilized dedicated men. But unfortunately due to Blackmen's faltering ego and deflated courage, many of today's male teens do not know, or have any contact with, their biological fathers. These boys have braced themselves against the eternal pain of their fathers' absence by an external facade of being tough, unfeeling, ruthless and daring. A relationship of truth and respect between generations must exist to make a transference of traditions or values possible. Today's Black teen boys do not have this frame of reference. It is not their haircuts, it is not their clothes and it is not their jokes that are the problem. The problem is that, as every Black adult fully knows, they are caught up in a circle with no doors or windows leading to the real world outside. And for most of them, even if they do escape, in their present condition, they will be helpless and unneeded because they do not know how to survive. They are trying to protect themselves. They are blind to any pursuit except that of money — to buy the things that advertisers promise and swear will dim the pain and make them feel better about themselves. It has already been pointed out that Black mothers, in the absence of Black fathers, tend to teach and train the girls, and love and spoil the Black son. This misdirected expression of extra love is the mother's failed attempt to give the Black boy freedom — the freedom she knows Blackmen have been denied in the past, and the opportunity she thinks he needs to become a man. So she replaces the male role model with irresponsible freedom. Freedom to run the streets, forfeit their chores and learn how to be a man "out there." She believes that if unhampered, he will automatically follow his natural instincts and assume the principles of manhood he needs. She erroneously believes that the best place for a Black boy to learn to be a man is by using his own wits to survive in the streets of America. This is based on an old lingering jungle idea of turning the Black boy loose in the wilderness wherein he must survive to be considered a man. Of course this came after training by male elders of the community and ended with certain commemorative ceremonies associated with this kind of rite of passage. The male ancestors of today's Blackman implemented levels of rites of passage for the male children in the community.

Physical accomplishment was only one aspect of the gradual adoption and growth into manhood. Support systems were in place to aid and guide the male youth, the expectations were explained to him and levels of acceptance outlined clearly. A supportive love and concern provided the emotional base that inspired the boy to achieve. None of these things are in place when a Black boy is turned out into the urban jungles of today's world. As mentioned, many times there is no masculine figure at all to mentor him or be an example of the result of surviving the jungle healthfully. So these boys look to media figures and each other for guidelines, and have to sort out the disorganized remote examples of the manhood goal. It appears as if the main achievement is to be care-less, unconcerned about other people, uncaring about the impression they make on people they don't know, and to place self-value over all others. So it is easy for them to curse in front of elderly people, women and small children. They do this and they do it loudly — and offer no apology. They seem to delight in stunning others with their brash sounds of cursing all hours of the night, in all places, at anyone. Since they are virtually valueless they have no behavioral thermometer. They don't understand respect outside of the distorted definitions acknowledged among their immediate peers, and since so much unnatural behavior is going on around them anyway there is no standard to adhere to or live by. Anything goes.

They actually are an excellent example to study because on questioning them one finds that many of the pressing questions about world affairs, social conduct, language, sexual responsibility and so forth, have not even occurred to them. They have very limited scopes of expression and usually have not given any thought to anything outside themselves, and perhaps their "girl" and their music. They have very narrow focuses mostly about subjects that have nothing to do with their survival. They are a futureless group. The apocalypse now.

Clothes are important to them, sneakers are important to them, their hair cuts are important to them, their jewelry is important to them, their physical image is important to them and beyond that they are not concerned with yesterday or tomorrow. They don't like being broke and will work five or six days a week and spend all their money in a couple of hours just to obtain a certain garment or experience the thrill of spending money any way they choose... or to impress a girl.

Many travel in packs, and the way they interact with each other demonstrates that their greatest threat is not the police, quite the contrary, their greatest threat is each other. Their emotions seem to escalate on the weekends when they fight, stand around waiting on someone else to fight, try to pick a fight, or plan one. Of course this description does not include all of them. Many live in terror that they will be put on the spot by another dude, be forced to defend themselves, or have their honor threatened. Their code of respect is interesting in that we have never seen it reduced to such base terms. It is not unusual to find that the issues they consider to be disrespectful are almost intangible. A few examples are:

1) It is considered disrespectful for someone to step on their sneakers (their foot).
2) To look or stare at them, their clothes, their shoes, their face or any other part of their anatomy.
3) For another brother to grit on (look at) his "girl" or female.
4) To bump into him, or any of his property.
5) To owe him money or property too long.
6) To get "new" (act differently to him) in front of other people.
7) To speak loudly to them in public.
8) To make him look bad or show him up in front of his "girl."
9) To laugh at him or make a spectacle of him in front of his "boys."
10) To walk through another "homeboy's" neighborhood (to cross their turf).

These are just a few of the statutes in their guidelines on respect. Note, the guidelines have nothing to do with neatness or cleanliness, decent language, scholastic intelligence or moral standards. These principles cannot be included because they have not been taught by their fathers. School has little value to them and the church even less. They are the children of the parents who made bad choices 20 to 30 years ago about which direction to take in their own lives. They are the children of the Black fathers who rejected the truth about their own identity and believed things would work out. They are the offspring of the Black fathers who weakly went on with their lives and forgot about them, gave them up so they could seek out an easier life filled with work and play, wrongdoings and contraband, short-lived involvements and futile pursuits. They did not even tell their sons that they were Black and must always be proud of that.

Back in 1964 a married team of Black sociologists constructed a testing system among five and six-year-old Black children by placing a Black and a white doll in front of them with instructions to choose the doll they liked the best and desired to own and play with. The majority of the Black children chose the white dolls. This testing resulted in the same Northern and Southern kindergarten age Black children. In 1991 the Research Director of *Sesame Street* performed the same test on preschoolers and found that both Black and white children only played with the white dolls. A more recent study announced that 65% of the Black children chose the white dolls, and 76% reported that the Black dolls "looked bad." Despite all that civil rights action, Black power statements and Kwanzas, Black babies still hate being Black, would rather be white, and continue to reject self and kind. Black boys have suffered the most from neglect.

Respect is often learned as a by-product of watching someone else live up to a set standard. So what happens when a Black boy doesn't have any visible standard? He chooses from the actions of those around him and most of these standards are based on some type of aggression if for no other reason than communal overcrowding. They set rules to set them apart from the women, the females in their area. They are the 1960-70's bred children who were born during a nationwide moral free-for-all so they weren't taught some basic rules about life. So many things are considered square business to them. Sometimes doing homework is square, staying in the house or going home at a reasonable time is square, respecting a parent, going to church, going to the library, not having sex with a girl, not experimenting with drugs and a host of other backward positions that destroy them further — are listed as being square, old time, corny, or dead.

They are bored so they create their own excitement based on what they know, and what they know has already been described. Some of their fun is warped, masochistic and sadistic. They are disappointed and angry. The over 500,000 Black men incarcerated are some of the absent fathers who voluntarily/intentionally gave up their sons (and daughters) for nothing. The genetic result of an attraction to violence is also manifested in the Blackman's son, he has the same urge.

Many of them are enthralled with weapons — hand guns, knives, uzis, razors, or anything else they can get their hands on. Sometimes they are seen standing around on corners with the guns cocked in their fists just waiting for a target. They might all stand around talking with the guns in their hands — just to feel the power they think the firearm gives them, the invincibility that weapons allegedly represent. They fill the emergency rooms with bullets in the foot, the legs, the thighs and the hands. Any value they have for life as a heart beating blood circulating organism is remote and instantly forgotten under the frailest of situations with a brother man. They persist in killing each other.

They drink alcohol and take drugs to give them a chance to behave or talk in a certain way, give them courage to do certain things and maybe even claim the next day that they don't remember it. Alcohol makes them even more impatient with each other and any outsiders they may encounter. If they use drugs they inspire them the same way. Much has been studied about why they sell drugs to members of their own neighborhoods, to women, men and children. Some reports say they do it for the money because they aren't qualified to get a real paying job, or that no jobs are available, or they need money to feed their poor families at home. Certainly these aspects deserve consideration but psychologically the main reason they sell drugs is:

1) To have an activity that involves cunning and courage.
2) For the "respect" and attention it gets them in the "hood."
3) For the satisfying feeling of being in charge of something.
4) Being able to be in a powerful position, give instructions or punish.
5) To be over the people, receive favors.
6) To belong.
7) And of course the material items, and to handle and make large sums of *easy* money.
8) To have a responsibility where he alone is accountable.

If a young Black boy or teenager has any encounter with the drug culture they eventually find that it is run by an adult Blackman, usually many. This is not to say that the white suppliers of drugs do not exist, but the Black youth never sees him. What he sees is his replica, a Blackman. He learns that the major requirement to sell drugs is to be cold hearted, have a "to hell with it" attitude and become unfeeling, shed any natural emotion of sympathy, caring or conscience. They disconnect — even further with themselves and with their Black sisters and brothers.

The disconnection from Blackhood started as a small child from watching too much television, too many violent movies, and fatherly deprivation. They were in the company of women too much, and the men they did come in contact with appeared weak or punks as compared with the examples of maleness they saw on T.V. They've been under pressure all their lives, constantly being put in positions to prove their stamina. Physical challenges took the place of value learning. And they practice vandalism and lying, playing hookey and gambling.

In school and in their neighborhood another rite of passage is to get in a fight and win. Win or lose he must demonstrate that he is not afraid to fist it out in front of all the people he values. In school the same thing may have to occur on or near the playground. The rules are set for his honor at that time. If he does not fight he may be labeled as a punk or a sissy. If he cries he earns the same title. And it can follow him all the way through elementary, high school and senior high school. The first fight can set the tone of how he will be dealt with by other Black boys for several years. Much of this he has to go through alone — without his father's hug, support and unwavering acceptance. He grew without experiencing admiration for a regular Blackman — sportsmen and entertainers took up the slack.

Many summers are spent perfecting the skill of riding a bike at great speed and doing tricks on them. Learning to play sports, run great distances, approach girls, curse, match colors for wardrobe, shoot dice, swim, and defy authority, are the activities he participates in and which often accelerate in later years if no organized, planned or self-benefitting program shows up. This lifestyle can also cause him to be in places that cause him to lose his life.

It is absolutely true that when packs of Black boys, thug-looking gangs, commence to invading a shopping mall, adult patronage (Black and white) declines. Many malls have become a place for them to congregate and conduct their social activities. They go there to shop, show off new clothes, meet girls, eat, settle scores, shoplift and fight. Shopping mall planners now know that if the mall is anywhere in the proximity of Black teens they will not put an arcade in it. The same goes for skating rinks, and multiple movie theatres. If they congregate, have to touch elbows, or confront each other in passing they may fight. Purchasing in shopping malls is expensive because of the high cost of rental for every square foot utilized by shop owners but Black teens go there because of the colors, sounds, activities, crowds and excitement. Most of their enjoyment is visible, only eye sight required. Other than shopping malls, they frequent amusement parks and movies.

Unfortunately they have few other nice brightly lit places to go to socialize. They make their dates there, exchange phone numbers, eat, are loud, unruly and boisterous. They are easily riled and take up more space than they spend money. Their presence, whether threatening or innocent, is what forces adult shoppers to seek other malls outside of downtown or inner-city areas. They say they do not feel safe.

Some work, some do not, but seemingly they often have amazing sums of money to spend on entertainment and related activities. They keep many shop owners happy because if they like a particular item and several of them purchase it, it may possibly become a fad at their school. If and when this happens, shop owners stand to make a great deal of money servicing the teen buyers of several high schools representing thousands of students who all desire to own and wear the "in" item. For this reason they are probably tolerated in the way that they are. It is a very natural act to them to buy everything they own from white or Korean-owned store establishments. They just want it — and it doesn't matter where it comes from. Sound familiar?

The word *rap* is derived from the word rapport — to be in agreement with, and from the Irish language where *rap* means practically worthless. Their rap music is like a new foreign language, a form of communication that only they understand. It has a different cadence, it's speeded up, and thunders and crackles. Rap music is consistent with their impatience and lack of training in creativity. They make up banging and clanging words to match the soulful tunes of their fathers. They are poets in the rawest sense of rhyme. While it sounds like gobbly-gook to adults, the Black boys understand every word and while most of them can't recite their name, address, zip code, date of birth and Social Security number in rapid succession — they can talk the words to the most confusing beat of a rap record. The topics of their rap music range from comedy to violence to abrasive references to sex. Their use of previously considered filthy language is compatible with their untrained and untaught brains. It is a part of their rebellion and their acceptance of vulgarity is a way to communicate and get attention. When informed that they have just rearranged the music of the 60's or 70's they become angered and deny any real connection to another Blackman's creation. They were not taught about cheating either. So they rob other musical artists and feel no compulsion to share any profits they may earn by using background music they did not design. The impact of this loud rap music is not yet known. However, loud screeching sounds have been known to interfere with the ability to concentrate and perform sequential thinking.

They often walk the streets with this blaring rap music stabbing into their brains on each side of their heads with portable radios and earphones. They play it all night on the radio or sleep in earphones — the same technique used to penetrate the unconscious of sleep during hypnosis. It seems that everything they think is theirs and everything they admire belongs to others. The ability to make up nasty poems and set them to repetitive dull beats is not usually the criteria for either unique talent or artistic creativity. But they sell their rap music to each other and make money so they believe they are successful. They know little of generational trends in styles or sounds, and have much to say in gobbly-gook lingo so they devised a way to appear on stage, talk, dance and walk back and forth, with minimal skills and a flicker of talent. Quite clever, but still untrained and still suffering from a lack of knowledge of the Blackman's real aim and purpose in life. Soon their monstrous semi-permanent rap music will end. They will have spent themselves in their gluttony for foul language and immoral expressions. And their heads will be consumed with the predictable indigestion of a diet of useless filth and imaginary heroes. They will continue their dissent and proceed to turn on themselves. Their kind of disregard for civilized standards and regulatory education can't help but increase their appetite to feed on each other. Their mother, despite all her crying, praying, cursing and threatening, has no value to them — because she does not understand. While she grieves over her futile attempts to keep him in school, to keep him in church and keep him off the streets — he is manifest proof that her systems do not work. He was unable to be molded by outside institutions, he needed and still needs a father. She can not shame him into submission as she did when he was a little boy. He has outgrown the restraints of fairy tale fantasy and the thick leather belt. He is wild with confusion and dissatisfaction. And he is the only remaining example of the Blackman's life on earth. While unqualified to go into the new world, he is the best that the Blackman could make. And if his untamed energy is not captured and redirected he will eventually kill both his parents, or cause them to die trying to defend his defenseless position. The Black boy thinks that he is different from everybody else in America but he is thoroughly indoctrinated with Americanism. Without the love of a Blackman he has no future.

These Black boys have not experienced the toil of trying to desegregate a fast food chain, or the labor of sit-ins and protests, or the fever in Black blood generated by desires for freedom, justice and equality. They have grown up in a society that has usually always been available to them. But since the torch was not passed to them by their fathers to inspire them to continue working for better education, economic empowerment and government representation, they are not aware of or interested in working for any Black cause. They intermingle and date white teenage girls with the greatest of ease. Interestingly enough, while their fathers demonstrate a tendency, verifiable by statistics, to abandon or dislike the decorum of their mothers, these Black boys have enacted a similar attitude towards the Black girls in their peer groups, and are attracted to white females in large numbers. It appears to be a fad of sorts and something to be proud of. Their fathers never explained to them about how to handle and recover from "white fever."

"White fever" is a period in the Blackman's life when he experiences an overwhelming attraction and curiosity of the white woman. If not guided through this natural stage of masculine development many of them become so intrigued with possessing white flesh that they imagine themselves to be in love with a white female and are willing to tackle all and any obstacles in order to be with or marry her. Blackmen say the white woman is quite appealing due to her lesser hostile attitude they say emits from Blackwomen. She seems to accept them as is and is not overly critical of every move he makes. He can relax around her and be free of the almost constant attacks they claim Blackwomen make on them. She appears to sooth their egos instead of berating them, and is quicker to defend him, try to help him express himself and is unaware of his horrid track record in relationships with the sisters. Be this real or imagined, Blackmen and Black boys report that there is a distinct difference between white and Blackwomen. They prefer the white.

Having a fancy car, van or jeep is of exaggerated importance to these Black boys. The Black girls are very selective about what he must have to get her attention and entertain her. The boys go to any extreme to make their car the most unique or the fastest vehicle on the street. A great deal of money and time is spent installing an ear drum-bursting sound system so that they can draw attention to themselves while driving down the street. This trend has earned the police department and city governments a new income because traffic fines for playing excessively loud music on public roadways run from $200 to $500 in some cities. They like a loud motor car or screeching tires for the power they think it gives them. Anything to get extra attention.

Mobs of them travel around robbing other youths of their fancy stylish clothes and accessories. Gold earrings and neck chains, name brand sneakers, Porsche or Alpine sunglasses, leather trenches or jackets are the bounty. Many teenagers have been robbed at gunpoint, shot, mugged, beaten or stabbed by other, usually Black, boys trying to forcefully take their designer property. Some even take name brand jeans — off the body of the wearer. These crimes take place near schools, in subways and at bus stops — or on any street. Some of them report that they have had their property taken or snatched several times and they just replace them and continue to show off their flashy expensive name brand items.

Such is the condition of the Blackman's teenage Black boys. They set their rage in motion and attack others. They do not always do this out of need, many times they resell the item or give it away. They mostly do it for the thrill of the event. It is very tenuous to get their attention away from this kind of negative behavior. There are so many layers of cultural confusion and social deprivation to wade through before reaching the core of their being. They have become so formidable that few Blackmen choose to enter their domain. They do not all belong to any organized gang as such. They sometimes travel in packs of three or four, but many are extremely volatile and dangerous. They turn a deaf ear to announcements about their endangerment. Having no future does not frighten or intimidate them because their brains are vacant, and according to them — they have no past either. They are in a pitiful state and they should not be blamed for it. They are the result of the Blackman's error. The adult Blackman, their fathers, must bear the blame and the shame of what they have made. And what they allowed others to make when he deserted his own seed. He let himself be bullied out of fatherhood — and he does not like the outcome. No one does.

The Blackman made no plans for his son between birth and adulthood so his boys have, in the interim, devised their own methods of filling up their time. They couldn't just exist in a vacuum, paused, waiting to grow up. They are too curious for that. So they developed their own secret language. None of the prohibitions have any reasoning to them and they are frustrated at not being able to discover by themselves some order or meaning for their life. Toys of all sorts have been shoved at them, records, tapes, video games, sports equipment, clothes, and social events, yet none of these have given them a reason to want to live or be. Social culture has changed so rapidly that they never understood how to judge which changes were best for them based on Black male standards because they are not aware of any standards. They were introduced to methods of providing them with continuous playtime with no break time to learn about adulthood responsibilities. Trying to start now in giving them the meaning of certain values failed because the message was too prolonged. Their rudimentary understanding of life has been learned in the streets and while they may have started out as amateur criminals they are quickly rising to become semi-professional murderers. Their behavior is not necessarily the result of inferior intelligence but a result of illogical guidance in the absence of having a father. Traditionally sons learn how to make a living from their fathers or other extended family male members, but in the Black boys' case, they have neither. On top of all this they have no knowledge of the philosophy or aims of their foreparents. They are in rebellion and distrust all adults. They are frighteningly pitiful and do not know which way is up. And they are disavowed by their Black fathers who haven't got it straight themselves.

These Black boys link no special significance to having sexual relations with a Black girl. They report that sometimes they are able to achieve this after knowing the girl for only a few hours in some cases. They are not overly-sexed, they crave the gratification of sole attention. They have a high nearly constant need for reaffirmation and heroism, whether real or imagined, and the sexual outlet provides them with fleeting glimpses of both physical pleasure and mental satisfaction of interacting with another human being, in unity of purpose and acceptance. They have no real roots or training in commitment so sexual validation is not enough to charm them permanently, especially when they believe it can't be all that special because it's too easily obtained.

Another way the Black boy makes a weak effort to express his understanding of unity with other Black boys is to make up very elaborate synchronized motions to use with each other when shaking hands. They have hand moves, finger signs and certain kinds of grips that often vary from coast to coast among Blackmen. They slap each others palms, give the high five sign, sometimes hug, and in sports slap each other on the behind. Communication of the sequence of the hand or elbow motions spreads quickly in the African-American male population. Just as their dance steps do. The younger ones spend a lot of time getting their dance moves just right. They practice day and night so that when they get on the dance floor they can move so smoothly that their routine looks impromptu and effortless. They are talented expert dancers who manage to remember long skits and devise interesting dance moves never seen before. Their energy is overwhelming. Too bad they have not been taught how to use that kind of creativity and stamina to accomplish more long lasting durable goals.

Black male teenagers now wear their pants hung low below their hips, kind of like the hip huggers of back in the 60's. They have a slouchy look whereby they droop their pants over their shoes at the cuff to facilitate wearing their jeans below their waist, sometimes showing off their underwear. This is considered a hip style. Cool.

Others walk around town sucking on pacifiers or with a

baby bottle hanging out of the side of their mouth. They claim this is a fad but the wise know that the sucking motion satisfies something in the psyche, a very basic impulse from the moment of birth, first shared with the mother by breast or bottle, and remains pleasurable throughout life. Could be these Black boys are trying to experience something they missed.

Black boys express themselves loudly in public places offering them the invisibility of a crowd. In movie theatres they yell out, curse, respond to the actors on the screen and react to emotional scenes. In many movie houses it is impossible to hear or understand what is being said on the big screen because of their loud responses to whatever is taking place. Fights erupt when one of them decides that someone in the dark disrespects them, keeps yelling in their ear or refuses to be quiet when requested. In some theatres the managers keep the lights on for the duration of the showing of the movie so they can be ready to address any disruptions likely to occur. This kind of behavior in movie theatres drives other Blacks further and further away from urban areas into suburb shopping mall theatres to escape the yelling and cursing going on in local venues. The so-called "homeboys" can make a night out at the movies pure hell just going in, and getting back into one's car. Depending on the subject of the movie, many will mill around outside the theatre until something jumps off — a fight or shoving match and maybe a shooting.

They are quick to choose up sides on negative encounters. They set a poor example for the smaller children who view them as the only close-by role models. The younger Blackman must see a living example of what he must do and he must see the results of legitimate efforts. He needs a pattern which demonstrates repetition that ends in success. He needs to see the adult Blackmen around him doing things that count. He must be touched, embraced and be able to depend on receiving attention from his elders. The young Blackmen who are conscious, and who are trying to make a difference by becoming educated, speaking out against wrong, not joining gangs or practicing juvenile crimes, are few in number and are themselves detached from the hard-core teen Black male who appears to be unreachable by all conventional methods.

NOTES

Chapter 12

LEADERSHIP

Leadership in the Black community has become blurry. As African-Americans have slumped into political empathy leaders find it increasingly burdensome to capture the hearts and minds of the people. Dissatisfaction with the government is rampant and any Blackman who aspires to a pontificated point of leadership by embracing variations of old political themes finds his path arduous and thorn ridden. It has been many years since a Blackman leader has emerged with a new refreshing political concept that appeals to the current nature of African-Americans. Blacks have lost faith in the politician's ability to solve their problems. And many are disappointed because they spent the wonder years of their careers pursuing and believing that the political system was the key to the door of every room of success they desired to enter. Ironically when these doors are finally pried open the Blackman finds other barriers more dense and equally immovable. While the Blackman was busy marching, desegregating lunch counters and petitioning for integration, other nationalities were setting up economic bases to provide for their futures. Ever since the early 1800's Blackmen have come forth with various agendas they devised as a solution to the complicated problems of Blacks in America. Each one hoisting their own placard, and each one systematically rejected, mocked or ignored. As a consequence, no major economic agenda was adopted as the main thrust of the people. Splintered, poorly financed, special interest groups of Blackmen have periodically altered their agendas when they found they could not be successful taking hard-line positions unvalidated by mass agreement of the people. The Blackman has always experienced difficulty trying to arouse the Black community into positive supportive action on any plan. This disunity and stagnation has caused many viable dockets to wilt and be discarded before their effectiveness could be measured. He warply expects the whiteman to give him a job and other benefits while he continues to maintain his long-standing feud with this same benefactor. His absolute dependency on the group he claims to hate makes no sense at all. He even circulates documents about his dissatisfaction in European owned newspapers and magazines.

The few Black-owned publications out that claim to cater to the Blackman are of little value for leadership development or for teaching respect or brotherhood to Blackmen. One of them unwholesomely caters to the low sensual desires of Blackmen by offering nude pictures of questionable Black females in a variety of contortions and activities. It is assumed that if whitemen have *Playboy* displaying pictures of naked white women, then certainly the Blackman, just as interested in porno stimulation as he, must have his own version of the same kind of filth. They are capitalizing on the Blackman's perverted disrespectful view of Blackwomanhood. He is proud to have his Black sisters uncovering their bodies publicly and he's proud that she's so fine. But a proper Blackman would not allow another Blackman to insult Blackwomen, and shame elders and mislead small children by seeking a market to prostitute the bodies of potential Black mothers. He should not be willing to sell his woman's respect for employment and money. The other slick magazine for Blackmen represents little of the kind of information Blackmen should receive in the mail each month. They contain the latest fashions, entertainers, fragrance and cosmetic news, trite advice about handling women with a light sprinkle of health and business news. They are both geared to the social advancement and high understanding of successful corporate Black. With times as tight as they are now, every Black-owned publication should be devoted to distributing advice on how to handle hard times. Realistically. Because Blackmen are more affected by unemployment disproportionately then any other nationality in America. But these publications attempt to carry on with their frivolous topics as if all Blackmen are enjoying sheer economic prosperity. How about printing some information suggesting jobs or work an unemployed Blackman can do to make some money? In place of this lifesaving section are countless articles about how to prepare the perfect resume, what to wear to work and how to break through the glass ceiling in middle management. Another magazine advertises Blackmen and Blackwomen who are interested in coupling with whites. Or, in some cases, homosexuals. They have classified columns advocating every kind of degenerate sexual decadence imaginable. And they have a healthy market they service to promote continued moral decay among Blackmen and Blackwomen. All of the aforementioned are accessible to Black children. The same Black children who are projected to be the most unconcerned, selfish, ill-prepared generation in the past 200 years. It is difficult to pick out any unique or revolutionary ideas among them. When young newly-started-out Blackmen are singled out for special recognition it's because he has excelled to some lofty remarkable position among white competitors in corporate or political America. Each one of them is willing to stand on the neck of their brothers to advance their position, and are opting for color blindness and neutrality. Is this representative of the kind of leadership teams delegated to inherit the Black world of tomorrow? Are they going to use the same obsolete tactics of their fathers and grandfathers? And if so, how do they rationalize it? More questions.

Something must be done about the slate dark denseness pervading the brains of the Blackman that forbids him from thinking clearly. It is as if his skull is frozen, brain dead. So much of his will has been emasculated. He is incapable of choosing right over wrong.

The Blackman's desperation for leadership has caused him to be overly impressed with emotion filled rugged sounding dialogue and outrageous platform suggestions of so-called politicians. The Blackman's leaders have come from the church, politics, law and education. Every so often a self-made Blackman rises to the podium, but unless he presents visible proof of his ability to get more entitlements, the credentialed educated class will not recognize him. And the uneducated, having been duped into believing that only the college trained Black is qualified to lead, are also prone to dismiss his findings. This chapter will discuss the doctrines and platforms of the top ten Blackmen who rose to prominence in leadership authority. An attempt will be made to explain their positions as briefly as possible. Other Blackmen who were, or continue to aspire, as wannabe leaders will also be mentioned as they too are a part of the history. All of the Blackmen listed were/are instrumental in either guiding the Blackman to success and respectability, or misleading them into unemployment, violence and self-hatred. To be clear, each Blackman is responsible for the result of what he chose and what he selected to reject. In other words, every Blackman has what he deserves. Unfortunately, his decisions impacted on his women, his children and his future generations. However sparse the group, many Blackmen in leadership positions over the past years have misrepresented the needs of the people and fostered inaccurate priorities. Every Blackman is a leader in his home, his community and nation. Whether or not he exercises the authority of his leadership is up to him. His ineffectiveness in the home is crystal clear by observing his offspring and women, and his incompetence in politics is proven by the inadequate temporary solutions he endorsed. It is the men in the African-American community who have not only failed themselves but forfeited their mothers, women and children in the process.

The ten most popular and influential Blackmen leaders in chief positions over the African-American nation during the past 175 years are:

1)	Frederick Douglass Politician/Orator	1817-1895
2)	Booker T. Washington Educator/Community Advocate	1856-1915
3)	Marcus M. Garvey Organizer/Nationalist	1887-1940
4)	W.E. Dubois Educator/Politician/Writer	1868-1963
5)	Elijah Muhammad Religious Messenger	1897-1975
6)	Adam Clayton Powell, Jr. Politician/Minister	1908-1972
7)	Stokely Carmichael Organizer/Civil Rights Advocate	1941-
8)	Malcolm X Muslim Minister/Orator/Militant	1925-1965

9) Martin Luther King, Jr.   1929-1968
   Civil Rights Activist/Minister

10) Jesse Jackson   1941-
    Minister/Politician

The purpose of studying leadership themes and political positions of Blackmen is to analyze their tactics, seek out their differences and similarities, and to trace the status of their ideas today. This analogy is not presented to dishonor their noble efforts because each one tried, in his own way, to alleviate the social, economic and religious problems Blacks still suffer from today. But this is a critical objective study of realistically dissecting their platforms so that future Blackmen leaders can benefit from potential remedies and avoid useless time consuming approaches already known to fail. There is no time left to expend pursuing goals which historically have proven to be pointless. Every effort is made to present their basic doctrines in a concise assessment. These top ten Blackmen leaders, their political theories and resultant practicum, will be judged by the following criteria on a conclusion sheet after each description of their teachings.

The criteria for evaluation are:
A) Did he seek advancement through politics and the right to vote?
B) Did he think that social integration was the solution?
C) Did he believe in the European religion of Christianity?
D) Did he design a life-plan for self-sufficiency and self defense?
E) Did he keep his former slavemaster's name while seeking freedom?
F) Did his program include retention of Black culture and traditions?
G) What is the status of his ideas today?

Frederick Douglass — 1817-1895
Was a house slave in Maryland. The white mistress of the house taught him to read. His father was a white man but they had no relationship. Later, making his way to New York he became involved in the anti-slavery crusade and quickly became a leader. After publishing his great speech *Narrative*, his life was threatened and he escaped to England where he

211

lectured for pay on slavery and women's rights. He returned to America and bought his freedom and founded the *North Star Newspaper* later changed to *Frederick Douglass' Paper* with a masthead that read: "Devoted to the Rights of all Mankind without Distinction of Color, Class or Clime." He had many friends — Black and white — in England and America. Frederick Douglass thought that slavery was not abolished until the Blackman had the ballot. His anti-slavery affiliations kept him on the run from law enforcement agencies. His first wife was Black. He met political activist John Brown who he described as "a white man who is in sympathy a Blackman, as deeply interested in our cause as though his own soul had been pierced with the iron of slavery." Douglass hoped for favorable action under the Constitution, which he felt was "in its letter and spirit an anti-slavery instrument."

During his career he was appointed to several governmental positions. He helped Lincoln recruit the 54th and 55th Massachusetts Negro regiments to fight in the Civil War. He worked to get the first Civil Rights Act passed in 1875 which opened public accommodations, vehicles and movies and helped to inspire the 13th, 14th and 15th Amendments. After working in the Legislature, being hired to work on foreign affairs and commissions, or Marshall, and Consul General in Haiti, he was weary and disappointed in the system. He often remembered the words of his white friend John Brown: "Slaves had the right to gain their liberty in any way they could." He did not believe that moral suasion would ever liberate the slave, or that political action would abolish the slave system. "Slavery was a state of war, the slave had the right to do anything necessary to get his freedom." Douglass was against violence but began to consider that the only way slavery could be destroyed was by bloodshed. However, until his death, Douglass continued to apply written words, moral and political pressure to end bondage of the Blackman in America without violence. He was a powerful orator and drew huge crowds whenever he spoke. In May of 1865 Douglass made a famous speech to the American Anti-Slavery Society. He ended his speech by saying, "Slavery has been fruitful in giving itself names. It has been called 'the peculiar institution,' 'the social system,' and the 'impediment,' as it was called by the General Conference of the Methodist Episcopal Church. It has been called by a great many names, and it will call itself by yet another name, and you and I and all of us had better wait and see what new form this old monster will assume, in what new skin this old snake will come forth."

The 13th Amendment prohibited slavery, the 14th gave citizenship to anyone born in the United States, and the 15th guaranteed the right to vote. In 1883 the U.S. Supreme Court cancelled the Civil Rights Act of 1875 and declared that exclusion of certain races from public accommodations was not against the Constitution of the United States. This ruling disappointed Douglass greatly and made way for Jim Crow segregation and informal laws and attacks against Negroes. Still he prodded through the system seeking job assignments or positions which he believed would aid him in creating laws through the government to ensure civil rights and protection by the courts for his brethren. After his first wife died and his children were grown, he met a white woman in Washington, DC while working at one of his government jobs. She was considerably younger than him and quit her job to follow him.

After Douglass' death he left property to his children in New York and the Washington area. He left his house in Anacostia Heights in DC to the white woman who had attended him up until his death. She attempted to turn the home into a national shrine to honor Douglass' work but encountered bitter legal battles from his children who did not believe that she should get anything out of Douglass' estate. Negro writers opposed his children and wrote articles in support of the white wife and expressed their outrage that Douglass' children were so prejudice against interracial marriage. They claimed that the white woman was a hard worker for Black rights and for white women to gain the right to vote. She and Douglass were close friends with Susan B. Anthony for years during his campaign for white women to have rights in society.

Conclusion: Mr. Douglass believed in intermingling with whites, sought donations and recognition from them, and often traveled abroad to instigate friendships. He believed that if the Blackman obtained the right to vote that he could use the ballot to change his position in American society. He constantly went before white politicians to plead for civil and social opportunities for Negroes. He staunchly believed in the validity of the Constitution and believed it to contain the foundation from which change could be enforced. He was proud to be invited and involved in American politics. Douglass had no plan for the Negro to use to help himself economically. He thought that if the

Negro was unhampered by lynchings and unwarranted attacks by whites that they would seek out employment for themselves. As a matter of priority he wanted them to have congressional representation and legislative authority.

He kept his slavemaster's name and was not concerned with linking himself in any way to the Negro's African past or traditions. He made no mention of holidays or celebrations to retain the Negro's heritage and attached no special meaning to being Black other than that it was a negative stigma resulting from slavery and continuing racism.

Frederick Douglass is most remembered for his proud physique and beautiful facial features. His speeches, especially his major narrative, are recorded in many history books and studied. He sired two sons but there is little information about the continuation of his political ideas by his four children. He was an impressive, strong and diligent Blackman leader who retired with his greatest memory being his failure to convince whites that the Negro deserved full citizenship rights in America. The Caucasian woman he married preserved his papers, souvenirs and documents for study by historians. His children did not approve of his marriage to a white woman.

Despite Douglass' tedious pleas for civil rights for Blacks, the Blackman today is still negotiating for a Civil Rights Act from the American government. Every few years this Bill comes up for discussion, reconsideration and debate. The Blackman still does not completely benefit from the 13th, 14th or 15th Amendments. Each new president is confronted with the sensitive task of deciding whether or not being forced to accommodate Blacks (he did not include the Indians) in public, privately owned places is constitutional. Douglass was appalled to find that in 1858 when questioned in the South about his position on Negro-white affairs, that Lincoln proudly alluded: "I am not, nor ever have been, in favor of bringing about in any way the social and political equality of the white and Black races... I am not nor ever have been in favor of making voters or jurors of negroes, nor of qualifying them to hold office, nor to intermarry with white people; and I will say in addition to this that there is a physical difference between the white and Black races which I believe will forever forbid the two races living together on terms of social and political equality. And inasmuch as they cannot so live, while they do remain together there must be the position of superior and inferior, as I as much as any other man, am in favor of having the superior position assigned to the white race." This clip is from the Lincoln–Douglass Debate of 1858. When in the North Lincoln, as politicians do, adjusted his views for his audience, and held fast to the Declaration of Independence which viewed all men as equal. For many years African-American children were taught that Lincoln freed the slaves and that he felt special compassion for their condition. It was implied to them, by educators, that Lincoln fought for the rights of Blacks and was on their side and should be honored and remembered for his efforts. It was a misrepresentation of the truth — an outright lie. Mr. Douglass and Mr. Lincoln were associates.

Booker T. Washington — 1856-1915

Was born as a plantation slave in Virginia. He qualified and became founder and president of Tuskegee Normal and Industrial Institute in Alabama. He called for Negro self-improvement geared toward being independent. He believed that the only way that Blacks would advance was through industrial education, small business and hard work. He is most famous for his Atlanta Exposition Address in 1895 wherein he made what were considered counter-revolutionary statements such as advising Negroes that "it is at the bottom of life we must begin, and not at the top," and "it is the Negroes' lack of knowledge and experience in survival that cause him to seek first a seat in Congress or legislature rather than in land or industrial skill," and "the opportunity to earn a dollar in a factory just now is worth infinitely more than the opportunity to spend a dollar in an opera house." He further told them to "Cast down your bucket where you are — cast it down in making friends in every *manly* way of the people of all races by whom you are surrounded." He promised the white political constituency that they would be "surrounded by the most patient, faithful, law-abiding, and unresentful people that the world has seen." He believed that agitation of questions of social equality were the "extremist folly" and that access for Negroes would be gained by "severe and constant struggle" and not by "artificial forcing," and that while privileges of the law were deserved by Negroes he felt it far more important that they be prepared for the exercise of these privileges.

He wanted Negroes to wage their biggest struggle in themselves to overcome economic deprivation by applying themselves to occupational skills to improve their conditions and restore their self-respect. He helped to establish a Negro bank in New York City and had the support of George Washington Carver, a Black agricultural chemist. He touted self-help and industrial training as ways to eventually break down prejudice. He earned the support of several presidents for his Atlanta Address. He established the National Negro Business League to address the concerns of Negro businesses. At Tuskegee he directed his first students on how to build their own school with their own hands so they would learn how to organize and be independent. They had to raise their own food and livestock. Shortly support in the form of money and supplies came to the school from all over the country. Many Blackmen leaders of that day came to the school from all over the country. Many Blackmen leaders of that day politically aligned themselves against Booker T. Washington claiming that he was an "Uncle Tom" crouching up to whites to get on their best side, and that he was sacrificing Negroes' democratic rights by suggesting they give up political power and go straight to work to support themselves. His opponents further cried that Washington's program would create civic inferiority in Negroes.

In 1900, Booker T. wrote his autobiography, *Up From Slavery.* His famous speech was recorded by many as "The Atlanta Compromise." He received great media coverage and was designated by whites as the official leader of the Negro race. His entire career was devoted to teaching Blacks to own and operate their own businesses and to shop among themselves. He dined in the White House with President Theodore Roosevelt and received an honorary degree from Harvard and was entertained by white royalty abroad for his work in helping the ex-slaves to improve themselves. A letter of congratulations sent to him by President Cleveland stated: "Your words cannot fail to delight and encourage all who wish well for your race; and if our colored fellow citizens do not from your utterances gather new hope and form new determinations to gain every valuable advantage offered by their citizenship, it will be strange indeed." Washington was a Christian.

He informed the white political system that, "In all things that are purely social, we can be as separate as the fingers, yet one as the hand in all things essential to mutual progress." Violent objections from other negro politicians followed this statement. Booker found that he could gain more support for his program by taking care of his own needs. When others saw this happening they began to chip in and send gifts and supplies to aid him in his work. He earned respect from others because he demonstrated determination, self-esteem, discipline and maturity — all of which insisted that he be recognized and honored as a "man" — in control of his own survival affairs. He had a Black wife.

Conclusion: Mr. Washington did not believe in social or sexual integration, to the contrary, he insisted that each race maintain relations mainly with each other, and only interact on a business and commerce level peacefully. He did not seek assistance from the government or try to influence whites to do anything but leave him and his people alone. Although he gained the attention and support of whites, it was not due to him asking them to love him. The whites contributed to his programs because they were in agreement with his methods of educating and preparing Negroes to be self-sufficient. Tuskegee Institute still stands today although many of Washington's ideas regarding self-help preparation have been altered and today's Tuskegee graduates pretty much seek jobs in the white business world as all other historically Black college graduates do. Currently, Tuskegee vies for Federal dollars as usual. All of Booker T.'s programs were designed to establish an economic base for Negroes through learning skills and trades to offer services to the general public. He was a Christian but religion was not his guiding factor. He kept his slavemaster's name and did not teach his students to study the effects of slavery or return to their African roots.

His curriculums included teachings of Black pride through self-respect gained from being useful and independent in acquiring food, clothing and shelter. Today many Blacks enjoy the benefits of his efforts to establish separate educational facilities designed to meet the special needs of ex-slaves. Booker T. gained the respect, recognition and admiration — including a type of non-integrational acceptance that other Negroes were seeking through political means. He was a strong, realistic and determined Blackman leader who desired to teach Negroes how to live without going back to the people who had enslaved them and begging for food, education and work.

Marcus Moses Garvey — 1887-1940

He organized and established the Universal Negro Improvement Association in Jamaica in 1914 and in Harlem in 1917. He was born in Jamaica and was politically active there as well. On his way to America in 1912 he traveled to England to raise funds for his ideas, and while there he studied African history regarding the exploitation of Blacks by white colonialism. He also studied the works of Booker T. Washington and liked the self-help theory as a way to make Blacks independent in America and around the world. He published his own U.N.I.A. newspaper, organized several chapters of his group around the country. His slogan was "Africa for Africans" and he touted suggestions on Negroes going back to Africa. The Ku Klux Klan approved of his idea of transporting all the Blacks back to Africa. He used Booker T.'s idea of appealing to the common ordinary negro. His ideas spread to the West Indies, Africa and South America. Negroes contributed financially to his repatriation ideas. Garvey said, "Be as proud of your race today as our fathers were in days of yore." He tried to instill a sense of collective pride and self-esteem by reminding Blacks of their history and culture. He taught that the "pale man" was evil and were not the chosen people of God. He told Blacks that their God was named Allah. Garvey was a Muslim at heart and wanted Blacks to return to Africa where they would have an opportunity to develop themselves. He said, "Teach the negro to do for himself, help him the best way possible in that direction; but to encourage him into belief that he is going to possess himself of things that others have fought and died for, is to build up in his mind false hopes never to be realized." He had no confidence in the ability of whites to treat the Negro fairly. He told them to rely on self-reliance and economic development. He informed Negroes that, "A race that is solely dependent upon another for its economic existence sooner or later dies..."

Garvey disagreed with W.E. Dubois and the NAACP for their sniveling unmanly-like methods for social equality with whites. He was critical of Dubois' efforts for negro acceptance into white society instead of just trying to leave. He called the white members of the NAACP hypocrites. Because Negroes were so entrenched into European Christianity, although a Muslim, Garvey created for the Negro their own version of Christianity and formed the African Orthodox Church. He decorated it with a Black Holy Trinity, a Black Jesus and Black Madonna. At one point, as a show of solidarity, over 50,000 Garveyites paraded down Lenox Avenue in New York and held a mass meeting at Madison Square Garden. Garvey established the colors of red, black and green for his flag and wore stunning brightly colored military type uniforms of mainly purple and gold.

He invested his followers' money into his back-to-Africa movement and purchased a few heavy freighters to transport Blacks back home to Africa. He had chosen Liberia as the promised land for Negroes but, due to political pressure applied by America and slightly opposing political viewpoints, the Liberians rejected him and withdrew their support of his project. The ships, never quite functional due to age, were wrought with labor and mechanical problems due to unqualified help.

Garvey wanted Nubians (Negroes) to found their own nation, businesses and military. He was so proud of his jet Black skin, referring to himself as a "full-blooded Blackman," that he insisted that all of his top laborers be dark skinned. He instructed Blackwomen to dress modest and involved them in study classes to learn nursing and other skills. His female followers dressed in all white.

Garvey charged Father Divine with "blasphemy of the worst kind" for his attempt to pose as God over the people. He charged Divine with being backed by the Ku Klux Klan and the Black Legion of Detroit. He was also not impressed with the efforts of Negroes to be in show business and star in movies. He denounced films such as *Green Pastures*, *Sanders of the River*, *Emperor Jones* and *Imitation of Life*. He said the movies represented "an international conspiracy to disparage and crush the aspirations of Negroes in American civilization and to impress them that they are inferior." He scolded the Negro actors and actresses in these films "for prostituting their manhood and womanhood and their self-respect for the enrichment of imperial masters and purveyors of race prejudice."

Garvey told Blacks they should return to Africa just like Jews were planning to return to Palestine. Many white organizations agreed with Garvey and his plans to deport Negroes back to Africa but he would accept no help from them and kept them out of the Universal Negro Improvement Association's business.

When asked what kind of government he planned for the Negroes when he got them back to Africa he replied, "I believe in democracy, not communism, neither am I a social extremist. Our state would not be a soviet state but a democracy fashioned after the United States, and yet suited for liberalism."

Conclusion: He did not believe in social or sexual integration and forbid whites from joining his organization and refused their donations. He was not interested in asking the American government for help or assistance of any kind. Garvey maintained that the only way the negro could become psychologically and economically free was to take them back to their roots in Africa. He was frustrated to learn that Blacks hated and despised themselves so much and he advised them to stay away from whites. He tried to tell the Negroes that if they did not organize and determine their own destiny — including food, clothing and shelter — that they would have no power or authority over their lives. He knew he could attract them with flashy uniforms and brightly colored garments and loud joyful music. Garvey kept the name he was born with which was not African. He taught Black pride, history and culture in his classes and sought to improve the negroes' opinions about themselves through revitalization of their ancient heritage and religion. He did not force Islam on them and remained secular himself. Garvey invested his followers' donations in the purchase of a few ships he intended to use to take them back to Africa. He wanted to get the Negro out of America as soon as possible because he felt the political climate was not conducive to resuscitating the ex-slaves into independence. He used portions of Booker T. Washington's self-help doctrine and strongly disagreed with W.E. Dubois about his claims that only 10% of Blacks, mainly mulattos — like Dubois — held the keys to African-American survival. Garvey's bloodline has survived, and his descendents have tried, to no avail, to reinstitute his program. There are a few scattered branches of the U.N.I.A. today. Garvey devised a huge project to convince Blacks to abandon America and go back "home" to be free. He did not have enough support or interest from uppity Negroes who had already decided to use politics and education to improve their conditions.

After Liberia pulled out and withdrew their agreement to allow Garvey to land his ships filled with negroes on their shores, his followers lost faith and began rejecting his entire program. Garvey started having problems with the IRS and licensure bureaus, and the newspapers, both Black and white, were against him and circulated stories that he was a con man and racist. In 1923 he was felled by conspiratorial trumped up charges that he was committing mail fraud. He was sentenced to five years in prison at the Alabama penitentiary. In 1927 he was deported in shame to Jamaica and died in London a dozen years later. He died grief-stricken about his failure to get Negroes to go back to Africa.

William Edward Dubois — 1868-1963

Was a scholar in every sense of the word. He attended several prestigious colleges and earned the first Ph.D. to be conferred on a Negro at Harvard University. He was spurred into political action because of his disagreement with Booker T. Washington's plan for the Negro which he termed a "Gospel of Work and Money." He claimed that Booker T.'s idea of education dissuaded Negroes from demanding civil rights and practically accepted the alleged inferiority of the Negro. He said, "Manly self-respect is worth more than land and houses, and... a people who voluntarily surrender such respect, or cease striving for it, are not worth civilizing." Dubois was on the faculty of several colleges and universities including Atlanta University and Morehouse (then called the Atlanta Baptist College). He worked for Negro advancement through acquiring academic skills in preparation to enter mainstream America. He saw America as "this common Fatherland." He is most known for his suggestion that the talented 10% of the Black race be academically trained to rise and pull behind it the rest of the Negroes. These ten percenters would represent the cream of the crop of the Negro race. He felt that sacrifices should be made to ensure their total education and urged Black parents to send their children to the best colleges. In a speech he made in 1903 called "The Training of Negroes for Social Power," he concluded, "The history of civilization seems to prove that no group or nation which seeks advancement and true development can despise or neglect the power of well-trained minds; and this power of intellectual leadership must be given to the talented tenth among American Negroes before this race can seriously be asked to assume the responsibility of dispelling its own ignorance." Part of his text was purposely used as a political ploy to counteract Booker T. Washington's ideas about industrial education as opposed to liberal arts. Dubois wrote and distributed serious papers objecting to Washington's weak-kneed attempt to merge with southern racists by vowing to stay away from them by working. He also feared Washington's tactics would promote the Negroes' political disfranchisement and pave the way for withdrawal of Federal Aid from institutions of higher learning for Blacks. He wrote viciously against Tuskegee and gathered together 29 Negro teachers, editors and professional men from fourteen states to meet with him in 1905 to discuss ways to dethrone the popularity of Booker T.'s self-help theory. These Blackmen leaders called their meeting the Niagara Movement. Part of the purpose of this meeting was to protest whites taking back their seats in government and discounting and refusing to recognize the Blackman's ballot. Dubois, having traveled abroad and partially educated in Berlin, believed that political empowerment was the only key to protecting Blacks from the wrath of angry whites, and ensuring their equal treatment, voting and civil right opportunities. He said, "We will not be satisfied to take one jot or little less than our full manhood rights. We claim for ourselves every single right that belongs to a freeborn American, political, civil and social; and until we get these rights we will never cease to protest and assail the ears of America. The battle we wage is not for ourselves alone but for all true Americans." The Niagara Movement committee met several times to address the political needs of Negroes. Although credited with stimulating the NAACP (National Association for the Advancement of Colored People), actually this organization developed from a conference of white liberals in protest against a local lynching. Their first meeting was held in New York City in 1909 to address a renewal of the struggle for civil and political liberty. Several Blacks were invited and Dubois was one of the eight who attended from the Niagara Movement committee. Dubois was eventually appointed as director of publicity and research, and edited their publication called *Crisis*. This first NAACP organized to "stand for the rights of men, irrespective of color or race, for the highest ideals of American democracy, and for reasonable but earnest and persistent attempt to gain these rights and realize these ideals." By 1921 the NAACP had more than 400 branches and was integrated. A white male still headed the NAACP up until the early 1940's. Dubois wrote several books about Negroes and many papers on the status of the race as a whole. He worked diligently for the goals of the NAACP, taught at various universities and continued protesting against ill treatment of

Negroes and continued to negotiate politically for the rights of Blackmen to vote. He had mild success in achieving his aims later emigrating to Africa in 1961 to work with a publishing firm. He left America frustrated and disappointed that he had not been able to sway all Negroes to his talented tenth idea for advancement. He was equally despaired about his inability to force the American government to give Negroes the same social and civil rights that whites enjoyed naturally.

Conclusion: Dubois was representative of today's bourgeois class of Blacks who still believe that only a certain segment of intelligent African-Americans are qualified to lead or remedy the Black condition. Most of those in Dubois' Talented Tenth representation were light skinned with straight hair and, like himself, appeared to come from mixed heritage containing precious Caucasian blood. He believed in social integration justifiable by media support, philanthropy and federal subsidy gains he sought through political means. He was a Christian.

He was not as much concerned with economic gain through self-help as he was with securing voting rights, judicial protection and equal representation in the annals of government. He was very proud of his French/Dutch ancestry and his unusual exotic sounding last name. His only concern for Black pride was his insistence that the Black male ego enjoy the satisfaction of full acceptance in the category of respect and recognition of his ability to excel academically. He felt that the everyday working Negro was primitive and unsophisticated and unqualified to compete with whites in the classroom or boardroom. Dubois' loud public disagreement with the ideas of Booker T. Washington set the stage for justification of other Negroes to organize to defeat any Black who they did not completely agree with in principle and cause. This kind of squabbling produced political disharmony, physical fighting and wasted energy on trying to wreck the progress of other Blackmen leaders. Dubois' ideas of creating separate factions inside a group already separated upheld the emotions of jealousy, envy and rivalry among Blackmen that still exists today. Obtaining the glorified overrated right-to-vote has proved to be ineffectual towards improving the quality of life for Blacks in America — or elsewhere.

Dubois himself recognized the futility of struggling against the white rule in America and decided to seek citizenship elsewhere. Thus he migrated to Africa and became a Communist. Plans to erect a statue in his hometown of Barrington,

Massachusetts were initially rejected because of his affiliation with the Communist Party. Dubois' ideas represented the foundation of ideas that give the Democratic party such attraction for Blacks because he stood for social rather than economic advancement — and he fostered class distinction among Negroes.

The Honorable Elijah Muhammad — 1897-1975

In 1933, Elijah Muhammad (formerly Elijah Poole) announced that he had been taught a new religion called Islam which had a plan for the ultimate salvation of the Negro. He described his teacher as Master W.D. Fard Muhammad, Allah (God) in Person, and said that he had been divinely commissioned by Allah to help Negroes secure freedom, justice, equality, money, good homes and friendships in all walks of life. Muhammad started small but quickly and progressively expanded his new religious teachings from border to border. He called the Negroes Muslims — and told them that "all Black people are Muslims, some of them just don't know it." He established Mosques (temples) of Islam and taught his followers a new Black history, respect for the family unit, identified whites as a race of devils — and told them that their God, Allah, was Black. Mr. Muhammad organized schools for the children of his followers, and separated the boys from the girls during the early years of their education. He directed the "Muslims" in opening their own businesses, how to pool their resources and build and operate decent institutions of their own. Muslims participated in weekly services and daily prayers, lived under strict behavioral codes and were required to abstain from eating pork in any form. Muslim men attended weekly manhood training meetings called the Fruit of Islam (FOI), which also provided military training. Mr. Muhammad, the Messenger of Allah, forbade his members to carry weapons — not even a pen knife. He told them to fight only if aggressed and to "obey those in authority over you as long as it does not conflict with the practice of your religion." He cleaned Blackmen up and salvaged and repaired many damaged personalities among them. He used Islam to mold them into neat, obedient, upright loyal workers and "brothers." They wore royal blue uniforms with matching bow ties. The women (the sisters) were required to attend weekly homemaking skill classes and Sunday or weekday services. They dressed in long dresses, usually white, with headpiece coverings similar to those of nuns. The sisters' section was called the "Muslim Girls Training and General Civilization Class," (MGT & GCC). They were taught cooking, sewing, child rearing, how to take care of their husbands and how to act at home and abroad. Muslim sisters were a very respected group because it was well-known that the FOI did not allow anyone to disrespect a member of the MGT & GCC.

Messenger Muhammad stressed Black culture, re-arranged white history to reveal the Blackman's contributions to civilization, called for separation in another state completely run by "the brothers" — who he described as the original man. Whites were not welcome at his temples and he declined participation in politics or voting. He frowned on social integration and told Blackmen to stop asking others to do things for him which he could do for himself. He insisted on self-reliance for his congregation and advised Blacks to "stop spending your money on fine clothes and fine shoes before you have a fine place to live." The Muslims had a large newspaper operation called *Muhammad Speaks*, and used the Holy Quran by Maulana Muhammad Ali as their guide. Members were also required to study documented (lessons) about God, Black history, world facts and general orders which they were instructed to learn verbatim. They completely rejected Christianity as a false whiteman-made-up religion and there was no singing, dancing, shouting or baptism, or white statuaries in their Islamic temples. Farmland was purchased, canneries set up and meat processing plants expanded to include fish from a foreign country. They had their strongest hold in Chicago. All members were required to give up their "slavemaster's name" and accept an "X" to replace their last names or they were given an Arabic name or chose one of their own. Blackmen in the FOI ranks were motivated to perfection by being told by Messenger Muhammad that "you are the best, the most powerful and the wisest." He told them that they were members of the lost-found tribe of Shabazz and that God, the supreme being, was a Blackman — a real living and breathing human in the Person of Master W.D. Fard Muhammad, to whom all praise is due forever. Muslims were told to stop using drugs and alcohol to get to work to support themselves. People who did not understand the teachings considered Muslims strange.

Conclusion: Uniquely, practically all of the religious doctrines taught by the Honorable Elijah Muhammad have been purposely omitted or removed from public record. Muhammad, and all he stood for, has been hidden and written out of history books despite all he helped Blacks to accomplish. When Black or white historians document African-American existence in this country they tend to conveniently leave out any detailed sketch of the Nation of Islam, what it stood for, what they believed in and their social and political positions. The success of his work is not recognized by the educated class and no thought or value is given to any of his teachings. Black teachers tend to treat Mr. Muhammad as if he were an embarrassing hindrance to progress instead of the Black lifesaver he actually was. His means and methods are considered outdated and too morally restricting for modern Blacks, and his ideas are also rejected because Muhammad was not for integration, taught against mixing with whites and pointed them out as the "open enemy of the Blackman." He maintained that Blacks did not need personal association or support from whites in order to be successful and happy. For over 40 years the Nation of Islam, under the leadership of the Honorable Elijah Muhammad, represented the only stable example of Blackmen working together to better their lives — without voting or integrating with Europeans.

After Muhammad's untimely death in 1975, his son Wallace Muhammad was elected to replace his father's leadership and inherit his power over the Muslims. Within one year his son set about dismantling, discrediting and changing every aspect of what his father had given his life to build for Black people. Imam Wallace Deen Muhammad chose eastern orthodox Islam for the Muslims and told them that it was the "real" Islam and that it was blasphemous to believe that God was a mortal man. The new Imam dispensed with the notion that whites were devils and allowed them to attend his services, gave them equality on the podium, and former FOI members began dating and marrying white women and bringing them to the temple. Wallace/ Warith also relaxed dress codes, beards for the brothers and make-up for the sisters. After several embarrassing years of internal administrative strife, complicated changes in religious belief and wavering temple attendance; the newly designed "American Muslim Mission" faltered as a national vibrant organization and are now seldom seen, existing only in a few disconnected locations. Over the years following Messenger Muhammad's death his family members fought brutal public legal battles in court over the money, land, furnishings, vehicles, equipment, literature and property that had been worked for and financed for 40 years by nearly five million Black Muslim followers registered in the Nation under Messenger Muhammad's ideas. His survivors used European law guidelines to divide the spoils, and the general believers were left out of any calculation for distribution of their investment. Muhammad's extended family and others split the profits and disappeared unhampered by demands for financial accountability. Rumors were also spread charging Messenger Muhammad with questionable conduct and secrecy regarding aspects of his personal life. Opposing groups have arisen and because of their squabbling and disunity caused the Nation to lose its credibility and respect from onlookers. Some have ravaged Muhammad's original teachings, added their own interpretations and eliminated any parts they disagree with. Muhammad's followers, after briefly trying to adhere to and understand the new confusing guidelines, pulled out dismayed and often returned to the Judeo-Christian mysterious religion Messenger Muhammad spent his entire life disproving. None of the Blackmen Muslim leaders who appointed themselves as his spiritual descendant are as recognized or respected as Messenger Muhammad. Possibly the most outstanding accomplishment of Mr. Muhammad was that he never changed a word of his teachings from the first day he started to the last. No matter what the social climate was or the political temperament of the people, he stuck to his position working to get the Blackman to reclaim his own name, religion and peaceful way of life.

Throughout his career other non-Muslim Blackmen leaders stole portions of his program to build their own political platforms. The remaining splinter groups are led by Blackmen leaders Minister Louis Farrakhan, Silas Muhammad, John Muhammad and a few lesser known others. The infamous Five Percenters are an alternate group organized by Brother Clarence 13X now deceased. They are mostly younger Black males who study secret teachings, perform rituals, learn poems and other activities that Clarence 13X made up to give them a unique cultural identity and inspirational information. All of the new Blackmen Muslim leaders offer a slightly modified rendition of the original Islam espoused by Messenger Muhammad. And their followers, due to youth, inexperience, or lack of knowledge; do not know the difference. None of the remaining groups operate or maintain the types of institutions or goals that Muhammad previously demonstrated.

Due to occasional clashes with the police and newspaper and T.V. stories depicting the Muslims as teaching racial hate and Black supremacy, many Negroes were frightened away from the Nation of Islam. Any Blackman leader who adopts any part of Mr. Muhammad's economic teachings shortly becomes successful. His ideas have endured and his predictions are coming true.

Adam Clayton Powell, Jr. — *1908-1972*

Started out as associate pastor of the largest Black Baptist church in the world, the Abyssinia Baptist Church in Harlem with his father, Adam Clayton Powell, Sr. As the civil rights movement began to pick up momentum during the 1940's, Rev. Powell became involved in picketing white-owned businesses in Black neighborhoods that depended on Negro patronage but had no "colored" employees. At that time groups employed boycotting tactics to force white establishments to hire Blacks. New York's famous 125th Street became the employment target of Rev. Powell. He claimed to represent the "new Negro" who was educated, politically astute and bold enough to demand equal treatment. He referred to his picketers as "Marching Blacks." He fought for the common man and woman who lived in New York. He participated in the Harlem Renaissance of revitalization of Negro artists, writers, poets, musicians and singers as an illumination of Negro life. He was a commanding speaker and drew huge crowds to his church sermons and was able to gain support from his membership to confront racism in America.

Powell was elected to Congress in 1945 and served until 1970. He was appointed Chairman of the House, Labor and Education Committee. During his services under President John F. Kennedy with his "New Frontier" ideas of civic and social responsibility of the government, Powell helped, between 1961-66, to push new rulings he felt would benefit Negroes. He endorsed minimum wage laws, entitlement projects, aid to elementary and secondary education, vocational rehab, school lunch programs, anti-juvenile delinquency acts and worked to eliminate discrimination against women. At that time practically every Negro in the land was in love with and supportive of President Kennedy. They viewed him as sensitive, sincere and on their side. They admired Rev. Powell, too.

Conclusion: Powell believed that he should mingle with the white power structure if they sympathized with his efforts to create better job opportunities or voting benefits for Negroes in Harlem. He was such a handsome and intelligent speaker that he was able to penetrate the ears of the Black middle class and the underclass. He was very much involved in American politics and thought that his presence in Congress would facilitate many long range advancements for his people. He organized marches and protests using nonviolent means of pressure. He was a Christian assistant minister of a popular church. He did not encourage Blacks to go into business for themselves and create their own jobs, he fought to get them employed in enterprises already built by whites. He believed it was simpler for them to use forced hirings since Blacks shopped and spent their money with white shopkeepers, than to tell them to open their own businesses and stop spending their money in white-owned establishments. He was quite proud of his dignified sounding name. He was not a separatist and talked harder than he really acted. Black culture was not on his agenda but he did want Blacks to believe that they were just as qualified to do a job as any white person was. The government is still dealing with many of the issues raised during the "War on Poverty" era of the 1960's and 1970's. Special interest groups espousing the need for women in politics, and more aid to needy families and parity of wages and promotion for both genders, prison reform, and other politically social issues are still debating the validity of enacting laws to support these positions. He became impressed with his personal achievements and believed he was in the "in crowd" in Washington until they ousted him for trying to have two women (one of which was famed jazz organist Shirley Scott — his wife), and for coming up funny with the money entrusted to his government budget.

Employment for Blacks in Harlem and other highly populated urban boroughs of New York have steadily declined over the years. 125th Street is filled with many boarded up businesses and landmarks and the majority of the remaining stores are owned by Asians, Latinos and whites offering commercial products to the African-American population living there. The so-called "War on Poverty" is lost. Poverty won. And few, if any, of Powell's political advancements remain viable today. His final fall from grace with the Negro public was when he was exposed by the media to be allegedly participating in immoral conduct with his secretary on the isle of Bimini and misappropriation of funds. However, Congressmen Powell was a dynamic, brave Blackman who just used his talents pursuing the wrong goals. There is an Adam Clayton Powell, III. Due to Congressman Powell dying so close on the heels of Martin Luther King, Jr. and having been out of the public's eye for a few years, he did not receive the kind of recognition he so well earned and deserved.

Stokely Carmichael (Kwame Toure) — 1941 - still living
Was born in Trinidad, brought up in America, experienced ghetto life and later graduated from Howard in 1964. His dissatisfaction with the treatment of Blacks in America prompted him to join the Student Nonviolent Coordinating Committee (SNCC), pronounced "snick." His talented vocal expressions soon landed him in a leadership role and he meticulously changed SNCC's policy from one of unaggressive nonviolent appeal to threats of disruption by riots and overthrow of white law makers. His simmering rage grew and was finally ignited after attending the 1964 Democratic Convention where he and his cohorts were discounted as having a vested interest in routine government affairs and practically ignored. SNCC was a popular Black student organization that sought to get Blacks to register to vote in the South and to desegregate public facilities. SNCC opened over 40 "Freedom Schools' established to teach Black youngsters about Negro American culture. These schools were staffed by Black and white volunteer teachers affiliated with the SNCC organization. Stokely told his group, "We must first define ourselves. Our basic need is to reclaim our history and our identity from what must be called cultural terrorism, from the depredation of self-justifying white guilt. We shall have to struggle for the right to create our own terms through which to define ourselves and our relationship to the society, and to have these terms recognized." Stokely spoke right up.

Stokely helped coin the popular phrase of "Black Power," which he screamed at the top of his lungs to every media in America. He defined "Black Power" as: "It is a call for Black people in this country to unite, to recognize their heritage, to build a sense of community. It is a call for Black people to begin to define their goals, to lead their own organizations and to support those organizations. It is a call to reject the racist institutions and values of this society."

Whites interpreted "Black Power" to mean a threat to oust the current government and replace it with strong revolutionary based Blacks. But "Black Power" became the battle cry of fed-up young Blacks all across America and many rioted, bombarded police with stones and Molotov cocktails — (a soda bottle filled with gasoline with a rag wick which could be easily assembled, lit, and thrown at the police) — and they staged unorganized riots and ravaged stores for merchandise in the process. The rioters mostly burned down dwellings in their own communities. After riots sporadically broke out in urban cities, Stokely lost control of his influence on his scattered followers and pandemonium ensued. All of this took place during the mid-60's while the Vietnam War was going on. Stokely quit SNCC because he felt their ideas of peaceful integration for political advancement was too slow moving so he next joined the Black Panthers, a more radical militant group of mainly young Black males. His involvement in the Black Panthers was not a successful mating either. He and the irrational egos of Huey P. Newton, Bobby Seale and Elderidge Cleaver were incompatible. Their youngness and quick rise to media popularity inflated their leadership abilities and each one wanted to be the boss. Their tactical and political views turned out to be vastly different. The Black Panthers, hosting a small mostly localized membership, had shot guns, rifles and hand weapons which they sported in clear public view; they said to protect themselves from unwarranted attacks by the police and to defend their turf. Being the most formally trained of the group, Stokely recognized the impossibility of the Panthers succeeding using such a violent stance. He also disagreed with internal factions who wanted to accept allegiance from sympathetic white extremists. Stokely resigned. Displaced. SNCC, after a brief leadership attempt by H. Rap Brown, another militant who wore a Black wool tam cap, slightly slanted, with dark sunglasses and a bushy mustache. Brown earned the name "Rap" Brown because he could talk so good. He unsuccessfully tried to revive SNCC and form some kind of economic base but their business attempts fizzled, too. SNCC was defunct. At that time any Blackman was considered a leader if he could describe the race problem with colorful metaphors and was referred to as a "Professional Rapper."

Stokely Carmichael (now Kwame Toure) was a brave Blackman leader who tried to mix portions of foreign nationalists Che Guevera and Frantz Fanon with the basic premises of Booker T. Washington to come up with a solidified mixture to provide salvation for Blacks. He said, "The goal of black people must not be to assimilate into middle class America, for that class — as a whole — is without a viable conscience as regards humanity. The values of the middle class permit the perpetuation of the ravages of the Black community. The values of that class are based on material aggrandizement, not the expansion of humanity." Stokely, who is primarily credited with fathering the "Black Power" movement, also produced from within his ranks the "Black is Beautiful" slogan of inspiration and the "clenched fist" sign still used by a few politicians to mean power and strength. They also came up with the saying, "all power to the people." Stokely was the voice of Black youth in America and they rallied behind him in support of his views and tactics. Stokely was also known for wearing dark sunglasses during his lectures or interviews. He saw the white power structure as the enemy of Blacks.

Conclusion: Carmichael was misplaced in his efforts from the very start. He was young and idealistic and believed that monumental change was possible in a short period of time. He also thought that as long as whites did not hold leadership or controlling positions over Blacks, that they should be allowed to work in his organizations as a support team. He found that white politicians were not willing to seriously negotiate with him and viewed him as a radical. Stokely was not willing to compromise any of his positions because he saw racism as morally indefensible and outright evil perpetrated on Blacks to subordinate them to whites. He wailed that he was in favor of violent self-defense and retaliation. He didn't realize that there was an uncontrollable element in the Black community who absorbed Stokely's "get 'em back" rantings but were not interested in sophisticated politics... and wanted to let off a little steam. And when this unruly irrational element exploded, Stokely was not able to control their riots because he failed to predict the outcome of his suggestions to rebel. His overall policies were so militantly radical in opposing whites in government that his theories have never been consulted for use as a method for Black advancement. His ideas evaporated along with the cries of "burn baby burn" chanted by rioters inspired by his messages. He was a proponent of Black liberation. He said: "This means that Black people must organize themselves without regard for what it is traditionally acceptable, precisely because Black people must make demands without regard to their initial 'respectability,' precisely because 'respectable demands have not been sufficient."

Stokely maintained his European name and did not introduce his followers to any particular religious doctrine. Carmichael's structural mistakes are attributed solely to his gross immaturity, and he had no acceptable adult Blackman mentor to direct his frenzied anger.

The Black Panthers made similar mistakes. Their collective failure was that they neglected to see the infeasibility of their task, and they had no qualified people waiting in the wings ready to revamp the institutions they wanted to tear down. They had no realistic agenda about what to do if and when America fell, and they began to hallucinate that things would automatically come together if they could just denounce the current political system. Even when they protected their communities from errant white outsiders, they had no plan on the inside to crate a new lifestyle for its inhabitants. They were repelled by almost everyone. The Panthers, after police attacks, FBI, IRS and CIA investigations, routine busts, search and seizures, unlawful attacks and killings; disbanded in a scurry.

Huey P. Newton, Bobby Seale, Elderidge Cleaver, Fred Hampton and Bobby Hutton — all frontline spokesmen for their group, unfortunately, have not left a sparkling legacy of their efforts. Some are dead, gone to prison, worked in the system, taught school, wrote books, opened bar-be-que pit operations, became a born-again Christian, completed college, embezzled, ran for mayor and live law abiding lives as regular American citizens. The Panthers' means and methods should be remembered today so that Black youth will not ever try to emulate them by evoking an armed revolutionary takeover of the government, their city or neighborhood. The media focused on the confusing activities of the Panthers to show the rest of the world how dangerous and frustrated leadership was among Blackmen. There is no proof today of any benefits that could remotely be linked to their existence. Carmichael maintained: "We are calling at this time for new political forms which will be the link between broadened participation (now occurring) and legitimate government. These forms will provide a means by whereby a newly politicized people can get what they need from the government." Despite his clouded appeals for the American government to cooperate with the needs of the Black community, between 1965 to 1967 there were 134 riots in major cities across America.

Stokely is the only one to survive the Black Panther history respectably intact. He met and married a South African singer named Miriam Mekeba and in 1969 they moved to Guinea in Africa, thus he changed his name and religion. He left disappointed and frustrated personally, and abandoned the ghettorized cities in post-riot shambles with damages estimated into the billions. Some of these cities were never rebuilt to their former status and have dilapidated further throughout the years. In 1970 Stokely returned one more time to try to awaken Blacks by Pan-Africanism consciousness. This, too, failed and since that time he may periodically show up in America to lecture to college students, but he does not take on any national forum about "Black Power."

On reflection, Stokely was like a bright shooting star, he rose quickly to a leadership position and fell with similar rapidity and is scarcely hard from today. He got out.

Malcolm X (Al-hajj Malik Shabazz) — 1925-1965

Malcolm X was born in the ghetto and said to be a dope dealer, pimp and thief who got caught and went to jail. He was an intelligent Blackman with an excellent memory. In prison (late 1940's) he studied the doctrines of the Black Muslims under the leadership of the Honorable Elijah Muhammad. He corresponded with Mr. Muhammad and was invited to visit his temple of Islam when he got out of jail. In the early 1950's he did just that. He was an avid student under his teacher, Mr. Muhammad. He delved into the Black Muslim beliefs hungrily. Their philosophy cleaned him up, gave him racial consciousness, educated and dignified him. He easily became a crowd attracting minister and generated new membership and enthusiasm among the followers. His national popularity earned by teaching Muslim self-help, how to be free of white devils, establish their own businesses and spend their money in the Black community, gained him the post of being the National Spokesman for the Nation of Islam. He was witty, articulate and informed. He made a stunning appearance with his sandy red hair and imposing height. He spoke out harshly against the slavemasters, demanded separation for Blacks from their oppressors, directed Blackmen to respect their women, and take responsibility for their children. Malcolm convinced everyone of his sincerity of belief in the Black Muslim doctrine in its totality and that he honestly believed that Caucasians were a race of devils. He daily expressed respectful allegiance to the Honorable Elijah Muhammad and always thanked him publicly for teaching him the truth and saving his life. Due to the strict regulations Mr. Muhammad required his ministers to adhere to, if one of his spokesmen, when representing the Nation of Islam, made public remarks that reflected badly on the entire group, they would be reprimanded. When this happened to Malcolm X he was at the peak of his public popularity and felt insulted and embarrassed. Punishment usually consisted of being "set down" which meant he was not allowed to teach from the rostrum for a designated period of time, customarily only a few months. This was in 1963 and the Nation of Islam was bulging with expanding memberships all over the country — partially due to the dramatic speaking efforts of Malcolm X.

Eventually Malcolm's ego got the best of him and he no longer felt obligated to obey instructions he perceived as unnecessary or wrong. After a disagreement of this sort with Messenger Muhammad, Malcolm angrily left the Nation. Malcolm's pull-out was carefully calculated because he was under the delusion that "his" following was large enough in and out of the Nation of Islam that his resignation would bust up the Muslims and gain him a lot of new converts from the streets. In other words, Malcolm tried, along with his inside supporters, to pull a coup — and it failed. The Nation of Islam, after a brief period of mumblings, continued on with their program as usual, hardly missing a beat. Malcolm defected from the Nation in March of 1964 and by summer was scrambling to put together his Organization for Afro-American Unity. After he failed at taking over the Nation from Messenger Muhammad, Malcolm was in immediate need for a platform (and a job). He began to respond to requests from colleges and speaking engagements. White classmates were in favor of student dissent and also sympathetic to the civil rights struggle. Malcolm began to lecture... "The young whites, and Blacks, too, are the only hope America has."

Next he went to Mecca. While in Mecca he experienced what he interpreted as spiritual revelations. He announced to the media, "In the past, yes, I have made sweeping indictments of all white people. I will not be guilty of that again — as I know now that some white people are truly sincere, that some are truly capable of being brotherly toward a Blackman. The true Islam has showed me that a blanket indictment of all white people is as wrong as when whites make blanket indictments against Blacks."

His statement about a "true Islam" resulted from his new exposure to Eastern Orthodox Islam. On returning from his pilgrimage he reported: "I have eaten from the same plate with people whose eyes were the bluest of blue, whose hair was the blondest of blond and whose skin was the whitest of white... and I felt the sincerity in the words and deeds of these 'whites' Muslims that I felt among the African Muslims of Nigeria, the Sudan and Chana." From that moment on began to doubt the full truth about what he had been taught about the natural opposition of whites to Blacks based on Blacks being God and whites being devils. This really was a trying time for Brother Malcolm. He was emotionally depressed about his ugly defection from the Nation of Islam and the bad blood between them over his parting.

He and his family were living in a house supplied to him by the Nation for senior ministers and special laborers. After Malcolm quit the Nation he was out of work and people started to say insulting things about the Messenger publicly — but still refused to move out of the Nation's house. Through some kind of mix-up Malcolm wouldn't leave. When his house got fire-bombed, he blamed it on the Muslims and took up weapons, later posing for the widely circulated picture of him standing at his window with a rifle in his hand. It was never proven that the Muslims bombed his house. The FOI denied it, claiming that they would never destroy the Nation's property. Malcolm had been traveling abroad familiarizing himself with African foreign governments and customs. He was searching for a new platform and it occurred to him that the Blackman's struggle for freedom was worldwide and after one of his trips decided that he was going to take the problems of Negroes politically before the United Nations to negotiate for freedom. He would use the tenets of Pan-Africanism. By this time the FBI had already secretly infiltrated the Nation of Islam and had spearheaded Malcolm for their major investigation searching for proof of illegal anti-government activities.

Malcolm also continued to lambast Mr. Muhammad publicly defaming his name insultingly in comments to the newspapers and bystanders. Many Blackmen were happy that Malcolm had left the Nation because they liked Malcolm but didn't agree with Messenger Muhammad's position regarding elimination of all social contact with whites.

Malcolm continued to lecture but decided, due to his new liberal views, that continuing to "search" attendees at his engagements, as he had always been required to do in the Nation — was no longer necessary. While speaking at the Audubon Ballroom in New York he was shot dead by some brothers who had smuggled weapons in the door. This happened in less than a year after his hostile break with the Nation of Islam. There was much mourning over his death across the country because he was a respected and admired Blackman leader. Alex Haley, a Blackman writer, completed an autobiography of his life and released it after his shocking death. Malcolm X was the most effective and powerful speaker the so-called Negro had ever seen. He was both admired and feared. He was married to a Muslim sister and sired four daughters.

Conclusion: Amazingly, while Malcolm's teacher and mentor, the Honorable Elijah Muhammad, and his ideas have been slowly erased from history books, and his achievements systematically ignored; Malcolm's name has almost been enshrined in gold. Rumors at the time of Malcolm's departure from the N.O.I. were that he had stumbled upon some personal information about the Messenger that shook his confidence and prompted him to judge his Muslim teacher by Christian precepts. He and other dissatisfied Muslim men used this incident to incite disharmony and disbelief among the FOI ranks. Internal struggles among various factions had been brewing for years. The strength of Malcolm's convictions as National Spokesman for the N.O.I., where he learned everything he knew, helped him spike his lectures with hints of impending racial war. This volatile mix, especially after he defected, continued to draw him an audience. The truth of this matter is that when Malcolm left the Nation, for whatever reason, he no longer had a program to improve the lives of African-American people. He then made the fatal mistake, as others before him had, of deciding that his mission was not to awaken Blacks religiously or economically, but one of obtaining civil rights for all humanity. He then concluded that the Blackman would have to take his freedom by force — or "by any means necessary." He abandoned his higher goals of teaching self-salvation and became a speaker lecturing on fatal strategies predicting illusionary results. The value of his life dwindled into being remembered only as a bold cryptic speaker. During the short time he had left after leaving the Nation he switched sides, changed his position, and attempted to introduce an entirely new, unfamiliar platform — grounded in Pan-Africanism. The majority of the Negroes didn't even know what Pan-Africanism was and greeted Malcolm with mild apprehension. Malcolm took on too much. He tried to leave the Nation, change his religion, rearrange his platform and earn a living all at the same time. He became confused, and while he had previously claimed to deplore American imperialism, decided to pursue democracy and politics at the U.N. He stopped teaching Black history, economic growth and about Yacub and changed his stance to one of attempting to save the entire world, especially Negroes, from mass world oppression. Malcolm loved his people but the thrill of applause pumped up his overblown ambition to override his common sense. And he bit the hand that fed him.

Today the only memory left of Malcolm's existence is an autobiography written by a non-Muslim, a few books of his speeches, a selection of taped lectures, the title "Malcolm X," a few photographs and his caption "By Any Means Necessary." Malcolm did not have a realistic program for the survival of Black people in America. His memory is laced with exaggerated deeds and emotional sentiment. Listening to Malcolm's tapes or wearing clothes with his name emblazoned across the front does not help or correct the wrongs in the African-American community. If the truth be told, if Malcolm X were alive today, Blackmen who claim they admire and believe in him, would not be his companions or supporters. Malcolm would be staunchly rejected by the educated class of Blacks, feared by the uneducated Blacks, and attacked as a radical by the media. Few Blacks would jeopardize their positions in society by announcing their allegiance to a perceived militant-like Malcolm X. This includes young Black males on campus, too. If Blackmen are so enthused and impressed with Malcolm, how come they are not teaching his theories, using his tactics or doing what he said to do — embrace Pan-Africanism? Furthermore, Malcolm would reject each and every Blackman leader on the scene today as being passive mentally dead hog eaters.

Few in his fan base consider the personal trauma that Malcolm suffered when he severed ties with Elijah Muhammad, his spiritual mentor and father image. He was like a fish out of water... with his bond broken with his guide, internal knowledge that he had failed the test, and abandonment by his fellow coup associates. He had a lot to deal with. But if remembering Malcolm today creates an emotional thrill of good feeling, or causes Blackmen to show respect for another Blackmen, then good. But carving out a special place of honor, reserved for those who willfully advanced the race as a martyr, is not called for — and is of no value. The new praise for Malcolm is another of the Blackman's attempts to uncover a Blackman to honor as a hero. Out of the sparse number available, Malcolm's turn just came around. Attempts to worship Malcolm X have not, and will not, benefit the Blackman in any way towards survival. X=Unknown.

Martin Luther King, Jr. — 1929-1968
Was an Atlanta Baptist Preacher who graduated from Morehouse College. He is the most famed civil rights activist in American history due to his use of non-violence to evoke social change. His reign began in the 50's in the deep south where he participated in sit-in and boycott efforts to desegregate public facilities and get the right to vote. He paid his dues to the movement through multiple arrests and brief jail time. He was a troubled man trying to do the right thing with God. He was an eloquent writer and enthralling speaker and soon rose to popularity in another hard working civil rights entity he co-founded; the Southern Christian Leadership Council (SCLC). King organized Blacks by appealing to them from the pulpit in churches all over America. He involved young Blacks, and armed them with his non-violent concepts as a way to remove civil barriers. King lead his followers in many marches, many ending in humiliation, injury, abuse and jail stints. He and his marchers often felt the vicious teeth of police dogs, iron tempered night sticks, cuts inflicted by stones and bottles, and the powerful thrust of high powered water hoses spraying 100 pounds of pressure per square inch. King managed to desegregate many institutions in the south, got Blacks on the ballot and organized other cities into action — and all was done by nonviolent passive resistance. While many believe that King

239

copied non-violence from Mahatma Gandhi, he actually embraced some ancient Greek ideas on the meaning of love — eros, philia and agape. After studying the definitions of these he settled on the agape method which he believed was supported by the teachings of Jesus in the Holy Bible. He defined agape to mean "one does not love another because they are necessarily worthy, but because God loves them." He told the press to inform his white racist opponents that: "We shall match your capacity to inflict suffering by our capacity to endure suffering. We will meet your physical force with soul-force. Do to us what you will and we will still love you... Bomb our homes and threaten our children, and, as difficult as it is, we will still love you. Send your hooded perpetrators of violence into our communities at the midnight hour and drag us out on some wayside road and leave us half-dead as you beat us, and we will still love you." This theme of obeying Jesus and "loving your enemy" became his major commitment.

He theorized: "We cannot solve this problem through retaliatory violence. We must meet violence with non-violence. Remember the words of Jesus, 'He who lives by the sword will die by the sword.' We must love our white brothers no matter what they do to us... We must make them know that we love them... We must meet hate with love." Amazingly, he found many cohorts in the Black male leadership pool who joined him and attracted others to this kind of rationale. Outspoken Black Power factions disagreed with him and were often responsible for retaliatory violence when attacked by whites for trying to integrate or march. To celebrate the centennial of 100 years of the signing of the Emancipation Proclamation and commemorate all the social advancements earned by Blacks between 1863 and 1963, Blackmen leaders decided to host their most notable event — The March on Washington. Hundreds of thousands of Blacks from all over the country and foreign shores — leaders, ministers, priests, educators, politicians, entertainers, students, white sympathizers, other civil rights agencies, government workers and people of all nationalities — mostly Black and white, convened at the Lincoln Memorial statue to express their solidarity. Their theme song, "We Shall Overcome," was sung in unison with much emotion and sincerity. It was here that King, the keynote speaker, gave his most famous and moving address — the "I Have A Dream" speech — where he promised: "Those who hope that the Negro needed to blow off steam and will now be content will have a rude awakening if the nation returns to business as usual. There will be neither rest nor tranquility in America until the Negro is granted his citizenship rights. The whirlwinds of revolts will continue to shake the foundations of our nation until the bright day of justice emerges." Dr. King was sincere in this idea, however, it didn't quite exactly happen the way he thought it would verified by the quiet inactivity of Blacks today.

King skillfully combined religion, conscience and law to challenge civil violations against Negroes. He was awarded many honorary degrees and citations for his dedicated work to eliminate racial prejudice by using nonviolent methods, love and prayer. He aided many in obtaining employment opportunities, better housing, education and legal representation. One of his greatest achievements was being nominated and receiving the 1964 Nobel Peace Prize, which was an international competition. It was King who brought the civil rights issue to national attention after he and his followers were set upon by excessive police brutality during a freedom march in the South. Some of his ideas were accommodated by President John Kennedy, Attorney General Robert Kennedy and President Lyndon B. Johnson. Federal troops were sent in to enforce government rulings against segregation on King's behalf. Martin Luther King, Jr. was shot dead on the balcony of a motel in Memphis, Tennessee on April 4, 1968 by a Caucasian sniper. After his reported death there were 126 riots in major cities during which 46 died, 21,000 were arrested and hundreds injured. King had a very mournful funeral with sympathizers expressing grief from all corners of the world. After his untimely death the civil rights movement slowed down somewhat due to the absence of its internationally known charismatic speaker. Many schools, streets, buildings, parks, gymnasiums, sport fields and libraries were named after him.

Conclusion: Obviously Dr. King believed in social and sexual integration and he prayed for it for his children because he saw it as a benefit. He had a sincere belief in politics and fought hard to gain voting rights for Blacks in the south and north. He was a devout Christian and gained strength and singleness of purpose from his religion. He made it the guiding factor to justify his actions of passive nonviolent resistance. He was not concerned with Negroes opening their own businesses but pleaded for them to be allowed to enjoy equal opportunity,

241

jobs, and humanitarian rights by acceptance into society. He definitely was not for self-defense of any kind. He was not concerned with names. His only connection to heritage was his belief that all people came from and were created by God, and Jesus loved everybody — equally. He was not in disagreement with Black pride but felt it would come from gaining civil rights guaranteed by the Constitution for every American. Today his wife, Coretta Scott King, continues to represent and preserve her husband's memory. She organized to build the now famous tourist spot, the Martin Luther King, Jr. Center for Nonviolent Social Change in Atlanta. This facility has a souvenir gift shop, day care center and offers community services much needed by the people in that area. As far as King's legacy of advancements — Blacks are riding anyplace they want to on public transportation, can eat in any restaurant, drink out of any water fountain, register and vote, attend any school, shop any store, frequent the movie house of their choice, live anywhere they please, participate in the political process, marry into white families, and apply for work anyplace they desire. If the aforementioned rights are the measure, then King indeed left a great legacy. It is quite plausible to infer that if it had not been for Dr. King's constant nonviolent protests against segregation that Blacks would not be able to have the public freedom of motion they currently enjoy. It is just as easily apparent that had Blacks used that same energy towards building their own facilities and institutions that they would be in a better economic and leadership position today. Because now they have access to all those integrated services and establishments — few can afford to patronize them. And these same "privileges" are the ones which take needed dollars out of the Black community almost faster than they come in.

Martin Luther King, Jr. introduced the Blackman to voluntary masochism. He, instead of uplifting their strength and dignity, required them to be weak, bombed, gassed and insulted — in the name of getting equality. He ushered Blackwomen, old and young, children of all ages, and adult Blackmen who should have known better, into humiliating, degrading, life threatening situations that caused much emotional suffering. He challenged Blacks to see how much abuse they could take from whites in order to eat, work, play and sleep with them. Had he lived, he, too, would have grieved over the oozing losses of what he had suffered to maintain. He obviously experienced sharp conflict internally in forcing himself to go against the natural instinct of any mammal — which is to retaliate when attacked. His eloquence of speech, his face of humility, dynamic terminology and his reference to Jesus and the Bible allowed him to hypnotize his followers into believing that unabiding, unwarranted and absolute love of the "white brothers" would tumble down the barriers of racism. His platform, deducted from the Greek history of Pythagoras and Mahatma Ghandi, mixed with a bit of Jesus Christ, put him on a mission.

He was an honorable, civilized, dedicated Blackman leader. He just applied all those excellent attributes to the wrong plan. If Martin Luther King is considered the greatest all-time Blackman hero, then African-American men are surely doomed. *A man must not just be judged by his sacrificial behavior, he must be judged by the sensibility of his ideas and the permanence of his agenda.* Dr. King is honored for his cause and not his effect. What are the benefits? Yes, Dr. King was persistent, persistent in goading Blacks into volunteering to get their heads cracked, ribs bruised and egos humiliated — all of which has turned out today to be of little or no value. His program inspired Blacks to turn all their good ideas and money over to whites. It made them think that there was no point in building anything for themselves because as long as they were permitted entry to white-owned facilities, there was no need to. It also made them think that as long as they were qualified that they would be guaranteed equal and fair treatment on a job.

King's so-called civil rights gains have ended up being the very foundation of the problems Blacks face today. When rejected for employment in white owned businesses they have no place to go, and it doesn't matter how much education they have. Attending school with whites and using their curriculum has removed the little bit of Black culture that Blacks tried to express in the early 60's, and prompted Blackmen to venture on an insatiable quest to integrate into white society. King is the major force credited for making all of these "advancements" available. Today, the Blackman is right back where he started during the pre-civil rights era — he is trying to find work, a place to live, a good education for his children, affordable food, reasonable clothing, goods and services, and a way to express and remember his Black culture. And he is still fumbling with issues about his name and religion. King thought he could shame racists into accepting Blacks by calling on the spiritual conscience of white Americans. He would be very sad today. When all sentimentality is put aside, the Blackman must make a decision and determination for himself who his heroes are, based upon their pertinent accomplishments and the useful longevity of their ideas.

Speculation arising after King's death that he was planning to take a more militant stand in his civil rights and anti-war protests remain unsubstantiated.

Jesse Jackson — 1941-still living

Is a graduate of a southern Black college and an ordained minister of the Christian faith. He has been active in the civil rights struggle for over 30 years. His tenure in the movement has been an exciting one. Starting with sit-ins in Greensboro, North Carolina, to membership in SCLC (Southern Christian Leadership Council) in Atlanta. He met Dr. King in 1965 while participating in the Selma March, rallied the Black clergy behind Dr. King's nonviolent curriculum, organized many human rights groups in Chicago and brought civil rights consciousness to Northern cities.

He launched Operation Breadbasket established by King to instigate better hiring policies for Blacks in Chicago. He was known for being colorful and capable. He became a magnificent speaker, often urging Blacks to form a separate political party and endorse their own candidates to represent their interests. He established Operation PUSH (People United to Save Humanity), a group formulated to organize groups made up of common laborers, farmers and women — a rainbow coalition. He designed PUSH–EXCEL to promote better academics for young children, and was elected by Black Enterprise Magazine in 1980 as the major spokesman for Blacks. His next major project was running for President of the U.S.A. His special way of articulating any idea by creating a catchy phrase or rhyming his words entertainingly drew attention from the public and the media. He toured the entire country in 1983 and 1984 touting his famous caption, "I am somebody." His travels took him to the campuses of historically Black colleges and universities where he used his lifelong talent of motivating and mobilizing people into action. He influenced students in record numbers to register to vote and to help him campaign through advertising and donations and raising money. He visited the pulpit and enjoined the Black church to support his nomination campaign and raise money for his quest to become the first Black President. He was greeted with enthusiasm, admiration and belief. His sparkling good looks and intelligent manners gain him acceptance by any audience and any media. Rev. Jackson did not get the Democratic nomination in 1984 but he certainly aroused the idea of the possibility — no matter how remote. During his political tenure Jackson has tried many approaches, peaked in some and failed miserably in others, but his unabashed determination kept him in the forefront. His announcement of seriously running for President of the United States was a modern receptive idea to the few remaining liberals and every disappointed Black. His revolutionary style of speaking garnered the ears of progressive Blacks and the poor. While it was plain to any political scientist that Jackson's bid for the presidency was just scrimmage, it soon became apparent four years later, in 1988, that Jesse had actually started to believe that he could be President of America. He made the campaign money-collecting rounds again, still basing his platform on demanding justice and attention to the little Americans — the disenfranchised. This time he received several electoral votes and persuaded Michael Dukakis, the real nominee, to allow him to present a speech and introduce his lovely family at the convention. It was Jackson's shining hour as he dramatically delivered his "yo' patch is not big enough" speech about the plight of the poor in America. After the real Democratic nominee (Dukakis) was chosen, Jackson embarrassingly flitted around trying to see if he would get an appointment. When this didn't materialize the entire Black population was crushed.

The deadly infection of AIDS penetrated the African-American community in 1984, and the debilitating crack-cocaine drug epidemic showed up in 1985 — both crucial years for Black leaders to arise and confront these issues and start stopgap measures. But none came forth.

Conclusion: Other than Stokely Carmichael, who no longer resides in America, Jesse Jackson is the only one of the top ten Blackmen leaders still alive. Due to his credibility of purpose while affiliated with the civil rights industry, coupled with his youth and quick thinking use of metaphors, he has been, for over 20 years, somewhat of a spokesman for Blacks. He makes a stunning appearance and is a beautiful specimen of a Blackman.

Jesse Jackson is what was termed in the 1960's as a

professional rapper. This was long before rap music gained its popularity with Black youth. Jesse can talk. He can say it right. He speaks the language with such flourish and spontaneity that his listeners get caught up in the fascinating way he arranges his words. He has fallen slightly in popularity resulting from his now predictable platform, and his inability to reach the goal for which he gained the most notoriety. Jackson fooled African-Americans into believing that he could be the first Blackman president of the United States. Twice now he has traveled the country pumping Blacks into emotional frenzies with his "I Am Somebody" yells, and inciting another cheer from his supporters of "Run Jesse Run" — ideally for the Presidency. He spent almost eight years pursuing this illusionary dream resulting in a waste of Black dollars and Black time spent on a project of futility. He gallantly went overseas to gain the release of American hostages and continued to function as if he was an American government dignitary. Studies say that a white American child's chance of growing up and becoming president are one in 27,773,000 — so a Black child's chance of accomplishing this increases the odds by at least nine times. Jesse has a greater chance of being struck by lightening, which is reported to be one in 650,000 people.

Any African-American who acknowledges this painful truism is spurned by other Blacks who, instead of dealing with reality, choose to participate in Jesse's fairy tale dream. Jesse used to expound proficiently very clearly on the needs of Blacks — politically, socially and economically. His involvement in playing like he was going to be president robbed the Black community because it drew his attention away from the torrential problems created by his so-called presidential opponent Ronald Reagan, who was succeeding in cancelling over $50 billion in social spending that mostly affected Black people. But Jesse was too busy getting ready to run, running, or recuperating from his loss of the nomination to give his serious attention to these issues. Due to his need to encompass all of the nationalities into his plan (which he expected to enact during his job as Chief of Staff), he chose to embrace a class struggle representation. Since that time he has ineffectually tried to mesh his message to include every group and every nationality. This he has continued to call his "Rainbow Coalition." He says this means he represents all colors of people. But there is no "black" in a rainbow, and thus there is no pot of political gold at the end of it for Jesse.

He has finally spread himself too thin. He has tried to be everything to everybody. He is no longer straightforward in his opinions or conclusions for he has grown afraid of losing his multi-cultural stance. Rev. Jackson is an excellent organizer with powerful influence which could be better utilized than chasing behind illusive bids for the presidency. Hopefully the good reverend will apply his vast talents to goals more grounded in the reality of the condition of his people — his own Black people. As soon as he gives up his quest for cross-racial acceptance the real Jesse will emerge stronger and more experienced and he will function as the kind of Blackman leader African-Americans need. He certainly has the potential. Jesse has remained in the public eye periodically and hosted a nighttime T.V. talk show out of Washington where he is also President-in-waiting. He is still very popular on the lecture circuit.

Overview Conclusions

After reading these brief analogies about the ideas of the major top ten Blackmen leaders in the past 175 years, it is apparent that only two of them provided solutions to the kinds of problems Blacks persist in having today. Those two are Booker T. Washington and the Honorable Elijah Muhammad. That's two out of ten. Not bad.

While Blackmen incessantly cry for justice, freedom, jobs, respect, recognition, protection, education, pride, unity and economic strength — few Blackmen, when put to the test, are willing to work for these rewards under the only programs they know of that provides them with ways and ideas to attain these goals. Today, recognizing the failure of the ballot, civil right gains and high education to improve their mental, emotional or financial conditions, Blacks are suggesting that striving for social goals is now passe. They are on the brink of developing new strategies different from the routine. Demands are being made for separate schools for Black children to address their special needs, instituting self-help programs for economic empowerment, and a return to traditional values and morals to repair the Black family. These basic goals are being recorded as the creative discoveries of the "New Black Leadership," but this is not true.

Blacks are being forced, by survival necessity, to use the

principles and foundation ideas first introduced by Booker T. Washington in the late 1800's and improved on and expanded by Elijah Muhammad in the mid-1930's. Over the next several crucial years Blackmen leaders will try to pick out various aspects of Washington's and Muhammad's programs and try to mold and adjust them to meet the current economic, social and cultural needs of the people, because Washington and Muhammad had the only complete programs not contingent on approval, finance or recognition from other races. Political party, sentimentality or personal desire will have nothing to do with it. These programs will be adopted based on bare necessity. Imagine how much time could have been saved, and how much deterioration of the Black community would have been prevented, had Blackmen leaders adopted Washington's or Muhammad's programs in their entirety 40 years ago. Especially since today Blacks are being forced to return to their ideas under the guise of calling them Black Republican or Democratic party ideologies. Selective amnesia is happening again.

The other eight Blackmen leaders promised their people personal recognition and social freedom in accord with the American dream. They choose to identify with a political idea instead of working for independence. Their idea was that Blacks must gain, by shrewd manipulation of the law and human protest, all civil rights, mainly integration, before anything else could be addressed. Their political dialogue relieved them of any responsibility to provide their followers with a real life plan. This also allowed them to grandstand media based on their sermons about humanitarian rights with no real accountability. These choices eliminated self-sufficiency and made Blacks crave for acceptance from the majority race in America. They violated all the laws of self preservation. Today, as yesterday, the Blackman needs a step program in the dynamics of pursuit — how to get things done. How to make proper choices and navigate the shortest distance between these two points. Planning is a specific function for these actions, and he must have foresight, adequate forecasting ability to measure the positive and negative potential of every plan considered. If after a predesignated date no progress is being made he must discipline his ego and quadruple his efforts to reach success. He cannot alibi. How do we ascertain the traits needed to become a Blackman leader? He must first realize that the basic premise of leadership lies in the proper development of men. The very structure of African-American disorganized daily life calls for special leadership. These Blackmen must have local goals whenever possible, their objectives must be clear because the effectiveness of good ideas vary in proportion to the people's understanding of what it is they need to do. This comes down to communication, in a language that the masses of the people can understand. Yes, it is necessary to have Blackmen leaders. Blackmen instinctively divide themselves into two classes — leaders and followers. The leaders must accept any rules required to reach the goals, and the followers must have something to do, preferably work. The base from which the Blackman will revive depends on the satisfaction he receives from his work. But he first must have some work, some principles to live by, and some rules to follow to keep him on target. The Blackman can reestablish the respect for his community only by being the example of change. And this is his last opportunity to do so. He must intelligently weigh the ideas of every Blackman leader, and consider them with the understanding that there is no plan available that all Blackmen agree with 100%. So he must choose a selected program and work for the good of it. Diligently.

Another example of wasted Black male leadership took the form of Nelson Mandela, a brilliant nationalist hero in South Africa. Mr. Mandela gave up 27 years of his life suffering in a rotten prison with few accoutrements for comfortable survival. He was a political prisoner in protest against apartheid in South Africa, and used his exile to gain the attention from other freedom fighters around the world. Nelson Mandela failed to reach his goal. After a quick flurry of media coverage, welcome home parades and a little special recognition from the U.S.A., his life has gone back to normal. Apartheid did not end. He is no longer a young man caught up in artificial visions, and he and his people are still faced with the organized cruelty of white rule, and the power and corruption therein. It is very difficult to get the Blackman to see, because of his misplaced emotionalism and abnormal desire to have a hero, that Nelson Mandela wasted his life. He gave his life based on his belief in the common good of all men, and their basic nature of justice and unselfishness. Those values did not show forth from present government. Mandela's people are still engaged in civil and community wars against each other. Whatever changes are happening in South Africa today they have nothing to do with

Nelson's prison term. While Mandela will be remembered for making such a personal and dignified sacrifice, what good did his sacrifice actually do to solve racism in South Africa? Granted he is a great inspiration of the courage and loyalty of a Blackman leader. But other than that. Unfortunately, Brother Nelson participated in 27 long, lonely years of an ineffective protest. He is not the leader of South Africa, he is one of the leaders. But at least Mandela and his people are fighting for social and political reform in their homeland. The Blackman has been fighting for the same thing in a land already claimed by the native Indians and the whiteman as theirs and theirs alone.

Currently there are trio photographs being offered to African-Americans. These are three-part photograph sets featuring Nelson Mandela, Martin Luther King, Jr. and Malcolm X. Back in the early 1970's, the Blackman was attracted to another trio photograph set featuring pictures of President John F. Kennedy, Martin Luther King, Jr. and Bobby Kennedy. Many African-Americans proudly purchased these often expensive photo sets and hung them conspicuously in their homes – for years. They have been continually searching for a Blackman to idolize and be worthy of their verbal support and artificial admiration. They have never emulated a Blackman leader beyond voicing their fondness for him. But the 65-70's version of the leaders they honored made more political sense because the Kennedys and King allegedly shared, on the surface, many of the same theories for different reasons.

Today's version of Mandela-King-Malcolm photos have no business being featured together as a trio because they all had opposing political ideas. While it seems harmless to salute a few notable Blackmen, it is psychologically impossible to sanely support all of them equally because each of their platforms conflict with each other.

As an example:
1) Nelson Mandela — believes in political resolution negotiations with attack and war as a last resort.
2) Martin Luther King, Jr. — stood for nonviolent protests, love for your enemy and prayer to Jesus.
3) Malcolm X — touted impending racial war, wanted Blacks to adopt Pan-Africanism and denounce Christianity for Islam.

The purpose of publicly promoting Black male heroes should be so their values can be used as an example of progress. The fact that many Blackmen claim to support all three of these Blackmen leaders is another example of their confusion regarding who to align themselves with. They do not know how to judge the value of the ideas of Blackmen leaders. Their philosophical concepts are clouded with faulty interpretations and emotions which prevent them from recognizing the real, instead of imagined, worth of a Blackman leader. Additionally, they think they are owed some kind of special consideration or adjusted treatment because they are Black.

Another mistake the Blackman made politically was to try to align himself with the Jewish community because of what they perceived as a unity based on both races being rejected by the Anglo-Saxon/Europeans. They had always heard about the anti-semitic behavior the gentiles practiced against the Jews because they accused them of killing Jesus. The Blackman and the Jewish man felt discriminated against in America. The Blackman, in his untiring search for an ally outside of himself, clasped hands with his Jewish brothers and looked forward to a long but inspirational march for freedom, respect and equality. However, the Jewish man spent no time in trying to convince the Europeans to accept them as equals, invite them to their parties, hire them on their jobs or fall in love with them. The Jewish community immediately went about determining their own internal priorities and ignored everyone else and went directly to work. They had talents and skills they brought with them from their homeland and through determination and sacrifice and being mocked and insulted; they have built an empire. And they enjoy admiration and respect even from those who disagree with their business tactics. They are not as monolithic as they were 40 years ago but it has not stopped them from persevering towards success individually. They are motivated high achievers while the Blackman got stuck in a gully he dug himself by never giving up on trying to force the Europeans to share America with them. The Jewish community have the same religion, same traditions and the same linkage to their homeland which they support vigorously. And the Jewish citizens in their homeland recognize and accept them as members in good standing of their tribe. Not so for the Blackman. The African citizens living in their motherland are quoted as saying "they don't want the American Negro back in

Africa because they practice too many of the whiteman's ways." Their own people do not want them in their present condition and do not recognize them because they have nothing in common anymore.

Had the Blackman been enslaved but allowed to keep his name and religion, things would be different today. There would be a connection. A bond. But their ideas come in as many variations as their European last names. Each of the previously listed Blackmen had opposing notions about how to go about obtaining freedom, justice and equality for the Blackman. Several of them did not even like each other.

The following additional list of an attempt to chart other Black male front liners who over the past years have attempted to bring forth their contribution to the Blackman leadership pool. Every Black mayor could conceivably be added to this list. While this list is not fully complete, it demonstrates the wide range of Blackmen leaders who rose to command attention. Some of them made sense, some made a little sense, and some made no sense at all. However, they represent the boldest ones who had the nerve to step forward with their ideas about how to ease the everyday pain of Black life.

A FEW OTHER NOTABLE BLACKMEN LEADERS

Each of these Blackmen leaders are, or were, in positions to advise African-Americans regarding strategies and priorities to develop jobs, prevent the dissolution of the family, and strengthen the moral foundation of the Black community.

1) Muhammad Ali
   Boxer/Conscientious War Objector

2) Rabbi Ben Ami
   Black Hebrew Israelites

3) Molefi Asante
   Educator of Afrocentricity

4) Amiri Baraka (Leroi Jones)
   Militant Social Activist/Writer

5) Yusef Bey
   Minister/Entrepreneur

6) Ralph Bunche
   U.N. Undersecretary/Politician

7) Ron Dellums
   Civil Activist/Politician

8) Medgar Evers
   Political Reformist/Com. Advocate

9) Earl Graves
   Publisher

10) William Gray
    Politician/UNCF Director/Minister

11) Dick Gregory
    Health Expert/Social Commentator

12) Nathan Hare
    Black Think Tank Founder

13) Benjamin Hooks
    NAACP Director/Lawyer/Minister

14) Yosef Ben Jochanon
    Historian/Educator

15) John H. Johnson
    Publisher/Cosmetic Manufacturer

16) Roy Innis
    CORE Director, Rights Activist

17) Maulana Ron Karenga
    KWANZA Founder/Educator

18) Arthur Lewis
    Nobel Prize in Economics

19) Joseph Lowery
    SCLC Director/Minister

20) Thurgood Marshall
    Supreme Court Justice

21) Clarence Pendleton
    Civil Rights Commissioner

22) Alvin Poussaint
    M.D./Psychiatrist/Social Researcher

23) A. Phillip Randolph
Labor Leader/Transportation

24) Paul Robeson
Communist/Lawyer/Actor

25) Carl Rowan
Journalist/U.S. Ambassador

26) Al Sharpton
Community Advocate/Minister

27) Shelby Steele
Professor/Social Commentator/Author

28) Leon Sullivan
OIC Founder

29) Louis Sullivan
M.D./U.S. Government Health Director

30) Clarence Thomas
Supreme Court Justice

31) Douglas Wilder
Governor/Virginia

32) Carter G. Woodson
Founder/Assoc. for Study of Negro Life

33) Andrew Young
U.N. Ambassador/Civil Rights Worker

34) Whitney Young, Jr.
Urban League Director

While the aforementioned list is admittedly only partial, few of them have been able to convey a message to help the Blackman improve his condition on a permanent ongoing basis. Most of the ideas these Blackmen leaders presented were only temporary. There has never been a major overriding agenda that all Blackmen agreed upon and worked for collectively regarding their survival. His citizenship remains in peril and every so often a Civil Rights Act or Civil Rights Bill must be endorsed by the government to determine if the Blackman will be allowed to continue benefiting from certain basic rights allegedly already guaranteed for every American in the

Constitution. He does not think it odd that he is periodically reevaluated or that it still takes federal statutes for him to be accepted on a marginal basis.

Rarely does a Blackman leader suggest to the Blackman that he stop forcing himself into places where he is not wanted, and use that energy to build something for himself. Blackmen leaders should be held accountable for their errors in judgment concerning the needs of the people who rely on them for guidance and truth. Partial proof of their mistake is visibly apparent based on the fact that 60% of the homeless are Blackmen, the rest are made up of Blackwomen, Black children and other races. These homeless Blackmen are in various states of mental disarray from drug addiction to alcoholism to insanity to sober poverty. Another half-million Blackmen are in jail. The numbers of homosexual Blackmen is growing daily and many others pursue interracial unions to escape the entire predicament. Employment reports say that approximately 2,000 jobs per week are being eliminated due to downsizing because of a stagnant economy. And as quiet as its been kept, embracing curriculums in Afrocentricity and celebrating Christmastime KWANZA does not help African-American men to enhance their survival or improve their lot. Racial incidents are on the rise throughout the country. Tempers are short.

The collapse of the Black family continues to impact on the development of Black males, and alienates him from Black females. The young claim that contemporary rap music serves as a catalyst for positive public change. But rap has not proven itself to prevent Black youth from inflicting crimes on each other. To the contrary, rap tends to stimulate ruthless behavior and barbaric language. Word.

Blackmen are dying in various stages of death in shocking recorded number daily — among all ages and social stratas. The remaining Blackmen have a big responsibility to take steps to save their own lives. Nobody cares whether he lives or dies but him. He has no more time to waste negotiating in the boardroom for crumbs from European controlled tables. He must rearrange his priorities and prepare to make a few personal sacrifices. He'll have to reject the built-in limitations of working by the hour for a regulated monetary boundary. So he should break the habit of the 9 to 5 treadmill and spend every waking hour thinking about how he can survive — on his own. Working 9 to 5 with preset guidelines about what he must do and when to do it stunts his brain and makes him mentally lazy. He functions as a robot of sorts. He is programmed when to rise and when to go to bed. What time to eat and what to do on Sunday. All of these systems are programming. They tell him what to think. He enjoys a regular 9 to 5 job because he doesn't have to give his schedule any special consideration. The Blackman must devise his own time frames — and stop shutting his brain off at 5pm sharp every day. It is time for him to cease leaning on other men for sustenance, and to stop begging the courts to pass laws forcing other races to cooperate with his shameful condition by supporting his woman and child. Statistical scientists predict that in less than 50 years the whiteman will be the minority in America. Who will the Blackman count on for jobs or blame for his condition then?

The Blackman's fight is with the wrong person. His fight should be with himself – because he is the only obstacle standing in the way of his success in life. He can sing, march, complain, or pray himself into a trance — it will not help him. He must help himself.

Yes, this book contains the final agenda. The Blackman can no longer escape his mistakes in misdirecting the entire African-American nation, by mismanagement of his leadership, and rejection of all paths leading to economic recovery. So while the Blackman thinks that he is refused respect based on slavery or the color of his skin, he is wrong.

He is denied respect and honor because he is inconsistent, disunified, and unproductive.

Thank you for reading this book.

CIVILIZED PUBLICATIONS

2019 S. 7th STREET • PHILADELPHIA, PA 19148

ORDER FORM

**ORDER TODAY!
...AND SEND ONE
TO A FRIEND!**

NAME _____

ADDRESS _____

CITY _____ STATE _____ ZIP _____ Pa. residents add 7% Sales Tax

# COPIES	TITLE	PRICE		SHIPPING & HANDLING		TOTAL
____	THE BLACKWOMAN'S GUIDE (The Book)	$10.	+	$2. (S&H)	=	$12.
____	*The Blackman's Guide* (The Book)	$10.	+	$2. (S&H)	=	$12.
____	*How Not To Eat Pork* (The Book)	$10.	+	$2. (S&H)	=	$12.
____	*The Blackman's Guide On Tour* (Video)	$20	+	$2. (S&H)	=	$24.

TOTAL AMOUNT ENCLOSED _____ CHECK _____ MONEY ORDER _____

MC, VISA & AMEX ACCEPTED

SIGNATURE _____ PHONE _____

CARD # _____ EXP. DATE _____ TYPE OF CARD _____

Thank You For Your Order. Please Allow 3 Weeks For Delivery
All Products Available Wholesale